Harcourt

Texas
GoMath!
Volume 1

Texas
GoMath!

Houghton Mifflin Harcourt.

Printed in the U.S.A.

ISBN 978-0-544-06097-5

13 14 15 16 0607 24 23 22

4500850980   C D E F G

Cover Image Credits: (building) ©MWaits/Shutterstock; (landscape) ©Radius Images/Corbis; (pier) ©Matthew Wakem/ Getty Images; (Ibis) ©Joel Sartore/Getty Images.

Dear Students and Families,

Welcome to **Texas Go Math!**, Grade 5! In this exciting mathematics program, there are hands-on activities to do and real-world problems to solve. Best of all, you will write your ideas and answers right in your book. In **Texas Go Math!**, writing and drawing on the pages helps you think deeply about what you are learning, and you will really understand math!

By the way, all of the pages in your **Texas Go Math!** book are made using recycled paper. We wanted you to know that you can Go Green with **Texas Go Math!**

Sincerely,

The Authors

Made in the United States
Printed on 100% recycled paper

Texas Go Math!

Authors

Juli K. Dixon, Ph.D.
Professor, Mathematics
  Education
University of Central Florida
Orlando, Florida

Edward B. Burger, Ph.D.
President
Southwestern University
Georgetown, Texas

Matthew R. Larson, Ph.D.
K-12 Curriculum Specialist for
  Mathematics
Lincoln Public Schools
Lincoln, Nebraska

Martha E. Sandoval-Martinez
Math Instructor
El Camino College
Torrance, California

Consultant

Valerie Johse
Math Consultant
Texas Council for Economic
  Education
Houston, Texas

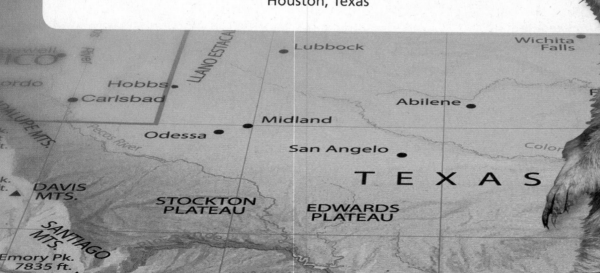

Volume 1

Unit 1 • Number and Operations: Place Value and Operations

Module 1) Place Value and Decimals

Module 2) Multiply and Divide Whole Numbers

Look for these:

Real World

H.O.T. Problems
Higher Order Thinking
Multi-Step Problems

Homework and Practice

Homework and TEKS Practice in every lesson.

 Resources

DIGITAL RESOURCES
Go online for the Interactive Student Edition with Math on the Spot Videos. Use *i*Tools, the Multimedia *e*Glossary, and more.

Look for these:

Real World

H.O.T. Problems
Higher Order Thinking
Multi-Step Problems

GO DIGITAL Resources

DIGITAL RESOURCES
Go online for the Interactive Student Edition with Math on the Spot Videos. Use *i*Tools, the Multimedia *e*Glossary, and more.

vi

Volume 1

Unit 2 • Number and Operations: Fractions

Module 5) Add and Subtract Fractions

Module 6) Multiply and Divide Unit Fractions and Whole Numbers

Volume 1

Unit 3 • Algebraic Reasoning

Module 7 Algebra • Expressions

Module 8 Algebra • Equations

Module 9 · Algebra · Formulas

Module 10 · Algebra · Patterns

Look for these:

H.O.T. Problems
Higher Order Thinking
Multi-Step Problems

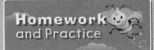

Homework and Practice

Homework and TEKS Practice in every lesson.

Volume 2

Unit 4 • Geometry and Measurement

Module 14 — Graphing

Volume 2

Unit 5 • Data Analysis

Look for these:

Real World

H.O.T. Problems
Higher Order Thinking
Multi-Step Problems

Homework and Practice

Homework and TEKS Practice in every lesson.

Module 15 — Categorical Data

Module 16 — Numerical Data

Volume 2

Unit 6 • Personal Financial Literacy

Module 17 Personal Financial Literacy

Number and Operations: Place Value and Operations

Show What You Know

Check your understanding of important skills.

Name _____

▶ **Meaning of Division** Use counters to solve.

1. Divide 18 counters into groups of 3. How many groups are there?

_____ groups

2. Divide 21 counters into groups of 7. How many groups are there?

_____ groups

▶ **Place Value of Decimals** Write the word form and the expanded form for each.

3. 3.4

_____

_____

4. 2.51

_____

_____

▶ **Estimate Quotients Using Compatible Numbers**
Estimate the quotients.

5. $2\overline{)312}$

6. $4\overline{)189}$

7. $6\overline{)603}$

8. $3\overline{)1,788}$

Vocabulary Builder

▶ **Visualize It** •••••••••••••••••••••••••••••••••••••

Use the ✓ words to complete the tree map.

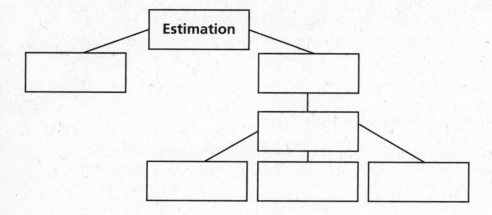

Estimation

▶ **Understand Vocabulary** •••••••••••••••••••••••••

Read the description. Which word do you think is described?

1. One of one hundred equal parts _____.

2. The value of each digit in a number based on the location of the digit _____.

3. To replace a number with one that is simpler and is approximately the same size as the original number _____.

4. A property that states that multiplying a sum by a number is the same as multiplying each addend in the sum by the number then adding the products _____.

5. One of ten equal parts _____.

6. A familiar number used as a point of reference _____.

7. One of one thousand equal parts _____.

8. Operations that undo each other _____.

GO DIGITAL
• Interactive Student Edition
• Multimedia eGlossary

Name _____

Reading When you read a story, you can look at the illustrations to help you visualize, or picture, what is happening. To visualize math, it can be helpful to show the information and numbers in a word problem in a different way.

Read the problem. Use the place-value charts to help you visualize the numbers.

United States Olympic athlete Brian Martin, from Palo Alto, CA, has won 2 medals in the luge event. Which of his practice times was better: forty-seven and sixty-nine thousandths seconds or forty-seven and two hundredths seconds?

Tens	Ones		Tenths	Hundredths	Thousandths
4	7	.	0	6	9

Tens	Ones		Tenths	Hundredths
4	7	.	0	2

Think

47.069 has 6 hundredths.
47.02 has 2 hundredths.
47.02 is the better time.

Writing Work with a partner to visualize the numbers in different ways. Here are four possibilities:

- Use place-value models.

- Use standard form.

- Use a number line.

Which way do you prefer to use to help you visualize the numbers and solve the problem? **Explain.**

_____

_____

_____

_____

Digit Challenge

Object of the Game Use your number cards to make the greatest number.

Materials

- Number/Symbol Cards: 4 sets labeled 0–9
- Strip of paper (1 per player; divided into 6 sections to represent the digits in the thousands, hundreds, tens, ones, tenths, and hundredths)

Set Up

Shuffle all the number cards and place them face down in a stack. Each player has a 6–section strip of paper.

Number of Players 2–4

How to Play

1 Each player draws a number card and places it on his or her strip of paper. Once placed, the card cannot be moved.

2 Repeat Step 1 until each player has placed 6 number cards. The player who makes the number with the greatest value scores one point.

3 Return all the cards to the stack and shuffle. Repeat steps 1–2. The first player to score a total of 10 points is the winner.

Name _____

1.1 Properties
ALGEBRA

Essential Question
How can you use properties of operations to solve problems?

You can use the properties of operations to help you simplify numerical expressions more easily.

Properties of Addition

Commutative Property of Addition If the order of addends changes, the sum stays the same.	$12 + 7 = 7 + 12$
Associative Property of Addition If the grouping of addends changes, the sum stays the same.	$5 + (8 + 14) = (5 + 8) + 14$
Identity Property of Addition The sum of any number and 0 is that number.	$13 + 0 = 13$

Properties of Multiplication

Commutative Property of Multiplication If the order of factors changes, the product stays the same.	$4 \times 9 = 9 \times 4$
Associative Property of Multiplication If the grouping of factors changes, the product stays the same.	$11 \times (3 \times 6) = (11 \times 3) \times 6$
Identity Property of Multiplication The product of any number and 1 is that number.	$4 \times 1 = 4$

Unlock the Problem

The table shows the number of bones in several parts of the human body. What is the total number of bones in the ribs, the skull, and the spine?

To find the sum of addends using mental math, you can use the Commutative and Associative Properties.

Part	Number of Bones
Ankle	7
Ribs	24
Skull	28
Spine	26

Use properties to find 24 + 28 + 26.

$24 + 28 + 26 = 28 + $ _____ $ + 26$ Use the _____ Property to reorder the addends.

$= 28 + (24 + $ _____ $)$ Use the _____ Property to group the addends.

$= 28 + $ _____   Use mental math to add.

$= $ _____

So, there are _____ bones in the ribs, the skull, and the spine.

Math Talk
Mathematical Processes
Explain why grouping 24 and 26 makes the problem easier to solve.

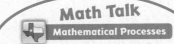

Distributive Property

Multiplying a sum by a number is the same as multiplying each addend by the number and then adding the products.

$5 \times (7 + 9) = (5 \times 7) + (5 \times 9)$

The Distributive Property can also be used with multiplication and subtraction. For example, $2 \times (10 - 8) = (2 \times 10) - (2 \times 8)$.

🔒 Example Use the Distributive Property to find the product.

One Way Use addition.

$8 \times 59 = 8 \times ($_____$+ 9)$ Use a multiple of 10 to write 59 as a sum.

$\quad = ($_____$\times 50) + (8 \times$_____$)$ Use the Distributive Property.

$\quad =$_____$+$_____   Use mental math to multiply.

$\quad =$_____   Use mental math to add.

Another Way Use subtraction.

$8 \times 59 = 8 \times ($_____$- 1)$ Use a multiple of 10 to write 59 as a difference.

$\quad = ($_____$\times 60) - (8 \times$_____$)$ Use the Distributive Property.

$\quad =$_____$-$_____   Use mental math to multiply.

$\quad =$_____   Use mental math to subtract.

Math Talk
Mathematical Processes
Explain how you could find the product 3×299 by using mental math.

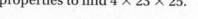 Share and Show MATH BOARD

1. Use properties to find $4 \times 23 \times 25$.

$23 \times$_____$\times 25$ _____ Property of Multiplication

$23 \times ($_____$\times$_____$)$ _____ Property of Multiplication

$23 \times$_____

_____

Use properties to find the sum or product.

2. $89 + 27 + 11$

_____

☑ 3. 9×52

_____

☑ 4. $107 + 0 + 39 + 13$

_____

6

Name _____

Problem Solving

Practice: Copy and Solve Use properties to find the sum or product.

5. 3×78

6. $4 \times 60 \times 5$

7. $21 + 25 + 39 + 5$

Complete the equation, and tell which property you used.

8. $11 + (19 + 6) = (11 + \underline{\hspace{1cm}}) + 6$

9. $25 + 14 = \underline{\hspace{1cm}} + 25$

_____

_____

10. **H.O.T.** Show how you can use the Distributive Property to rewrite and find $(32 \times 6) + (32 \times 4)$.

_____

Problem Solving *Real World*

11. **Multi-Step** Three friends' meals at a restaurant cost $13, $14, and $11. Use parentheses to write two different expressions and find how much the friends spent in all. Which property does your pair of expressions demonstrate?

_____

_____

Fancy Guppy Prices	
Blue neon	$11
Red blond	$22
Sunrise	$18
Yellow	$19

12. **Multi-Step** Jacob is designing an aquarium for a doctor's office. He plans to buy 6 red blond guppies, 1 blue neon guppy, and 1 yellow guppy. The table shows the price list for the guppies. How much will the guppies for the aquarium cost?

_____

13. **H.O.T.** **Sense or Nonsense?** Julie wrote $(15 - 6) - 3 = 15 - (6 - 3)$. Is Julie's equation sense or nonsense? Do you think the Associative Property works for subtraction? **Explain.**

_____

_____

_____

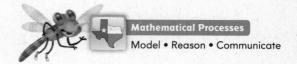

Daily Assessment Task

Fill in the bubble completely to show your answer.

14. **Connect** In a flea circus, 12 fleas pull carts, 23 fleas ride on tiny bicycles, and 18 fleas sit on seesaws. You can add $12 + 23 + 18$ to find the total number of fleas. Which equation shows the Commutative Property of Addition?

    (A) $12 + 23 + 18 = 23 + 12 + 18$

    (B) $12 + 23 + 18 = (12 + 23) + 18$

    (C) $12 + 23 + 18 = 12 + (23 + 18)$

    (D) $12 + 23 + 18 = 35 + 18$

15. **Use Symbols** Complete the equation.

$$15 + (25 + 27) = (15 + \underline{\hspace{1cm}}) + 27$$

    (A) 40

    (B) 25

    (C) 10

    (D) 52

16. **Multi-Step** Nick read 24 pages in his book one day, 29 pages the next day, and 16 pages on the third day. Megan read 26 pages for three days in a row. Who read more pages? How many more?

    (A) Megan read 9 more pages.

    (B) Megan read 11 more pages.

    (C) Nick read 9 more pages.

    (D) Megan read 11 more pages.

⭐ TEXAS Test Prep

17. Canoes rent for $29 per day. Which expression can be used to find the cost in dollars of renting 6 canoes for a day?

    (A) $(6 + 20) + (6 + 9)$

    (B) $(6 \times 20) + (6 \times 9)$

    (C) $(6 + 20) \times (6 + 9)$

    (D) $(6 \times 20) \times (6 \times 9)$

8

Homework and Practice

Name _____

1.1 Properties

Use properties to find the sum or product.

1. 4×47

2. $3 \times 40 \times 6$

3. $34 + 21 + 84 + 7$

_____   _____   _____

Complete the equation, and tell which property you used.

4. $103 + 21 = $ _____ $ + 103$

5. $16 + (70 + 8) = (16 + $ _____ $) + 8$

_____   _____

Problem Solving Real World

6. Maggie's class bought three books at the book fair. The books cost $15, $9, and $12. Use parentheses to write two different expressions and find how much the class spent in all. Which property does the pair of expressions demonstrate?

_____

_____

7. Leo's basketball team makes 16 points in the first game, 22 points in the second game, and 18 points in the third game. Use the Associative Property of Addition to show two different ways Leo can group the addends to show the total number of points.

_____

_____

Fill in the bubble completely to show your answer.

8. Which property is shown by the following equation?

$$44 + (13 + 11) = (44 + 13) + 11$$

(A) Commutative Property of Addition

(B) Associative Property of Addition

(C) Identity Property of Addition

(D) Distributive Property

9. Janel rakes leaves for $8 per lawn. Which expression can be used to find the amount she earns if she rakes 14 lawns?

(A) $(8 + 10) \times (8 + 4)$

(B) $(8 + 10) + (8 + 4)$

(C) $(8 \times 10) \times (8 \times 4)$

(D) $(8 \times 10) + (8 \times 4)$

10. Sara bought 7 tickets to the school play. Each ticket costs $11. To find the total cost in dollars, she added the product 7×1 to the product 7×10, for a total of $77. Which property did Sara use?

(A) Commutative Property of Multiplication

(B) Associative Property of Multiplication

(C) Identity Property of Multiplication

(D) Distributive Property

11. There are 6 granola bars in each box. Which expression can be used to find the number of granola bars in a dozen boxes?

(A) $(6 + 10) \times (6 + 2)$

(B) $(6 \times 10) + (6 \times 2)$

(C) $(6 + 10) + (6 + 2)$

(D) $(6 \times 10) \times (6 \times 2)$

12. **Multi-Step** Kara's garden has 4 sections. Each section has 7 rows of carrots and 9 rows of celery. How many rows are in the garden?

(A) 64

(B) 56

(C) 20

(D) 36

13. **Multi-Step** Max's school bought boxes of pencils. Each box holds 12 pencils. The fourth grade classes need 25 boxes. The fifth grade classes need 22 boxes. How many pencils are needed by both grades?

(A) 300

(B) 264

(C) 564

(D) 600

1.2 Thousandths

TEKS Number and Operations—5.2.A

MATHEMATICAL PROCESSES
5.1.D, 5.1.F

? Essential Question

How can you describe the relationship between two decimal place-value positions?

Investigate

Materials ■ color pencils ■ straightedge

Thousandths are smaller parts than hundredths. If one hundredth is divided into ten equal parts, each part is one thousandth.

Use the model at the right to show tenths, hundredths, and thousandths.

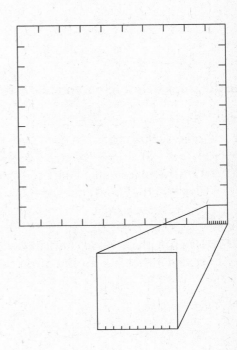

A. Divide the larger square into 10 equal columns or rectangles. Shade one rectangle. What part of the whole is the shaded rectangle? Write that part as a decimal and a fraction.

_____

B. Divide each rectangle into 10 equal squares. Use a second color to shade in one of the squares. What part of the whole is the shaded square? Write that part as a decimal and a fraction.

_____

C. Divide the enlarged hundredths square into 10 equal columns or rectangles. If each hundredths square is divided into ten equal rectangles, how many parts will the model have?

_____

Use a third color to shade one rectangle of the enlarged hundredths square. What part of the whole is the shaded rectangle? Write that part as a decimal and a fraction.

_____

Math Talk

There are 10 times as many hundredths as there are tenths. **Explain** how the model shows this.

Make Connections

The relationship of a digit in different place-value positions is the same with decimals as it is with whole numbers. You can use your understanding of place-value patterns and a place-value chart to write decimals that are 10 times as much as or $\frac{1}{10}$ of any given decimal.

Ones	•	Tenths	Hundredths	Thousandths
0		0	4	
		?	0.04	?

10 times as much

$\frac{1}{10}$ of

_____ is 10 times as much as 0.04.

_____ is $\frac{1}{10}$ of 0.04.

Use the steps below to complete the table.

STEP 1 Write the given decimal in a place-value chart.

STEP 2 Use the place-value chart to write a decimal that is 10 times as much as the given decimal.

STEP 3 Use the place-value chart to write a decimal that is $\frac{1}{10}$ of the given decimal.

Decimal	10 times as much as	$\frac{1}{10}$ of
0.03		
0.1		
0.07		

Math Talk
Mathematical Processes

Describe the pattern you see when you move one decimal place value to the right and one decimal place value to the left.

Share and Show

1. Write the decimal shown by the shaded part of the model.

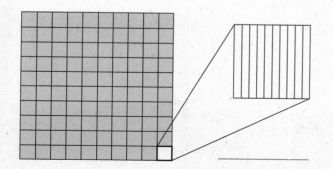

_____

Use place-value patterns to complete the table.

	Decimal	10 times as much as	$\frac{1}{10}$ of
2.	0.06		
3.	0.9		
4.	0.3		
5.	0.08		

Name _____

Problem Solving · Real World

Use the table for 6–9.

6. What is the value of the digit 2 in the carpenter bee's length?

   _____

7. If you made a model of a bumblebee that was 10 times as large as the actual bee, how long would the model be in meters? Write your answer as a decimal.

   _____

Bee Lengths (in meters)	
Bumblebee	0.019
Carpenter Bee	0.025
Leafcutting Bee	0.014
Orchid Bee	0.028
Sweat Bee	

8. **Record** The sweat bee's length is 6 thousandths of a meter. Complete the table by recording the sweat bee's length.

Write Math ▶ **Show Your Work** · ·

9. **H.O.T.** An atlas beetle is about 0.14 of a meter long. How does the length of the atlas beetle compare to the length of a leafcutting bee?

   _____

   _____

10. **H.O.T.** **Multi-Step** Terry, Sasha, and Harry each chose a number. Sasha's number is 10 times as much as Harry's number. Terry's number is 10 times as much as Sasha's number. Harry's number is 0.075. What number did each person choose?

    _____

11. **Write Math** ▶ **Explain** how you can use place value to describe how 0.05 and 0.005 compare.

    _____

    _____

    _____

    _____

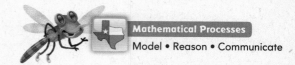
Daily Assessment Task

Fill in the bubble completely to show your answer.

12. A squirrel is 1.1 feet tall. The squirrel shrinks to $\frac{1}{10}$ of its height. How tall is the squirrel now?

    Ⓐ 11.0 feet

    Ⓑ 0.11 feet

    Ⓒ 1.10 feet

    Ⓓ 0.011 feet

13. **Use Diagrams** Write the decimal shown by the model.

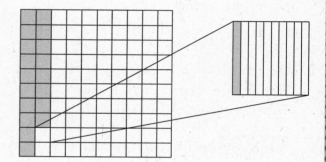

    Ⓐ 18.1

    Ⓑ 1.18

    Ⓒ 0.181

    Ⓓ 0.118

14. **Multi-Step** A chef uses 0.03 liter olive oil to make soup. He uses 10 times as much chicken broth as olive oil. He uses 10 times as much vegetable broth as chicken broth. How much vegetable broth does he use?

    Ⓐ 0.003 liter

    Ⓑ 0.03 liter

    Ⓒ 0.3 liter

    Ⓓ 3 liters

 TEXAS Test Prep

15. What is the relationship between 1.0 and 0.1?

    Ⓐ 0.1 is 10 times as much as 1.0

    Ⓑ 1.0 is $\frac{1}{10}$ of 0.1

    Ⓒ 0.1 is $\frac{1}{10}$ of 1.0

    Ⓓ 1.0 is equal to 0.1

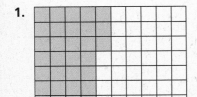
Name _____

1.2 Thousandths

Write the decimal shown by the shaded part of the model.

1.

_____

2.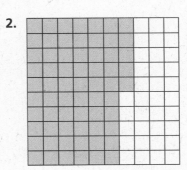

_____

Use place-value patterns to complete the table.

3.

Decimal	10 times as much as	$\frac{1}{10}$ of
0.08		
0.5		
0.2		
0.06		

4.

Decimal	10 times as much as	$\frac{1}{10}$ of
0.3		
0.07		
0.09		
0.1		

Problem Solving Real World

5. Andy makes a model of a new tool that is 0.24 meter long. His model is 10 times as large as the actual tool. How big is the model?

_____

6. Jamie makes a necklace with beads that are 0.08 meter long. Her next necklace will have beads that are $\frac{1}{10}$ the size of the beads of the first necklace. What will be the length of the beads for the second necklace?

_____

Fill in the bubble completely to show your answer.

7. What is the value of the digit 1 in the number 0.413?

  Ⓐ 1 tenth

  Ⓑ 1 hundredth

  Ⓒ 1 hundreds

  Ⓓ 1 tens

8. How does 0.03 compare to 0.003?

  Ⓐ 0.03 is 10 times as much as 0.003

  Ⓑ 0.03 is 100 times as much as 0.003

  Ⓒ 0.03 is $\frac{1}{10}$ of 0.003

  Ⓓ 0.03 is $\frac{1}{100}$ of 0.003

9. The ice on a pond is 0.03 meter thick. If the ice were 10 times as thick, how many meters thick would the ice be?

  Ⓐ 0.003 meter

  Ⓑ 0.3 meter

  Ⓒ 3 meters

  Ⓓ 3.03 meters

10. How does 0.008 compare to 0.08?

  Ⓐ 0.008 is 10 times as much as 0.08

  Ⓑ 0.008 is 100 times as much as 0.08

  Ⓒ 0.008 is $\frac{1}{10}$ of 0.08

  Ⓓ 0.008 is $\frac{1}{100}$ of 0.08

11. **Multi-Step** A green ribbon is 9 inches long. A red ribbon is $\frac{1}{10}$ the length of the green ribbon. A purple ribbon is 10 times as long as the red ribbon. What is the length of the purple ribbon?

  Ⓐ 0.09 inch

  Ⓑ 9 inches

  Ⓒ 0.9 inch

  Ⓓ 90 inches

12. **Multi-Step** Alan lives 10 times as far from school as Linda. Linda lives 0.7 mile from school. Jenny lives $\frac{1}{10}$ as far from school as Alan. Pedro lives $\frac{1}{10}$ as far from school as Jenny. How far from school does Pedro live?

  Ⓐ 7 miles

  Ⓑ 0.07 mile

  Ⓒ 70 miles

  Ⓓ 0.7 mile

1.3 Place Value of Decimals

 TEKS Number and
Operations—5.2.A
Also 5.2.B
MATHEMATICAL PROCESSES
5.1.D

? Essential Question

How do you read, write, and represent decimals through thousandths?

🔑 Unlock the Problem

The Brooklyn Battery Tunnel in New York City is 1.726 miles long. It is the longest underwater tunnel for vehicles in the United States. To understand this distance, you need to understand the place value of each digit in 1.726.

You can use a place-value chart to understand decimals. Whole numbers are to the left of the decimal point. Decimals are to the right of the decimal point. The thousandths place is to the right of the hundredths place.

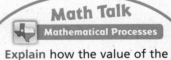
▲ The Brooklyn Battery Tunnel passes under the East River.

Tens	Ones	Tenths	Hundredths	Thousandths	
	1 •	7	2	6	
	1×1	$7 \times \frac{1}{10}$	$2 \times \frac{1}{100}$	$6 \times \frac{1}{1,000}$	} Value
	1.0	0.7	0.02	0.006	

The place value of the digit 6 in 1.726 is thousandths. The value of 6 in 1.726 is $6 \frac{1}{1,000}$, or 0.006.

Standard Form: 1.726
Word Form: one and seven hundred twenty-six thousandths

Expanded Form: $1 + 0.7 + 0.02 + 0.006$

Math Talk
Mathematical Processes

Explain how the value of the last digit in a decimal can help you read a decimal.

Try This! Use place value to read and write decimals.

Ⓐ **Standard Form:** 2.35
Word Form: two and _____

Expanded Form: 2 + _____

Ⓑ **Standard Form:** _____
Word Form: three and six hundred fourteen thousandths

Expanded Form: _____ + 0.6 + _____ + _____

1 **Example** Use place value to compare.

The silk spun by a common garden spider is about 0.003 millimeter thick. A commonly used sewing thread is about 0.3 millimeter thick. How does the thickness of the spider silk and the thread compare?

Count the number of decimal place-value positions to the digit 3 in 0.3 and 0.003.

0.3 has _____ fewer decimal places than 0.003

2 fewer decimal places: $10 \times 10 =$ _____

0.3 is _____ times as much as 0.003

0.003 is _____ of 0.3

So, the thread is _____ times as thick as the garden spider's silk. The thickness of the garden spider's silk is

_____ that of the thread.

Share and Show

1. Complete the place-value chart to find the value of each digit.

Ones	Tenths	Hundredths	Thousandths
3 •	5	2	4
3×1		$2 \times \frac{1}{100}$	
	0.5		

} Value

Write the value of the underlined digit.

2. 0.5<u>4</u>3

_____

3. 6.<u>2</u>34

_____

✅ **4.** 3.95<u>4</u>

_____

Write the number in two other forms.

5. 0.253

_____

_____

✅ **6.** 7.632

_____

_____

Name _____

7. Connect You can use place-value patterns to rename a decimal. Complete the chart to rename 0.3 using other place values.

8. **Write Math** ▶ **Explain** how you know that the digit 6 in the numbers 3.675 and 3.756 does not have the same value.

0.300	3 tenths	$3 \times \frac{1}{10}$
0.300	_____ hundredths	_____ $\times \frac{1}{100}$
0.300	_____	_____

_____

_____

_____

Problem Solving · Real World

Use the table for 9–11.

9. What is the value of the digit 7 in New Mexico's average annual rainfall?

_____

10. The average annual rainfall in Maine is one and seventy-four thousandths meters per year. Complete the table by writing that amount in standard form.

11. Which of the states has an average annual rainfall with the least number in the thousandths place?

Average Annual Rainfall (in meters)	
California	0.564
New Mexico	0.372
New York	1.041
Wisconsin	0.820
Maine	

Write Math ▶ **Show Your Work**

_____

12. **H.O.T.** **Multi-Step** Dan used a meter stick to measure some seedlings in his garden. One day, a corn stalk was 0.85 m tall. A tomato plant was 0.850 m. A carrot top was 0.085 m. Which plant was shortest?

_____

13. **H.O.T.** **What's the Error?** Damian wrote the number four and twenty-three thousandths as 4.23. **Describe** and correct his error.

_____

_____

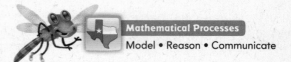
Daily Assessment Task

Fill in the bubble completely to show your answer.

14. Although the average turkey sandwich in Turkeyton costs 3.456 dollhorts, the cost of a gourmet turkey sandwich at Sandwich Palace is 5.032 dollhorts. What does the 3 in 5.032 dollhorts represent?

   (A) 3 dollhorts

   (B) 3 tenths of a dollhort

   (C) 3 hundredths of a dollhort

   (D) 4 hundredths of a dollhort

15. **Use Math Language** One meter is equal to about 3.281 feet. What is the word form of this decimal?

   (A) three and twenty-eight hundredths and one thousandth

   (B) three and two hundred eighty-one thousandths

   (C) three and two tenths and eighty-one thousandths

   (D) three point two eighty-one

16. **Multi-Step** Sam had a piece of ribbon 8.469 centimeters long. He cut off exactly one tenth of a centimeter from the ribbon. Then he cut off two hundredths of a centimeter. How long is the ribbon now?

   (A) 8.169 cm

   (B) 8.269 cm

   (C) 8.349 cm

   (D) 8.466 cm

TEXAS Test Prep

17. In 24.736, which digit is in the thousandths place?

   (A) 4

   (B) 7

   (C) 3

   (D) 6

Name _____

1.3   Place Value of Decimals

Rename 0.6 using other place values.

1.

0.600	6 tenths	$6 \times \frac{1}{10}$
0.600	_____ hundredths	_____ $\times \frac{1}{100}$
0.600	_____	_____

Rename 0.2 using other place values.

2.

0.200	2 tenths	$2 \times \frac{1}{10}$
0.200	20 _____	20 × _____
0.200	_____	_____

Write the number in two other forms.

3. 0.632

_____

_____

_____

4. 4.293

_____

_____

_____

Problem Solving Real World

5. A weather reporter reads aloud the number of meters of snowfall. The amount is 0.103 meter. What words should the reporter use on the air to explain the amount of snowfall?

_____

_____

6. Amil says that the snow on the ground is $5 \times \frac{1}{100}$ meter high. How can this number be expressed as a decimal?

_____

_____

Fill in the bubble completely to show your answer.

7. In the number 5.923, which number is in the thousandths place?

(A) 5

(B) 9

(C) 2

(D) 3

8. Which number has the same value as $7 \times \frac{1}{1,000}$?

(A) 0.7

(B) 0.007

(C) 0.07

(D) 7.0

9. **Multi-Step** Which value correctly represents the number that is 10 times as great as five hundred eighty-one thousandths?

(A) 5.81

(B) 581

(C) 0.581

(D) 500.81

10. Which number has the same value as $3 \times \frac{1}{10}$?

(A) 0.003

(B) 3.10

(C) 0.3

(D) 0.03

11. Jack's baby sister crawled three and five tenths meters today. Which number represents that distance?

(A) 3.5

(B) 3.05

(C) 3.510

(D) 3.005

12. **Multi-Step** Leon measured the distance each of his four toy cars rolled across the floor. Which car measurement that has a 4 in the thousandths place represents the shortest distance rolled?

(A) 0.741 meter

(B) 0.714 meter

(C) 0.224 meter

(D) 0.213 meter

Name _____

 1.4 **Compare and Order Decimals**

 Essential Question

How can you use place value to compare and order decimals?

🔑 Unlock the Problem

The table lists some of the mountains in the United States that are over two miles high. How does the height of Cloud Peak in Wyoming compare to the height of Boundary Peak in Nevada?

Mountain Heights	
Mountain and State	**Height (in miles)**
Boundary Peak, Nevada	2.488
Cloud Peak, Wyoming	2.495
Grand Teton Peak, Wyoming	2.607
Wheeler Peak, New Mexico	2.493

🔒 One Way Use place value.

Line up the decimal points. Start at the left. Compare the digits in each place-value position until the digits are different.

STEP 1 Compare the ones.

2.495
↓   2 = 2
2.488

STEP 2 Compare the tenths.

2.495
↓   4 ◯ 4
2.488

STEP 3 Compare the hundredths.

2.495
↓   9 ◯ 8
2.488

Since 9 ◯ 8, then 2.495 ◯ 2.488, and 2.488 ◯ 2.495.

So, the height of Cloud Peak is _____
the height of Boundary Peak.

🔒 Another Way Use a place-value chart to compare.

Compare the height of Cloud Peak to Wheeler Peak.

Ones	•	Tenths	Hundredths	Thousandths
2	•	4	9	5
2	•	4	9	3

2 = 2   4 = _____   9 = _____   5 > _____

Since 5 ◯ 3, then 2.495 ◯ 2.493, and 2.493 ◯ 2.495.

So, the height of Cloud Peak is _____
the height of Wheeler Peak.

Math Talk

Mathematical Processes

Explain why it is important to line up the decimal points when comparing decimals.

Order Decimals You can use place value to order decimal numbers.

🔒 Example

Mount Whitney in California is 2.745 miles high, Mount Rainier in Washington is 2.729 miles high, and Mount Harvard in Colorado is 2.731 miles high. Order the heights of these mountains from least to greatest. Which mountain has the least height? Which mountain has the greatest height?

STEP 1

Line up the decimal points. There are the same number of ones. Circle the tenths and compare.

2.745   **Whitney**

2.729   **Rainier**

2.731   **Harvard**

There are the same number of tenths.

STEP 2

Underline the hundredths and compare. Order from least to greatest.

2.745   **Whitney**

2.729   **Rainier**

2.731   **Harvard**

Since ◯ < ◯ < ◯ , the heights in order from least to

greatest are _____ , _____ , _____ .

So, _____ has the least height and

_____ has the greatest height.

Math Talk

Mathematical Processes

Explain why you do not have to compare the digits in the thousandths place to order the heights of the 3 mountains.

Share and Show

 MATH BOARD

1. Use the place-value chart to compare the two numbers. What is the greatest place-value position where the digits differ?

Ones	Tenths	Hundredths	Thousandths
3	4	7	2
3	4	4	5

_____

Compare. Write <, >, or =.

2. 4.563 ◯ 4.536

3. 5.640 ◯ 5.64

☑ 4. 8.673 ◯ 8.637

Name the greatest place-value position where the digits differ. Name the greater number.

5. 3.579; 3.564

_____

6. 9.572; 9.637

_____

☑ 7. 4.159; 4.152

_____

Name _____

Order from greatest to least.

8. 2.007; 2.714; 2.09; 2.97

9. 0.386; 0.3; 0.683; 0.836

_____

_____

 Algebra Find the unknown digit to make each statement true.

10. 3.59 > 3.5 ☐ 1 > 3.572

11. 6.837 > 6.83 ☐ > 6.835

12. 2.45 < 2. ☐ 6 < 2.461

13. Dawn keeps track of her softball batting average each year. The first year, her batting average is .783. The second year, her batting average is .81. In which year did she have the greater batting average?

_____

Problem Solving (Real World)

Use the table for 14–16.

14. Use Math Language How does the height of Steele Mountain compare to the height of Blackburn Mountain? Compare the heights using words.

Mountains Over Three Miles High	
Mountain and Location	**Height (in miles)**
Blackburn, Alaska	3.104
Bona, Alaska	3.134
Steele, Yukon	3.152

_____

_____

15. Write Math ▶ **Explain** how to order the height of the mountains from greatest to least.

_____

_____

_____

16. H.O.T. Multi-Step What if the height of Blackburn Mountain were 0.05 mile greater. Would it then be the mountain with the greatest height? **Explain.**

_____

_____

Daily Assessment Task

Fill in the bubble completely to show your answer.

17. The length of a piece of plastic for a science kit needs to be greater than 22.4 inches and less than 22.5 inches. Which length of plastic can be used?

    (A) 22.35 in   (C) 22.47 in.

    (B) 22.51 in   (D) 22.40 in.

18. Louis is comparing the numbers 8.402 and 8.451. What is the least place value he needs to compare to decide which number is greater?

    (A) ones

    (B) tenths

    (C) hundredths

    (D) thousandths

19. **Multi-Step** Melinda compares four numbers. Which shows the numbers from least to greatest?

    (A) 3.04; 3.10; 3.529; 3.685

    (B) 3.10; 3.04; 3.529; 3.685

    (C) 3.10; 3.04; 3.685; 3.529

    (D) 3.04; 3.685; 3.529; 3.10

 TEXAS Test Prep

20. Mount Logan in the Yukon is 3.702 miles high. Mount McKinley in Alaska is 3.848 miles high and Pico de Orizaba in Mexico is 3.571 miles high. Order these mountains by height from greatest to least.

    (A) Logan, McKinley, Pico de Orizaba

    (B) McKinley, Logan, Pico de Orizaba

    (C) Pico de Orizaba, Logan, McKinley

    (D) Logan, Pico de Orizaba, McKinley

Name _____

1.5 Round Decimals

? Essential Question

How can you use place value to round decimals to a given place?

🔑 Unlock the Problem (Real World)

The Gold Frog of South America is one of the smallest frogs in the world. It is 0.386 of an inch long. What is this length rounded to the nearest hundredth of an inch?

• Underline the length of the Gold Frog.
• Is the frog's length about the same as the length or the width of a large paper clip?

_____

🔓 One Way Use a place-value chart.

• Write the number in a place-value chart and circle the digit in the place value to which you want to round.

• In the place-value chart, underline the digit to the right of the place to which you are rounding.

• If the digit to the right is less than 5, the digit in the place value to which you are rounding stays the same. If the digit to the right is 5 or greater, the digit in the rounding place increases by 1.

• Drop the digits after the place to which you are rounding.

So, to the nearest hundredth of an inch, a Gold Frog is

about _____ of an inch long.

Ones	Tenths	Hundredths	Thousandths
0	3	8	6

Think: Does the digit in the rounding place stay the same or increase by 1?

🔓 Another Way Use place value.

The Little Grass Frog is the smallest frog in North America.
It is 0.437 of an inch long.

A **What is the length of the frog to the nearest hundredth of an inch?**

0.437   7 > 5
↓
0.44

So, to the nearest hundredth of an inch, the frog is

about _____ of an inch long.

B **What is the length of the frog to the nearest tenth of an inch?**

0.437   3 < 5
↓
0.4

So, to the nearest tenth of an inch, the frog is about

_____ of an inch long.

Write the place value of the underlined digit. Round each number to the place of the underlined digit.

1. 0.6<u>7</u>3

✓ 2. 4.<u>2</u>82

3. 1<u>2</u>.917

_____

_____

_____

_____

_____

_____

Name the place value to which each number was rounded.

4. 0.982 to 0.98

5. 3.695 to 4

✓ 6. 7.486 to 7.5

_____

_____

_____

Problem Solving

Write the place value of the underlined digit. Round each number to the place of the underlined digit.

7. 0.<u>5</u>92

8. <u>6</u>.518

9. 0.8<u>0</u>9

_____

_____

_____

_____

_____

_____

Round 16.748 to the place named.

10. tenths _____

11. hundredths _____

12. ones _____

13. **Write Math** ▶ **Explain** why any number less than 12.5 and greater than or equal to 11.5 would round to 12 when rounded to the nearest whole number.

_____

_____

_____

14. **Write Math** ▶ **Explain** what happens when you round 4.999 to the nearest tenth.

_____

_____

30

Name _____

Problem Solving Real World

Use the table for 15–18.

Insect Speeds (meters per second)	
Insect	**Speed**
Dragonfly	6.974
Horsefly	3.934
Bumblebee	2.861
Honeybee	2.548
Housefly	1.967

15. The speeds of two insects when rounded to the nearest whole number are the same. Which two insects are they?

_____

16. What is the speed of the housefly rounded to the nearest hundredth?

_____

17. The speed of an insect is about 3.9 meters per second. Which insect could it be?

_____

Write Math ▶ **Show Your Work** · · · · · ·

18. **H.O.T.** **What's the Error?** Mark said that the speed of a dragonfly rounded to the nearest tenth was 6.9 meters per second. Is he correct? If not, what is his error?

_____

_____

19. **H.O.T.** **Multi-Step** A rounded number for the speed of an insect is 5.67 meters per second. What are the fastest and slowest speeds to the thousandths that could round to 5.67? **Explain**.

_____

_____

_____

_____

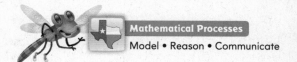
Daily Assessment Task

Fill in the bubble completely to show your answer.

20. Chef Round uses 1.257 kilograms of meat for his famous meatballs. There are four packages at the market. Which amount is closest to 1.257 kilograms?

    (A) 1.26 kg

    (B) 1.2 kg

    (C) 1.3 kg

    (D) 1.35 kg

21. **Representations** The table shows the neck lengths for four giraffes in the Long-Necked Friends Sanctuary. Which two giraffes have necks that are the same length when rounded to the nearest tenth?

    (A) Spot and Stretch

    (B) Mittens and Spot

    (C) Mittens and Stretch

    (D) Spot and Zippy

Giraffe's Name	Neck Length (feet)
Mittens	5.632
Spot	5.725
Stretch	5.405
Zippy	5.657

22. **Multi-Step** Janis sells friendship bracelets at a fair. She has three bracelets that are 16.53 cm, 16.755 cm, and 16.55 cm long. She wants to label the lengths to the nearest tenth of a centimeter. In order, how should she label the bracelets?

    (A) 16.5 cm, 16.76 cm, 16.6 cm

    (B) 16.6 cm, 16.7 cm, 16.5 cm

    (C) 16.5 cm, 16.8 cm, 16.6 cm

    (D) 16.3 cm, 16.5 cm, 16.5 cm

⭐ TEXAS Test Prep

23. To which place value is the number rounded?

    6.706 to 6.71

    (A) ones

    (B) tenths

    (C) hundredths

    (D) thousandths

32

Name _____

1.6 Estimate Decimal Sums and Differences

TEKS Number and Operations—5.3.A
MATHEMATICAL PROCESSES
5.1.C

Essential Question

How can you estimate decimal sums and differences?

Unlock the Problem

A singer is recording a CD. The lengths of the three songs are 3.4 minutes, 2.78 minutes, and 4.19 minutes. About how much recording time will be on the CD?

 Use rounding to estimate.

Round to the nearest whole number. Then add.

$$
\begin{array}{rr}
3.4 & 3 \\
2.78 & \\
+\,4.19 & + \\
\hline
&
\end{array}
$$

Remember

To round a number, determine the place to which you want to round.

- If the digit to the right is less than 5, the digit in the rounding place stays the same.
- If the digit to the right is 5 or greater, the digit in the rounding place increases by 1.

So, there will be about _____ minutes of recording time on the CD.

Try This! Use rounding to estimate.

A Round to the nearest whole dollar. Then subtract.

$$
\begin{array}{rr}
\$27.95 & \\
-\,\$11.72 & - \\
\hline
&
\end{array}
$$

To the nearest dollar,
$27.95 − $11.72 is about _____.

B Round to the nearest ten dollars. Then subtract.

$$
\begin{array}{rr}
\$27.95 & \\
-\,\$11.72 & - \\
\hline
&
\end{array}
$$

To the nearest ten dollars,
$27.95 − $11.72 is about _____.

- Do you want an overestimate or an underestimate when you estimate the total cost of items you want to buy? **Explain**.

_____

_____

Use Benchmarks Benchmarks are familiar numbers used as points of reference. You can use the benchmarks 0, 0.25, 0.50, 0.75, and 1 to estimate decimal sums and differences.

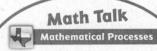 **Example** Use benchmarks to estimate. 0.76 − 0.22

Locate and graph a point on the number line for each decimal. Identify which benchmark each decimal is closer to.

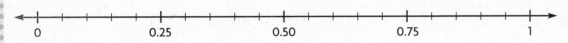

0	0.25	0.50	0.75	1

Think: 0.76 is between _____ and

_____. It is closer to _____.

Think: 0.22 is between 0 and 0.25. It is

closer to _____.

$$0.76 - 0.22$$
$$\downarrow \qquad \downarrow$$
$$\_\_\_\_\_ - \_\_\_\_\_ = \_\_\_\_\_$$

So, 0.76 − 0.22 is about _____.

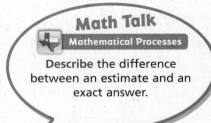

Math Talk
Mathematical Processes
Use the Example to **explain** how using rounding or benchmarks to estimate a decimal difference can give you different answers.

Share and Show MATH BOARD

Use rounding to estimate.

1.
```
   2.34
   1.9
 + 5.23
```

2.
```
  10.39
 − 4.28
```

3.
```
  $19.75
 + $ 3.98
```

Use benchmarks to estimate.

4.
```
   0.34
   0.1
 + 0.25
```

5.
```
  10.39
 − 4.28
```

Math Talk
Mathematical Processes
Describe the difference between an estimate and an exact answer.

36

Name _____

Problem Solving

Use rounding or benchmarks to estimate.

6.
$$0.93$$
$$+0.18$$

7.
$$8.12$$
$$+5.52$$

8.
$$9.75$$
$$-3.47$$

Practice: Copy and Solve Use rounding or benchmarks to estimate.

9. $12.83 + 16.24$

10. $\$26.92 - \$11.13$

11. $9.41 + 3.82$

 Estimate to compare. Write < or >.

12. $2.74 + 4.22$ ◯ $3.13 + 1.87$

_____ _____
estimate   estimate

13. $6.25 - 2.39$ ◯ $9.79 - 3.84$

_____ _____
estimate   estimate

Problem Solving

Use the table to solve 14. Show your work.

14. **Representations** For the week of April 4, 1964, the Beatles had the top four songs. About how long would it take to listen to these four songs?

_____

Use the table and estimation to solve 15–16.

15. **Representations** Gina had a scrambled egg, an oat bran muffin, and a cup of low-fat milk for breakfast. About how many grams of protein did Gina have at breakfast?

_____

16. **H.O.T.** **Multi-Step** Pablo had a cup of shredded wheat cereal, a cup of low-fat milk, and one other item for breakfast. He had about 21 grams of protein. What was the third item Pablo had for breakfast?

_____

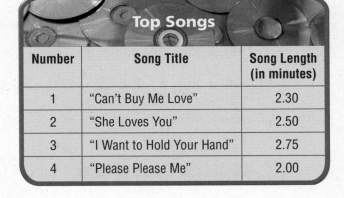

Top Songs

Number	Song Title	Song Length (in minutes)
1	"Can't Buy Me Love"	2.30
2	"She Loves You"	2.50
3	"I Want to Hold Your Hand"	2.75
4	"Please Please Me"	2.00

Grams of Protein per Serving

Type of Food	Protein (in grams)
1 scrambled egg	6.75
1 cup shredded wheat cereal	5.56
1 oat bran muffin	3.99
1 cup low-fat milk	8.22

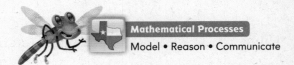
Daily Assessment Task

Fill in the bubble completely to show your answer.

17. **Multi-Step** Marco has room for 15 more minutes of songs on his mp3 player. He has three songs to upload with the following lengths: 5.15 minutes, 3.8 minutes, and 4.4 minutes. After uploading all three songs, about how many minutes will he have left?

    (A) 3 minutes   (C) 2 minutes

    (B) 1 minute   (D) 0 minutes

18. **Connect** Geoff and Andrea want to combine their money to buy pizza. Geoff has $5.95. Andrea has $8.30. Which benchmarks should they use to estimate the money they have?

    (A) $6.00 + $8.25   (C) $6.00 + $8.50

    (B) $5.75 + $8.00   (D) $5.00 + $8.00

19. **Multi-Step** Maiko wrote two songs. The first song was 2.9 minutes long. Then he added 0.4 minute. The second song was 5.6 minutes long. Then he subtracted 1.1 minutes from it. Use benchmarks to estimate the length of each song.

    (A) first song: 2.5 minutes, second song: 4 minutes

    (B) first song: 3.5 minutes, second song: 4.5 minutes

    (C) first song: 3.5 minutes, second song: 7 minutes

    (D) first song: 2.5 minutes, second song: 5.5 minutes

 TEXAS Test Prep

20. Fran bought sneakers for $54.26 and a shirt for $34.34. If Fran started with $100, about how much money does she have left?

    (A) $35

    (B) $20

    (C) $5

    (D) $80

Homework and Practice

Name _____

1.6 Estimate Decimal Sums and Differences

Use rounding or benchmarks to estimate.

1. 3.39
    + 4.58

2. 6.77
    + 3.23

3. 2.09
    + 5.92

4. 9.76
    − 3.28

5. 7.36
    − 0.83

6. 5.55
    − 0.25

Estimate to compare. Write < or >.

7. 8.23 + 2.22 ◯ 3.21 + 5.89

    _____   _____
    estimate   estimate

8. 7.32 − 3.76 ◯ 9.23 − 4.28

    _____   _____
    estimate   estimate

9. $18.25 + $5.50 ◯ $10.75 + $15.00

    _____   _____
    estimate   estimate

10. 6.2 − 4.8 ◯ 7.23 − 5.08

    _____   _____
    estimate   estimate

Problem Solving

11. Li is running a race around the school track. He runs 0.327 kilometer during the first half of the race. What is the distance that he travels in the first half of the race, rounded to the nearest hundredth?

    _____

12. A video lasts 6.44 minutes. About how long does the video last, rounded to the nearest minute?

    _____

Fill in the bubble completely to show your answer.

13. Dylan wants to buy a book for $16.95 and a magazine for $4.50. About how much will he need to buy the items without having to round down to the nearest benchmark?

Ⓐ $15

Ⓑ $30

Ⓒ $25

Ⓓ $20

14. Sasha downloads a song that is 4.32 minutes long and one that is 8.28 minutes long. About how many minutes will it take all of her songs to play if she already has 13.8 minutes of songs?

Ⓐ 15 minutes

Ⓑ 30 minutes

Ⓒ 20 minutes

Ⓓ 26 minutes

15. Mike spends $23.40 on a present for his mom and a $18.95 on a present for his dad. If Mike started with $75, about how much money does he have left?

Ⓐ $30

Ⓑ $50

Ⓒ $20

Ⓓ $40

16. Danielle and Raj want to combine their money to buy a soccer ball. Danielle has $7.95. Raj has $6.35. Which benchmarks should they use to estimate the money they have?

Ⓐ $7.75 + $6.50

Ⓑ $8.00 + $6.25

Ⓒ $7.50 + $6.50

Ⓓ $6.00 + $6.50

17. **Multi-Step** Jesse, Max, and Kalel each ate 0.32 of a pizza pie. Which number shows the best estimate of how much of the pie they ate together?

Ⓐ 1.0

Ⓑ 0.5

Ⓒ 0.25

Ⓓ 0.10

18. **Multi-Step** George is giving two speeches at school. The first was 3.4 minutes long. Then he added 0.9 minutes to the speech. The second speech was 4.1 minutes long. Then he subtracted 1.4 minutes from it. Use benchmarks to estimate the length of each speech.

Ⓐ first speech: 4.0 minutes; second speech: 3.5 minutes

Ⓑ first speech: 4.0 minutes; second speech: 3 minutes

Ⓒ first speech: 4.5 minutes; second speech: 2.5 minutes

Ⓓ first speech: 4.5 minutes; second speech: 3.5 minutes

1.7 Add and Subtract Decimals Through Thousandths

TEKS Number and Operations—5.3.K
Also 5.3.A

MATHEMATICAL PROCESSES
5.1.C, 5.1.E

? Essential Question

How can you record addition and subtraction of decimals through thousandths?

🔑 Unlock the Problem

At the 2010 Winter Olympics, Armin Zoeggeler won the bronze medal in the men's luge event. In his fastest run, he completed the first interval in 21.261 seconds. It took him another 27.198 seconds to reach the finish line. What was Zoeggeler's finish time?

- Underline the sentence that tells you what you are trying to find.
- Circle the numbers you need to use.

🔒 **Add decimals through thousandths. 21.261 + 27.198**

THINK	RECORD
• Line up the numbers in each place.	
• First, add the thousandths.	
• Then, add the hundredths, tenths, ones, and tens. Regroup as needed.	
• Place the decimal point in the sum.	

So, Zoeggeler's finish time was _____ seconds.

Math Talk

Mathematical Processes

Why would you use paper and pencil instead of mental math to solve this problem?

Try This! **Use subtraction to check your work. Subtract one of the addends from the sum.**

Addition and subtraction are opposite, or **inverse operations**. You can use subtraction to check your answer to an addition problem.

← The difference should equal the other addend.

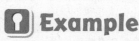 **Example**

Zoeggeler finished the first half of the run in 31.116 seconds. The second half took only 17.343 seconds. How many seconds faster was the second half of the run?

Estimate. 31 − 17 = _____

STEP 1	**STEP 2**	**STEP 3**
Line up the place values. Subtract the thousandths.	Subtract the hundredths. Subtract the tenths. Regroup as needed.	Subtract the ones and tens. Place the decimal point in the difference.
$$\begin{array}{r} 31.116 \\ -17.343 \\ \hline 3 \end{array}$$	$$\begin{array}{r} 31.116 \\ -17.343 \\ \hline 3 \end{array}$$	$$\begin{array}{r} 31.116 \\ -17.343 \\ \hline 773 \end{array}$$

So, Zoeggeler was _____ seconds faster in the second half of the run.

To check subtraction using the inverse operation, add the number you subtracted to the difference. The sum should equal the number you subtracted from.

 **Math Talk**

Mathematical Processes

Explain how you know without adding that the sum of 2.475 and 6.43 will result in a 5 in the thousandths place.

Try This! Subtract. Then check your work.

$$\begin{array}{r} 4\ 2.7\ 8\ 4 \\ -\ \ \ 6.9\ 8\ 0 \\ \hline \end{array}$$

$$\begin{array}{r} +\ \ \ 6.9\ 8\ 0 \\ \hline \end{array}$$

Share and Show

Find the sum or difference.

1.
$$\begin{array}{r} 1.845 \\ -0.357 \\ \hline \end{array}$$

2. $3.46 + 6.834$

☑ **3.** $13 - 0.943$

☑ **4.**
$$\begin{array}{r} 0.254 \\ 1.3 \\ +0.79 \\ \hline \end{array}$$

Name _____

Problem Solving

Find the sum or difference.

5. 3.704
    −1.325

6. 14.467
    +12.33

7. 23.002
    − 1.74

8. 9.94
    0.318
    + 1.283

Practice: Copy and Solve Find the sum or difference.

9. $21.54 + 4.758$

10. $6.328 − 3.62$

11. $15.87 − 3.274$

12. $2.45 + 3.247 + 1.8$

 Algebra Find the unknown numbers in the pattern.
Then write a description for the pattern.

13. 2.1, 3.3, 4.5, 5.7, _____, 8.1, _____

Description: _____

14. 4.05, 4.00, 3.95, _____, 3.85, _____

Description: _____

Problem Solving Real World

Use the table to solve 15–16.

15. **Evaluate** Apolo Ohno won the men's 500-meter speed skating final at the 2006 Winter Olympics. His time for the race was 41.935 seconds. Francois-Louis Tremblay came in second, finishing 0.067 second behind Ohno. What was Tremblay's time?

_____

Men's 500-Meter Speed Skating Final	
Skater	**Time (in seconds)**
A. Ohno	41.935
F. Tremblay	▪
H. Ahn	42.089
E. Bedard	42.039
J. Eley	42.497

16. **Apply** Jon Eley came in fifth in the men's speed skating final. How many seconds after Apolo Ohno did Eley finish?

Write Math ▶ **Show Your Work** · · · · · · ·

17.  **Multi-Step** The sum of two numbers is 4.004. One number has a 4 in the tenths place and a 3 in the thousandths place. The other number has a 1 in the ones place and an 8 in the hundredths place. What are the two numbers?

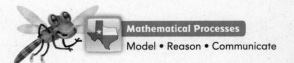

Daily Assessment Task

Fill in the bubble completely to show your answer.

18. **Multi-Step** Team A spent 61.242 seconds and 59.438 seconds running a relay race. Team B spent 60.561 seconds and 60.289 seconds running the relay race. Which statement is true?

    (A) Team A won by 0.17 second.　　(C) Team A won by 1.17 seconds.

    (B) Team B won by 0.17 second.　　(D) Team B won by 1.17 seconds.

19. Manuel is walking from his home to his school. He has walked 0.142 mile so far and has 0.088 mile left to walk. How far is Manuel's home from school?

    (A) 0.054 mile

    (B) 0.12 mile

    (C) 0.23 mile

    (D) 1.022 miles

20. **Multi-Step** Music & Movie Mart is selling used CDs for $6.99 each and used DVDs for $8.49 each. You have $30 to spend. Which of these combinations could you buy?

    (A) Two CDs and two DVDs

    (B) Three CDs and one DVD

    (C) Three CDs and three DVDs

    (D) One CD and three DVDs

⭐ TEXAS Test Prep

21. Toni has a ribbon that is 2.75 meters long. She cuts off 0.345 meter. How much of the ribbon does Toni have left?

    (A) 3.095 meters

    (B) 2.715 meters

    (C) 2.785 meters

    (D) 2.405 meters

1.7 Add and Subtract Decimals Through Thousandths

Find the sum or difference.

1. 13.87
    + 6.06

2. 26.25
    − 5.73

3. 2.50
    + 0.926

4. 43.66
    − 9.08

5. 6.27
    0.133
    + 4.31

6. 25.75
    − 8.2

Find the sum or difference.

7. 6.389 + 17.39

8. 8.747 − 4.8

9. 2.09 + 12.639

**Find the unknown numbers in the pattern.
Then write a description for the pattern**

10. 1.0, 2.1, 3.2, 4.3. _____ 6.5, 7.6

Description: _____

11. 5.03, 5.00, 4.97, 4.94 _____ 4.88

Description: _____

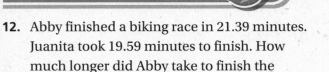

Problem Solving Real World

12. Abby finished a biking race in 21.39 minutes. Juanita took 19.59 minutes to finish. How much longer did Abby take to finish the race than Juanita?

_____

13. The sum of two numbers is 5.036. One number has a 4 in the tenths place and a 7 in the thousandths place. The other number has a 1 in the ones place and an 2 in the hundredths place. What are the two numbers?

_____

Fill in the bubble completely to show your answer.

14. Dara spends $13.02 on sandals, $9.85 on shorts, and $15.20 on a hat. How much change does she receive back from $50?
- (A) $10.93
- (B) $11.93
- (C) $11.34
- (D) $12.67

15. Ling's relay team ran the first part of the race in 28.134 seconds, the second part in 17.922 seconds, and the third part in 34.023 seconds. By how much did the relay team beat the champions, who ran the race in 83.736 seconds?
- (A) 3.412 seconds
- (B) 3.657 seconds
- (C) 3.327 seconds
- (D) 4.073 seconds

16. Juan has a batting average of 0.334. Gary has a batting average of 0.284. What is the difference between the batting averages of the two baseball players?
- (A) 0.50
- (B) 0.05
- (C) 0.028
- (D) 0.042

17. Jonas is jogging from the park to the school. He has jogged 0.424 mile so far. He has 0.384 mile left to jog. How far is the park located away from the school?
- (A) 0.730 mile
- (B) 0.808 mile
- (C) 1.032 miles
- (D) 0.40 mile

18. **Multi-Step** Jimmie adds 3.24, 4.294, and 2.073. How much more than 5.31 is the sum?
- (A) 4.297
- (B) 9.607
- (C) 4.607
- (D) 4.477

19. **Multi-Step** A gallon of milk costs $3.32 and a container of orange juice costs $2.95. Max buys two gallons of milk and two containers of orange juice. How much does Max spend?
- (A) $123.69
- (B) $6.64
- (C) $12.54
- (D) $6.27

Name _____

 Essential Question

How can the strategy *make a table* help you organize and keep track of your bank account balance?

Unlock the Problem (Real World)

At the end of May, Mrs. Freeman had an account balance of $442.37. Since then, she has written a check for $63.92 and made a deposit of $350.00. Mrs. Freeman says she has $729.45 in her account. Make a table to determine if Mrs. Freeman is correct.

Read

What do I need to find?

I need to find _____

_____

What information am I given?

I am given the _____

_____

_____

Plan

What is my plan or strategy?

I need to make a table and use the information to

_____

_____

_____

Solve

Mrs. Freeman's Checkbook			
May balance			$442.37
Check	$63.92		−$63.92
Deposit		$350.00	

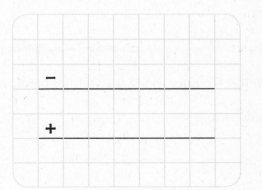

Mrs. Freeman's correct balance is _____.

---

1. How can you tell if your answer is reasonable? _____

_____

Nick is buying juice for himself and 5 friends. Each bottle of juice costs $1.25.
How much do 6 bottles of juice cost? Make a table to find the cost of
6 bottles of juice.

Use the graphic below to solve the problem.

Read	Solve
What do I need to find?	
What information am I given?	
Plan	
What is my plan or strategy?	
	So, the total cost of 6 bottles of juice is _____.

2. **What if** Ginny says that 12 bottles of juice cost $25.00? Is Ginny's

statement reasonable? **Explain.** _____

_____

_____

3. If Nick had $10, how many bottles of juice could he buy?

_____

Math Talk
Mathematical Processes

Explain how you could use another strategy to solve the problem.

Name _____

Share and Show

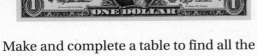

1. Sara wants to buy a bottle of apple juice from a vending machine. She needs exactly $2.30. She has the following bills and coins:

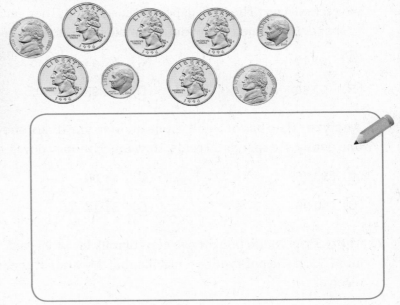

Make and complete a table to find all the ways Sara could pay for the juice.

First, draw a table with a column for each type of bill or coin.

Next, fill in your table with each row showing a different way Sara can make exactly $2.30.

2. **What if** Sara decides to buy a bottle of water that costs $1.85? What are all the different ways she can make exactly $1.85 with the bills and coins she has? Which coin must Sara use?

_____

Problem Solving Real World

Use the following information to solve 3–4.

At Open Skate Night, admission is $3.75 with a membership card and $5.00 without a membership card. Skate rentals are $3.00.

3. **H.O.T.** **Multi-Step** The Moores paid $6 more for skate rentals than the Cotters did. Together, the two families paid $30 for skate rentals. How many pairs of skates did the Moores rent?

_____

4. **H.O.T.** **Multi-Step** Jennie and 5 of her friends are going to Open Skate Night. Jennie does not have a membership card. Only some of her friends have membership cards. What is the total amount that Jennie and her friends might pay for admission?

_____

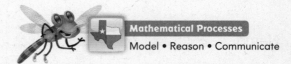
Daily Assessment Task

Fill in the bubble completely to show your answer.

5. **Apply** Sherry and Mario want to buy a pack of pencils to split for the new school year. The pack of pencils costs $3.68. They each have $1.25 to spend. How much more money do they need to buy the pencils?

   (A) $1.18   (C) $2.43

   (B) $2.50   (D) $4.93

6. **Analyze** Marc has one dollar, one quarter, one dime, one nickel, and one penny. He spends 35 cents. How much money does he have left?

   (A) $0.76   (C) $1.06

   (B) $0.96   (D) $1.16

7. **Multi-Step** Maria bought two cups of milk for $1.09 each, and a salad for $7.75. If she pays with a ten-dollar bill, how much change does she receive?

   (A) $0.07

   (B) $1.16

   (C) $2.25

   (D) $7.82

 TEXAS Test Prep

8. Sean and Hope are going bowling. For each person, a game costs $4.25. Shoe rentals are $3.00. Sean gives the clerk $20 for their admission and shoe rental. How much change should he receive?

   (A) $12.75

   (B) $5.50

   (C) $9.75

   (D) $14.50

Homework and Practice

Name _____

1.8 PROBLEM SOLVING • Add and Subtract Money

1. Sam wants to buy a snack from a vending machine. He needs exactly $3.20. Complete the table to find the different ways Sam could pay for the snack.

$1 bills	Quarters	Dimes	Nickels	Value
3				$3.20
2				$3.20
2				$3.20
2				$3.20

2. Mandy is buying popcorn for herself and 5 friends. Each bag of popcorn costs $0.95. How much do 6 bags of popcorn cost? Complete the table to find the total cost.

Bags of Popcorn	1	2	3	4	5	6
Total	$0.95					

3. Orlando is buying 6 bottles of water. Each bottle of water costs $1.19. How much do 6 bottles of water cost? Complete the table to find the total cost.

Bottles of Water	1	2	3	4	5	6
Total	$1.19					

Problem Solving

4. At the end of September, Ms. Diaz had an account balance of $623.41. Since then, she has written checks for $149.00 and $27.50, and made a deposit of $299.00. Ms. Diaz says her balance is $845.91. Find Ms. Diaz's correct balance.

_____

Fill in the bubble completely to show your answer.

5. One shirt costs $7.90. What is the price of 4 shirts?

Ⓐ $31.60

Ⓑ $28.36

Ⓒ $32.10

Ⓓ $31.42

6. **Multi-Step** Jorge's checking account balance is $458.00 He writes a check for $89.20 and donates $20.00 to a local charity. Then he makes a deposit for $92.19. What is his new checking account total?

Ⓐ $440.99

Ⓑ $398.80

Ⓒ $480.99

Ⓓ $256.61

7. **Multi-Step** Theodore buys a sandwich for $4.47 and two salads for $5.10 each. If he pays with a $20 bill, how much change does he receive?

Ⓐ $5.24

Ⓑ $5.21

Ⓒ $5.19

Ⓓ $5.33

8. **Multi-Step** Carleen has three quarters, four dimes, and three nickels. She spends 55 cents. How much money does she have left?

Ⓐ $0.80

Ⓑ $0.75

Ⓒ $0.60

Ⓓ $0.85

9. **Multi-Step** Mr. Lee has a balance of $237.35 after he wrote two checks. One check was for $350.40 and the other was for $211.25. What was his balance before he wrote the checks?

Ⓐ $597

Ⓑ $799

Ⓒ $561

Ⓓ $780

10. **Multi-Step** Andrew bought balloons for his dad's birthday for $5.30. The tax on the balloons is $0.83. If he pays with a $10 bill, how much change does he receive?

Ⓐ $3.78

Ⓑ $3.97

Ⓒ $3.87

Ⓓ $3.56

Name _____

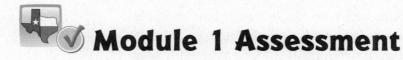
Vocabulary

Choose the best term from the box.

Vocabulary
Commutative Property
Distributive Property
inverse operation
thousandth

1. The _____ states that multiplying a sum by a number is the same as multiplying each addend in the sum by the number and then adding the products. (p. 4)

2. If one hundredth is divided into ten equal parts, each part is one

   _____. (p. 7)

Concepts and Skills

Write the value of the underlined digit. ⬤ TEKS 5.2.A

3. 6.5<u>4</u>

4. 0.8<u>3</u>7

5. 8.70<u>2</u>

6. <u>9</u>.173

_____

_____

Compare. Write <, >, or =. ⬤ TEKS 5.2.B

7. 6.52 ◯ 6.520

8. 3.589 ◯ 3.598

9. 8.463 ◯ 8.483

Write the place value of the underlined digit. Round each number to the place of the underlined digit. ⬤ TEKS 5.2.C

10. 0.<u>7</u>24

11. <u>2</u>.576

12. 4.7<u>6</u>9

_____

_____

Complete the equation, and tell which property you used. ⬤ TEKS 5.3.K

13. $8 \times (14 + 7) =$ _____ $+ (8 \times 7)$

14. $7 + (8 + 12) =$ _____ $+ 12$

_____

_____

Find the sum or difference. ⬤ TEKS 5.3.K

15. $14.85 - $4.63

16. 12.325 + 8.274

17. 7.423 − 5.15

_____

_____

Fill in the bubble completely to show your answer.

18. Maya uses rope to make decorative necklaces for her friends. She has a total of 3.75 yards of rope. If she uses 0.48 yard of rope to make a necklace for her friend, how much rope does Maya have left?

    ⬇ TEKS 5.3.K

    (A) 4.13 yards

    (B) 3.27 yards

    (C) 3.17 yards

    (D) 4.23 yards

19. Stacy has $75 in her account. On Monday, she deposits $19.75 she earned babysitting. If Stacy buys a new pair of shoes for $40.35, about how much money does Stacy have left in her account? ⬇ TEKS 5.3.A

    (A) $40

    (B) $95

    (C) $55

    (D) $35

20. A honeybee can fly up to 2.548 meters per second. Which choice shows that number in expanded form? ⬇ TEKS 5.2.A

    (A) 2 + 5.4 + 0.008

    (B) 2 + 0.5 + 0.48

    (C) 2 + 0.5 + 0.04 + 0.008

    (D) 2 + 0.5 + 0.04 + 0.08

21. Jan ran 1.256 miles on Monday, 1.265 miles on Wednesday, and 1.268 miles on Friday. What were her distances from greatest to least? ⬇ TEKS 5.2.B

    (A) 1.268 miles, 1.256 miles, 1.265 miles

    (B) 1.268 miles, 1.265 miles, 1.256 miles

    (C) 1.265 miles, 1.256 miles, 1.268 miles

    (D) 1.256 miles, 1.265 miles, 1.268 miles

Name _____

TEKS Number and Operations—5.3.B
Also 5.3.A
MATHEMATICAL PROCESSES 5.1.B

2.1 Multiply by 1-Digit Numbers

? Essential Question

How do you multiply by 1-digit numbers?

🔑 Unlock the Problem 🌎 Real World

Each day an airline flies 9 commercial jets from New York to London, England. Each plane holds 293 passengers. If every seat is taken on all flights, how many people fly on this airline from New York to London in 1 day?

🔒 **Use place value and regrouping.**

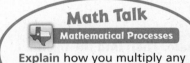

Math Talk
Mathematical Processes

Explain how you multiply any number by a 1-digit number.

STEP 1 Estimate: 293 × 9

  Think: 300 × 9 = _____

_____

STEP 2 Multiply the ones.

$$\begin{array}{r} \overset{2}{29}3 \\ \times\ \ 9 \\ \hline 7 \end{array}$$

9 × 3 ones = _____ ones

Write the ones and the regrouped tens.

_____

STEP 3 Multiply the tens.

$$\begin{array}{r} \overset{8\,2}{29}3 \\ \times\ \ 9 \\ \hline 37 \end{array}$$

9 × 9 tens = _____ tens

Add the regrouped tens.

_____ tens + 2 tens = _____ tens

Write the tens and the regrouped hundreds.

_____

STEP 4 Multiply the hundreds.

$$\begin{array}{r} \overset{8\,2}{29}3 \\ \times\ \ 9 \\ \hline 2{,}637 \end{array}$$

9 × 2 hundreds = _____ hundreds

Add the regrouped hundreds.

_____ hundreds + 8 hundreds = _____ hundreds

Write the hundreds.

So, in 1 day, _____ passengers fly from New York to London.

- How can you tell if your answer is reasonable? _____

_____

Share and Show

Complete to find the product.

1. $6 \times 2{,}796$　　　**Estimate:** $6 \times$ _____ = _____

Multiply the ones and regroup.	Multiply the tens and add the regrouped tens. Regroup.	Multiply the hundreds and add the regrouped hundreds. Regroup.	Multiply the thousands and add the regrouped thousands.
2,796 × 6	³ 2,796 × 6 ‾‾‾‾‾‾ 6	⁵³ 2,796 × 6 ‾‾‾‾‾‾ 76	⁴⁵³ 2,796 × 6 ‾‾‾‾‾‾ ,776

Estimate. Then find the product.

2. Estimate: _____

608
×   8

3. Estimate: _____

556
×   4

4. Estimate: _____

1,925
×   7

Problem Solving

H.O.T. **Algebra** Solve for the unknown number.

5.
396
×   6
‾‾‾‾‾
2,3 6

6.
5,12▢
×   8
‾‾‾‾‾
▢▢16

7.
8,5▢6
×   7
‾‾‾‾‾
60,03▢

Practice: Copy and Solve Estimate. Then find the product.

8. 116×3 　　**9.** 338×4 　　**10.** 6×219 　　**11.** 7×456

12. $5 \times 1{,}012$ 　　**13.** $2{,}921 \times 3$ 　　**14.** $8{,}813 \times 4$ 　　**15.** $9 \times 3{,}033$

16. **Multi-Step** A commercial airline makes a flight each day from New York to Paris, France. The aircraft seats 524 passengers and serves 2 meals to each passenger per flight. How many meals are served in one week?

56

Name _____

H.O.T. What's the Error?

17. The Plattsville Glee Club is sending 8 of its members to a singing contest in Cincinnati, Ohio. The cost will be $588 per person. How much will it cost for the entire group of 8 students to attend?

Both Brian and Jermaine solve the problem. Brian says the answer is $40,074. Jermaine's answer is $4,604.

Estimate the cost. A reasonable estimate is _____.

Although Jermaine's answer seems reasonable, neither Brian nor Jermaine solved the problem correctly. Find the errors in Brian's and Jermaine's work. Then, solve the problem correctly.

Brian	**Jermaine**	**Correct Answer**
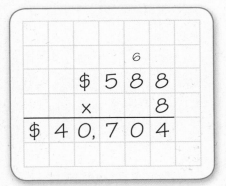	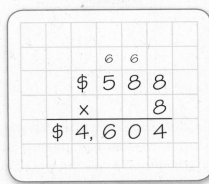	

18. What error did Brian make? **Explain.** _____

_____

_____

19. What error did Jermaine make? **Explain.** _____

_____

20. **Multi-Step** How could you predict that Jermaine's answer might be incorrect using your estimate?

_____

_____

_____

Daily Assessment Task

Fill in the bubble completely to show your answer.

21. A minivan weighs 4,275 pounds. You would need 6 minivans to balance 2 elephants on a balance scale. Which could be the combined weight of the 2 elephants?

   Ⓐ 25,650 pounds

   Ⓑ 12,825 pounds

   Ⓒ 24,650 pounds

   Ⓓ 25,620 pounds

22. A small sports arena can hold 274 people in each section. The arena has 7 sections. Estimate how many people the arena can hold, and then give the exact total.

   Ⓐ estimate: 1,400; exact: 1,818

   Ⓑ estimate: 1,400; exact: 1,918

   Ⓒ estimate: 2,100; exact: 1,898

   Ⓓ estimate: 2,100; exact: 1,918

23. **Multi-Step** The 133 students in the fifth grade each made 6 bookmarks for the school library. The 128 students in the fourth grade each made 7 bookmarks for the school library. Which class made more bookmarks and how many more did they make?

   Ⓐ fourth grade, 108   Ⓒ fifth grade, 108

   Ⓑ fourth grade, 98   Ⓓ fifth grade, 98

TEXAS Test Prep

24. The Memorial School has 1,362 students enrolled for the current school year. The school is purchasing 5 notebooks for each student. How many notebooks does the school need to purchase for the students?

   Ⓐ 6,800   Ⓒ 6,810

   Ⓑ 6,510   Ⓓ 5,810

Homework and Practice

Name _____

2.1 Multiply by 1-Digit Numbers

Solve for the unknown number.

1.
$$
\begin{array}{r}
5\ \ 4 \\
\times\ \ \ 4 \\
\hline
2{,}296
\end{array}
$$

2.
$$
\begin{array}{r}
3{,}852 \\
\times\quad\ \ 7 \\
\hline
26{,}9\ \
\end{array}
$$

3.
$$
\begin{array}{r}
1{,}\ \ 73 \\
\times\quad\ \ 5 \\
\hline
6{,}865
\end{array}
$$

4.
$$
\begin{array}{r}
7{,}593 \\
\times\quad\ \ 2 \\
\hline
\ ,186
\end{array}
$$

5.
$$
\begin{array}{r}
\ \ 79 \\
\times\ \ 3 \\
\hline
537
\end{array}
$$

6.
$$
\begin{array}{r}
835 \\
\times\ \ \ 4 \\
\hline
3{,}\ \ 0
\end{array}
$$

Estimate. Then find the product.

7. 4×923

8. 227×3

9. $4 \times 1{,}238$

10. 384×2

11. $2{,}831 \times 3$

12. $4 \times 2{,}899$

Problem Solving Real World

13. Mrs. Sampson is buying new tires for her car. Each tire costs $129.00. What is the total cost of four tires? Estimate. Then solve.

14. The drama club sold 386 tickets to the school play. Each ticket costs $7. How much money did the club raise for the school? Estimate. Then solve.

Fill in the bubble completely to show your answer.

15. A baker sold 1,246 cakes in November. He sold three times as many cakes in December. How many cakes did he sell in December?

- (A) 3,729
- (B) 3,738
- (C) 3,728
- (D) 3,628

16. Wendy earned $1,645.00 each month for 6 months. How much had Wendy earned at the end of 6 months?

- (A) $9,670.00
- (B) $9,640.00
- (C) $9,840.00
- (D) $9,870.00

17. A commercial airline makes several flights each week from New York to Paris, France. If the airline serves 1,978 meals each day, how many meals are served the entire week?

- (A) 13,796
- (B) 13,346
- (C) 13,846
- (D) 1,985

18. Leo's penny jar holds 386 pennies. Leo has set a goal to save 8 jars full of pennies. Estimate how many pennies Leo will have if he saves 8 jars of pennies and then give the exact total.

- (A) estimate: 2,400; exact 2,448
- (B) estimate: 2,400; exact 3,048
- (C) estimate: 3,200; exact 3,088
- (D) estimate: 3,200; exact 3,048

19. **Multi-Step** Jefferson School held a fitness contest during the month of April. The 168 fifth grade students each ran a total of 3 miles during the contest. The 154 fourth grade students each ran a total of 2 miles during the contest. What is the total number of miles run by all students in the contest?

- (A) 802 miles
- (B) 792 miles
- (C) 812 miles
- (D) 712 miles

20. **Multi-Step** Mr. Benson is buying supplies for his office. He bought 8 boxes of large rubber bands, which come 195 to a box. He bought 6 boxes of small rubber bands, which come 256 to a box. What is the total number of rubber bands that Mr. Benson bought?

- (A) 3,096
- (B) 4,576
- (C) 3,066
- (D) 3,520

TEKS **Number and Operations—5.3.B**
Also 5.3.A
MATHEMATICAL PROCESSES
5.1.B, 5.1.D

2.2 Multiply by 2-Digit Numbers

 Essential Question

How do you multiply by 2-digit numbers?

🔑 Unlock the Problem

A Siberian tiger sleeps as much as 18 hours a day, or 126 hours per week. About how many hours does a tiger sleep in a year? There are 52 weeks in one year.

 Use place value and regrouping.

STEP 1 Estimate: 126 × 52

Think: 100 × 50 = _____

_____

STEP 2 Multiply by the ones.

$$\begin{array}{r} 126 \\ \times\ 52 \\ \hline \end{array}$$

126 × 2 ones = _____ ones

_____

STEP 3 Multiply by the tens.

$$\begin{array}{r} 126 \\ \times\ 52 \\ \hline \end{array}$$

126 × 5 tens = _____ tens, or _____ ones

_____

Math Talk
Mathematical Processes

Are there different numbers you could have used in Step 1 to find an estimate that is closer to the actual answer? Explain.

STEP 4 Add the partial products.

$$\begin{array}{r} 126 \\ \times\ 52 \\ \hline \end{array}$$

← 126 × 2

← 126 × 50

+ _____

Remember

Use patterns of zeros to find the product of multiples of 10.

$$3 \times 4 = 12$$

$$3 \times 40 = 120 \qquad 30 \times 40 = 1{,}200$$

$$3 \times 400 = 1{,}200 \qquad 300 \times 40 = 12{,}000$$

So, a Siberian tiger sleeps about _____ hours in one year.

Complete to find the product.

1.

			6	4
	×		4	3
+				

← 64 × _____
← 64 × _____

2.

		5	7	1
	×		3	8
+				

← 571 × _____
← 571 × _____

Estimate. Then find the product.

3. Estimate: _____

$$\begin{array}{r} 24 \\ \times\, 15 \\ \hline \end{array}$$

 4. Estimate: _____

$$\begin{array}{r} 37 \\ \times\, 63 \\ \hline \end{array}$$

 5. Estimate: _____

$$\begin{array}{r} 384 \\ \times\, 45 \\ \hline \end{array}$$

Problem Solving

Practice: Copy and Solve Estimate. Then find the product.

6. 54×31

7. 42×26

8. 38×64

9. 63×16

10. 204×41

11. 534×25

12. 722×39

13. 957×43

14. When you multiply 235 and 4 tens in 235×43, why does its product have a zero in the ones place? **Explain.**

_____

_____

15. **Write Math** ▶ **Communicate** How is multiplying a number by a 2-digit number similar to multiplying the number by a 1-digit number? How is it different?

_____

_____

_____

TEKS Number and Operations—5.3.C

MATHEMATICAL PROCESSES 5.1.C

2.3 Division with 2-Digit Divisors

? Essential Question How can you use base-ten blocks to model and understand division of whole numbers?

Investigate

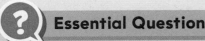

Materials ■ base-ten blocks

There are 156 students in the Carville Middle School chorus. The music director wants the students to stand with 12 students in each row for the next concert. How many rows will there be?

A. Use base-ten blocks to model the dividend, 156.

B. Place 2 tens below the hundred to form a rectangle. How many groups of 12 does the rectangle show? How much of the dividend

is not shown in this rectangle? _____

C. Combine the remaining tens and ones into as many groups of 12

as possible. How many groups of 12 are there? _____

D. Place these groups of 12 on the right side of the rectangle to make a larger rectangle.

E. The final rectangle shows _____ groups of 12.

So, there will be _____ rows of 12 students.

Draw Conclusions

1. Explain why you still need to make groups of 12 after Step B.

_____

_____

2. Describe how you can use base-ten blocks to find the quotient 176 ÷ 16.

_____

_____

_____

_____

Make Connections

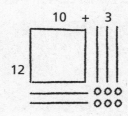

The two sets of groups of 12 that you found in the Investigate are partial quotients. First you found 10 groups of 12 and then you found 3 more groups of 12. Sometimes you may need to regroup before you can show a partial quotient.

You can use a quick picture to record the partial products.

Divide. 180 ÷ 15

MODEL Use base-ten blocks.

STEP 1 Model the dividend, 180, as 1 hundred 8 tens.

Model the first partial quotient by making a rectangle with the hundred and 5 tens. In the Record, cross out the hundred and tens you use.

The rectangle shows _____ groups of 15.

STEP 2 Additional groups of 15 cannot be made without regrouping.

Regroup 1 ten as 10 ones. In the Record, cross out the regrouped ten.

There are now _____ tens and _____ ones.

STEP 3 Decide how many additional groups of 15 can be made with the remaining tens and ones. The number of groups is the second partial quotient.

Make your rectangle larger by including these groups of 15. In the Record, cross out the tens and ones you use.

There are now _____ groups of 15.

So, 180 ÷ 15 is _____.

RECORD Use quick pictures.

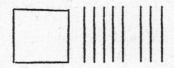

Draw the first partial quotient.

Draw the first and second partial quotients.

Share and Show

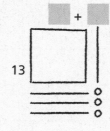

Use the quick picture to divide.

1. 143 ÷ 13

Math Talk

Mathematical Processes

Explain how your model shows the quotient.

Name _____

Use base-ten blocks or a quick picture to divide.

2. $168 \div 12$

 3. $187 \div 11$

 4. $182 \div 13$

5. $228 \div 12$

Problem Solving Real World

The Pony Express used men riding horses to deliver mail between St. Joseph, Missouri, and Sacramento, California, from April 1860 to October 1861. The trail between the cities was approximately 2,000 miles long.

Write Math ▶ Show Your Work · · · ·

6. **H.O.T.** **Multi-Step** Two Pony Express riders each rode part of a 176-mile trip. Each rider rode the same number of miles. They changed horses every 11 miles. How many horses did each rider use?

_____

7. Suppose a Pony Express rider was paid $192 for 12 weeks of work. If he was paid the same amount each week, how much was he paid for each week of work?

_____

8. **H.O.T.** **Multi-Step** It took 19 Pony Express riders a total of 11 days 21 hours to ride from St. Joseph to Sacramento. If they all rode the same number of hours, how many hours did each rider ride?

_____

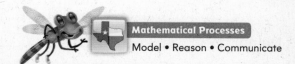

Daily Assessment Task

Fill in the bubble completely to show your answer.

9. **Use Diagrams** A rover brings 144 rock samples back from Mars. The samples will be divided among 12 teams of scientists for analysis. Which quick picture shows the correct division of the samples between the 12 teams?

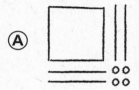 Ⓐ

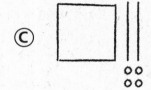 Ⓒ

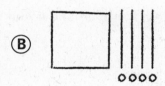 Ⓑ

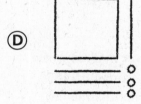 Ⓓ

10. **Analyze** The Mars rover is going to travel across a crater that is 360 cm (about 12 ft) in diameter. The rover must stop every 15 cm to recharge its batteries. How many times will the rover recharge while it crosses the crater?

Ⓐ 24 Ⓒ 30

Ⓑ 15 Ⓓ 25

11. **Multi-Step** On Monday, the rover traveled 330 cm. On Tuesday, it traveled 180 cm. If the rover stopped every 15 cm to recharge, how many more times did it need to recharge on Monday than on Tuesday?

Ⓐ 24 Ⓒ 12

Ⓑ 22 Ⓓ 10

 TEXAS Test Prep

12. **Analyze** Three Pony Express riders each rode part of a 252-mile trip. If they used a total of 18 horses, and rode each horse the same number of miles, how many miles did they ride before replacing each horse?

Ⓐ 54 miles Ⓒ 84 miles

Ⓑ 14 miles Ⓓ 42 miles

Homework and Practice

Name _____

2.3 Division with 2-Digit Divisors

Use base-ten blocks or a quick picture to divide.

1. $180 \div 12$

2. $216 \div 18$

3. $224 \div 16$

4. $176 \div 16$

Problem Solving Real World

5. Ryan read 145 pages of his book. If he read 29 pages every night, how many nights did it take him to complete the book?

6. Mrs. McDonald passed out 189 photos that she had taken during the school year. If each of her 21 students received the same number of photos, how many did each receive?

_____

_____

Fill in the bubble completely to show your answer.

7. Susanna made a total of $132 for the school fundraiser. She sold pizza combo meals for $12 each. How many combo meals did Susanna sell?

   (A) 10

   (B) 11

   (C) 13

   (D) 12

8. Carlos' horse ran around the track a total of 336 times. If the horse ran 21 laps each day, how many days did it take the horse to complete all of the laps?

   (A) 20

   (B) 16

   (C) 18

   (D) 12

9. Milos rode his bicycle in a marathon for 154 miles. He took a rest stop every 22 miles. How many rest stops did Milos take during the marathon?

   (A) 8

   (B) 7

   (C) 10

   (D) 9

10. There are 325 books on the library wall. There are 13 rows of books, each with an equal number of books. How many books are in each row?

    (A) 28

    (B) 21

    (C) 25

    (D) 19

11. **Multi-Step** Lilly was paid $308 for 14 weeks of work. If she was paid the same amount each week, how much did she earn after 2 weeks?

    (A) $38

    (B) $28

    (C) $22

    (D) $44

12. **Multi-Step** Manny drove 910 miles during a two-week period. If he drove the same number of miles each day, how many miles had he driven after 5 days?

    (A) 182 miles

    (B) 250 miles

    (C) 650 miles

    (D) 325 miles

Name _____

2.4 Partial Quotients

? Essential Question

How can you use partial quotients to divide by 2-digit divisors?

🔓 Unlock the Problem

People in the United States eat about 23 pounds of pizza per person every year. If you ate that much pizza each year, how many years would it take you to eat 775 pounds of pizza?

• Rewrite in one sentence the problem you are asked to solve.

_____

_____

🔑 Divide by using partial quotients.

$775 \div 23$

STEP 1

Subtract multiples of the divisor from the dividend until the remaining number is less than the multiple. The easiest partial quotients to use are multiples of 10.

_____

STEP 2

Subtract smaller multiples of the divisor until the remaining number is less than the divisor. Then add the partial quotients to find the quotient.

COMPLETE THE DIVISION PROBLEM.

$$23\overline{)775}$$
$$-$$
$$545$$

10×23 | 10

$775 \div 23$ is _____ r _____.

So, it would take you more than _____ years to eat 775 pounds of pizza.

Remember

Depending on the question, a remainder may or may not be used in answering the question. Sometimes the quotient is adjusted based on the remainder.

 **Example**

Myles is helping his father with the supply order for his pizza shop.
For next week, the shop will need 1,450 ounces of mozzarella cheese.
Each package of cheese weighs 32 ounces. Complete Myles's work to
find how many packages of mozzarella cheese he needs to order.

```
32)1,450
  - 320        _____ × 32        [    ]
   1,130
  -  320       _____ × 32        [    ]
     810
  -  320       _____ × 32        [    ]
     490
  -  320       _____ × 32        [    ]
     170
  -  160       _____ × 32    + [    ]
      10
```

1,450 ÷ 32 is _____ r _____.

So, he needs to order _____ packages of mozzarella cheese.

Math Idea

Using different multiples of the
divisor to find partial quotients
provides many ways to solve a
division problem. Some ways
are quicker, but all result in the
same answer.

Math Talk
Mathematical Processes

What does the remainder
represent? Explain how
the remainder will affect
your answer.

 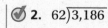

Divide. Use partial quotients.

1. $18\overline{)648}$

✓ 2. $62\overline{)3,186}$

✓ 3. $858 \div 57$

© Houghton Mifflin Harcourt Publishing Company

Name _____

Practice: Copy and Solve Divide. Use partial quotients.

4. 653 ÷ 42   **5.** 946 ÷ 78   **6.** 412 ÷ 18   **7.** 871 ÷ 87

8. 1,544 ÷ 34   **9.** 2,548 ÷ 52   **10.** 2,740 ÷ 83   **11.** 4,135 ÷ 66

12. What is the greatest possible whole-number remainder if you divide any number by 23? **Explain**.

_____

_____

Problem Solving Real World

Use the table to solve 13–16.

13. How many years would it take for a person in the United States to eat 1,120 pounds of turkey?

_____

14. **Multi-Step** If 6 people in the United States each eat the average amount of popcorn for 5 years, how many quarts of popcorn will they eat?

_____

15. **Multi-Step** In a study, 9 people ate a total of 1,566 pounds of potatoes in 2 years. If each person ate the same amount each year, how many pounds of potatoes did each person eat in 1 year?

_____

16. **Write Math** ▸ **Sense or Nonsense?** In the United States, a person eats more than 40,000 pounds of bread in a lifetime if he or she lives to be 80 years old. Does this statement make sense, or is it nonsense? **Explain**.

_____

_____

Each year each person in the U.S. eats about…
• 68 quarts of popcorn
• 53 pounds of bread
• 19 pounds of apples
• 14 pounds of turkey

Write Math ▸ **Show Your Work**

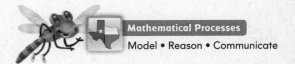
Daily Assessment Task

Fill in the bubble completely to show your answer.

17. You want to design a new calendar system. You decide that there will be 384 days in one year. Each month will have 24 days. How many months will be in one year in your calendar system?

 Ⓐ 18

 Ⓑ 16

 Ⓒ 17

 Ⓓ 15

18. **Analyze** David Blaine set a world record for holding his breath for 1,024 seconds. Which partial quotients can you use to find out how many minutes he held his breath (1 minute = 60 seconds)?

 Ⓐ 5 + 5 + 2

 Ⓑ 10 + 5 + 2

 Ⓒ 20 + 5 + 2

 Ⓓ 20 + 2

19. **Multi-Step** The fifth grade is having a picnic this Friday. There will be 182 students and 274 adults. Each table seats 12 people. How many tables are needed?

 Ⓐ 23

 Ⓑ 15

 Ⓒ 11

 Ⓓ 38

 TEXAS Test Prep

20. The school auditorium has 448 seats arranged in 32 equal rows. How many seats are in each row?

 Ⓐ 480   Ⓒ 416

 Ⓑ 14,336   Ⓓ 14

Homework and Practice

Name _____

2.4 Partial Quotients

Divide. Use partial quotients.

1. $723 \div 34$

2. $372 \div 22$

3. $682 \div 31$

4. $290 \div 52$

5. $284 \div 32$

6. $672 \div 15$

7. $643 \div 35$

8. $816 \div 62$

9. $781 \div 26$

10. $283 \div 66$

11. $754 \div 23$

12. $855 \div 36$

13. What is the greatest possible whole-number remainder if you divide any number by 41? **Explain**.

_____

_____

_____

Problem Solving

14. The PTA is ordering planners for each of the 154 fifth grade students. The planners come in packages of 6. How many packages will the PTA need to order? **Explain**.

_____

_____

15. Mr. Lee's science class needs 250 large clips for a project. The clips come in boxes of 24. How many boxes of clips will the class need for the project? **Explain**.

_____

_____

Fill in the bubble completely to show your answer.

16. Sierra uses 468 golf balls in a display at the sporting goods store. She uses 47 golf balls in each display case. Which answer shows the number of display cases she fills and the number of balls left over?

   Ⓐ 8 r2

   Ⓑ 9 r13

   Ⓒ 8 r31

   Ⓓ 9 r45

17. Kaj has 1,342 marbles in his collection. How many bags does he need if he is going to put 42 marbles in each bag, and have one with fewer marbles?

   Ⓐ 32

   Ⓑ 30

   Ⓒ 31

   Ⓓ 29

18. Hal has 558 cans of soup to put on a shelf. The shelf can hold 72 cans in each row. How many rows can Hal make with the soup cans?

   Ⓐ exactly 7 rows

   Ⓑ fewer than 7 rows

   Ⓒ more than 7 rows

   Ⓓ exactly 6 rows

19. Mr. Amos has a bill of $1,260 to pay. He will make 21 equal payments. How much will each payment be?

   Ⓐ $61

   Ⓑ $60

   Ⓒ $6

   Ⓓ $600

20. **Multi-Step** Max delivers 8,520 pieces of mail in one year. How many pieces of mail are delivered in two months?

   Ⓐ 710

   Ⓑ 1,420

   Ⓒ 7,200

   Ⓓ 700

21. **Multi-Step** The principal is arranging school buses for the spring field trip. There will be 109 students and 17 adults going on the trip. Each bus holds 54 people. How many buses will the group need?

   Ⓐ 4

   Ⓑ 5

   Ⓒ 3

   Ⓓ 2

Name _____

TEKS Number and Operations—5.3.A

MATHEMATICAL PROCESSES
5.1.F, 5.1.G

2.5 Estimate with 2-Digit Divisors

Essential Question

How can you use compatible numbers to estimate quotients?

Connect You can estimate quotients using compatible numbers that are found by using basic facts and patterns.

$$35 \div 5 = 7 \quad \leftarrow \text{basic fact}$$
$$350 \div 50 = 7$$
$$3,500 \div 50 = 70$$
$$35,000 \div 50 = 700$$

Unlock the Problem

The observation deck of the Willis Tower in Chicago, Illinois, is 1,353 feet above the ground. Elevators lift visitors to that level in 60 seconds. About how many feet do the elevators travel per second?

▶ Willis Tower, formerly known as the Sears Tower, is the tallest building in the United States.

Estimate. 1,353 ÷ 60

STEP 1

Use two sets of compatible numbers to find two different estimates.

$$1,353 \div 60$$
$$\downarrow$$
$$1,200 \div 60$$

$$1,353 \div 60$$
$$\downarrow$$
$$1,800 \div 60$$

STEP 2

Use patterns and basic facts to help estimate.

$$12 \div 6 = \underline{\hspace{1cm}}$$
$$120 \div 60 = \underline{\hspace{1cm}}$$
$$1,200 \div 60 = \underline{\hspace{1cm}}$$

$$18 \div 6 = \underline{\hspace{1cm}}$$
$$\underline{\hspace{1cm}} \div \underline{\hspace{1cm}} = \underline{\hspace{1cm}}$$
$$\underline{\hspace{1cm}} \div \underline{\hspace{1cm}} = \underline{\hspace{1cm}}$$

The elevators travel about _____ to _____ feet per second.

The more reasonable estimate is _____ because

_____ is closer to 1,353 than _____ is.

So, the observation deck elevators in the Willis Tower travel

about _____ feet per second.

Example Estimate money.

Miriam has saved $650 to spend during her 18-day trip to Chicago. She doesn't want to run out of money before the trip is over, so she plans to spend about the same amount each day. Estimate how much she can spend each day.

Estimate. $18\overline{)\$650}$

$600 \div \underline{\hspace{1cm}} = \$30$ or $\underline{\hspace{2cm}} \div 20 = \$40$

So, Miriam can spend about \underline{\hspace{1.5cm}} to \underline{\hspace{1.5cm}} each day.

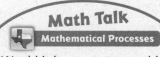

Math Talk
Mathematical Processes

Would it be more reasonable to have an estimate or an exact answer for this example? **Explain** your reasoning.

- Given Miriam's situation, which estimate do you think is the better one for her to use? **Explain** your reasoning.

_____

_____

Try This! Use compatible numbers.

Find two estimates.	Estimate the quotient.
$52\overline{)415}$	$38\overline{)\$2,764}$

 Share and Show MATH BOARD

Use compatible numbers to find two estimates.

1. $22\overline{)154}$

$140 \div 20 = \underline{\hspace{1cm}}$

$160 \div 20 = \underline{\hspace{1cm}}$

2. $68\overline{)503}$

3. $81\overline{)7,052}$

4. $33\overline{)291}$

5. $58\overline{)2,365}$

6. $19\overline{)5,312}$

© Houghton Mifflin Harcourt Publishing Company

Name _____

Problem Solving

Use compatible numbers to estimate the quotient.

7. 19)228

8. 25)$595

9. 86)7,130

Practice: Copy and Solve Use compatible numbers to estimate the quotient.

10. 462 ÷ 83

11. 9,144 ÷ 27

12. 710 ÷ 68

13. 1,607 ÷ 36

14. **Write Math** ▶ **Explain** how you know whether the quotient of 298 ÷ 31 is closer to 9 or to 10.

_____

_____

Problem Solving Real World

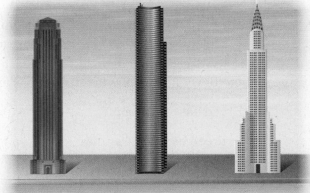

| 275 meters, 64 floors, Williams Tower, Texas | 295 meters, 76 floors, Columbia Center, Washington | 319 meters, 77 floors, Chrysler Building, New York |

Use the picture to solve 15–16.

15. About how many meters tall is each floor of the Chrysler Building?

_____

16. **H.O.T.** **Multi-Step** Use estimation to decide which building has the tallest floors. About how many meters is each floor?

_____

17. **H.O.T.** Eli needs to save $235. He plans to mow lawns and charge $21 for each. Write two estimates for the number of lawns he needs to mow. Decide which estimate you think is the better one for Eli to use. **Explain** your reasoning.

_____

_____

_____

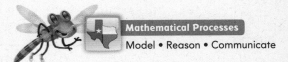

Daily Assessment Task

Fill in the bubble completely to show your answer.

18. A meteoroid travels 18 miles per second and is 2,863 miles away from the moon. Estimate how long it will take the meteoroid to reach the moon.

   (A) 120 seconds   (C) 200 seconds

   (B) 150 seconds   (D) 280 seconds

19. **Apply** A playground is 5,583 feet away from Jake's house. Jake runs 17 feet per second. Which is the best estimate of the amount of time it will take Jake to run to the park?

   (A) 5,000 ÷ 20 = 260 seconds

   (B) 6,000 ÷ 20 = 300 seconds

   (C) 6,000 ÷ 10 = 600 seconds

   (D) 5,000 ÷ 10 = 500 seconds

20. **Multi-Step** At an orchard, 486 green apples are to be organized into 12 green baskets, and 633 red apples are to be organized into 31 red baskets. Use estimation to decide which color basket has more apples. About how many apples are in each basket of that color?

   (A) red basket, 50 apples

   (B) green basket: 20 apples

   (C) red basket, 20 apples

   (D) green basket: 50 apples

TEXAS Test Prep

21. Anik built a tower of cubes. It was 594 millimeters tall. The height of each cube was 17 millimeters. About how many cubes did Anik use?

   (A) 10

   (B) 300

   (C) 30

   (D) 16

TEKS Number and Operations—5.3.A
MATHEMATICAL PROCESSES 5.1.F, 5.1.G

Name _____

2.5 Estimate with 2-Digit Divisors

Use compatible numbers to find two estimates.

1. $42\overline{)396}$

2. $59\overline{)413}$

3. $88\overline{)6,078}$

Use compatible numbers to estimate the quotient.

4. $7,233 \div 84$

5. $568 \div 34$

6. $938 \div 57$

7. $4,479 \div 89$

_____

8. $1,238 \div 57$

9. $5,587 \div 77$

10. $4,192 \div 55$

11. $1,847 \div 24$

_____

Problem Solving Real World

12. Alec needs to save $376. He plans to rake fall leaves for $12 per lawn. Using compatible numbers, write an estimate that shows the number of lawns he will need to rake.

_____

13. Mr. Rodriguez's construction company built an office building that is 1,848 feet tall. Each floor of the building is 14 feet high. About how many floors are in the building? Write an estimate.

_____

Fill in the bubble completely to show your answer.

14. Which number sentence with compatible numbers is the most reasonable estimate of the quotient for 478 ÷ 47?

   Ⓐ $500 \div 25 = 20$

   Ⓑ $500 \div 50 = 10$

   Ⓒ $400 \div 50 = 8$

   Ⓓ $600 \div 40 = 15$

15. Cameron wants to buy a bike for $268. He saves $53 each month from his job. Which is the best estimate of the number of months it will take him to save enough to buy the bike?

   Ⓐ $150 \div 50 = 3$ months

   Ⓑ $300 \div 60 = 5$ months

   Ⓒ $300 \div 50 = 6$ months

   Ⓓ $240 \div 60 = 4$ months

16. Leo has 279 comic books in his collection. He puts 34 comic books in each box. About how many boxes of comic books does Leo have?

   Ⓐ 6

   Ⓑ 11

   Ⓒ 9

   Ⓓ 5

17. The Alam family has saved $260 to spend on entertainment activities for one week. They want to spend about the same amount of money each day. Which is the best estimate of how much they can spend each day?

   Ⓐ $\$280 \div 7 = \$40$

   Ⓑ $\$260 \div 10 = \$26$

   Ⓒ $\$240 \div 6 = \$40$

   Ⓓ $\$270 \div 9 = \$30$

18. **Multi-Step** At the recycling center, 394 cans are to be organized into 10 green bins, and 560 bottles are to be organized into 12 blue bins. Use estimation to decide which type of bin has more items. About how many items are in this bin?

   Ⓐ blue bin, 60

   Ⓑ blue bin, 40

   Ⓒ green bin, 60

   Ⓓ green bin, 40

19. **Multi-Step** Farmer Theo sells cases of chicken eggs with 30 dozen eggs in a case. If he has 9,370 eggs, about how many cases of eggs does he have?

   Ⓐ 20

   Ⓑ 17

   Ⓒ 30

   Ⓓ 35

TEKS Number and Operations—5.3.C
Also 5.3.A
MATHEMATICAL PROCESSES
5.1.B

2.6 Divide by 2-Digit Divisors

? Essential Question

How can you divide by 2-digit divisors?

Unlock the Problem

Mr. Yates owns a smoothie shop. To mix a batch of his famous smoothies, he uses 18 ounces of orange juice. Each day he uses 560 ounces of orange juice. How many batches of smoothies can Mr. Yates make in a day?

- Underline the sentence that tells you what you are trying to find.
- Circle the numbers you need to use.

🔑 **Divide.** 560 ÷ 18   **Estimate.** _____

STEP 1 Use the estimate to place the first digit in the quotient.

$$18\overline{)560}$$

The first digit of the quotient will be in the _____ place.

STEP 2 Divide the tens.

$$\begin{array}{r} 3 \\ 18\overline{)560} \\ -54 \\ \hline 2 \end{array}$$

Divide. *56 tens ÷ 18*

Multiply. _____

Subtract. _____

Check. 2 tens cannot be shared among 18 groups without regrouping.

STEP 3 Divide the ones.

$$\begin{array}{r} 31r2 \\ 18\overline{)560} \\ -54\downarrow \\ \hline 20 \\ -18 \\ \hline 2 \end{array}$$

Divide. _____

Multiply. _____

Subtract. _____

Check. _____

_____

Math Talk
Mathematical Processes
Explain what the remainder 2 represents.

Since _____ is close to the estimate of 30, the answer is reasonable.

So, Mr. Yates can make _____ batches of smoothies each day.

Example

Every Wednesday, Mr. Yates orders fruit. He has set aside $1,250 to purchase Valencia oranges. Each box of Valencia oranges costs $41. How many boxes of Valencia oranges can Mr. Yates purchase?

You can use multiplication to check your answer.

Divide. 1,250 ÷ 41

DIVIDE

CHECK YOUR WORK

Estimate. _____

$$\begin{array}{r} 30 \text{ r}20 \\ 41\overline{)1{,}250} \end{array}$$

$$\begin{array}{r} 30 \\ \times 41 \\ \hline 30 \\ + 1{,}200 \\ \hline \end{array}$$

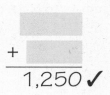

$$\begin{array}{r} + \\ \hline 1{,}250 \checkmark \end{array}$$

So, Mr. Yates can buy _____ boxes of Valencia oranges.

Share and Show

Divide. Check your answer.

1. $28\overline{)620}$

2. $64\overline{)842}$

3. $53\overline{)2{,}340}$

4. 723 ÷ 31

5. 1,359 ÷ 45

6. 7,925 ÷ 72

Name _____

Practice: Copy and Solve Divide. Check your answer.

7. $775 \div 35$ 8. $820 \div 41$ 9. $805 \div 24$

10. $1,166 \div 53$ 11. $1,989 \div 15$ 12. $3,927 \div 35$

13. Why can you use multiplication to check division? **Explain**.

_____

_____

Problem Solving (Real World)

Use the list at the right to solve 14–16.

14. A smoothie shop receives a delivery of 980 ounces of grape juice. How many Royal Purple smoothies can be made with the grape juice?

_____

15. **H.O.T.** **Multi-Step** The shop has 1,260 ounces of cranberry juice and 650 ounces of passion fruit juice. If the juices are used to make Crazy Cranberry smoothies, which juice will run out first? How much of the other juice will be left over?

Smoothie Main Ingredients

Orange Tango Smoothie
18 ounces orange juice
12 ounces mango juice

Royal Purple Smoothie
22 ounces grape juice
8 ounces apple juice

Crazy Cranberry Smoothie
20 ounces cranberry juice
10 ounces passion fruit juice

_____

16. **H.O.T.** In the refrigerator, there are 680 ounces of orange juice and 410 ounces of mango juice. How many Orange Tango smoothies can be made? **Explain** your reasoning.

_____

_____

Mathematical Processes
Model • Reason • Communicate

Daily Assessment Task

Fill in the bubble completely to show your answer.

17. A shipment of 572 scented erasers has arrived at the school store. You want to sell them in sets of 15. How many full sets of erasers can you make?

   (A) 40   (C) 39

   (B) 38   (D) 37

18. Darius counted that he walks 864 steps from his house to the bookstore. If Darius takes 52 steps each minute, about how long will it take him to reach the bookstore?

   (A) 31 minutes

   (B) 17 minutes

   (C) 13 minutes

   (D) 20 minutes

19. **Multi-Step** The school store has 1,262 bouncy balls. The bouncy balls are packaged in sets. Any single bouncy ball is sold for $1. If all the bouncy balls sell, which of the following will give the store the best profit?

   (A) Sets of 25 for $13

   (B) Sets of 16 for $9

   (C) Sets of 12 for $7

   (D) Sets of 10 for $6

 TEXAS Test Prep

20. James has 1,836 marbles. He decides to divide them equally among 23 boxes. How many marbles will James have left over?

   (A) 19

   (B) 23

   (C) 90

   (D) 79

Name _____

2.7 Adjust Quotients

? **Essential Question**

How can you adjust the quotient if your estimate is too high or too low?

Connect When you estimate to decide where to place the first digit, you can also try using the first digit of your estimate to find the first digit of your quotient. Sometimes an estimate is too low or too high.

Divide. 3,382 ÷ 48 **Estimate.** 3,000 ÷ 50 = 60

Try 6 tens.

If an estimate is too low, the difference will be greater than the divisor.

$$\begin{array}{r} 6 \\ 48\overline{)3,382} \\ -2\ 88 \\ \hline 50 \end{array}$$

Since the estimate is too low, adjust by increasing the number in the quotient.

Divide. 453 ÷ 65 **Estimate.** 490 ÷ 70 = 7

Try 7 ones.

If an estimate is too high, the product with the first digit will be too large and cannot be subtracted.

$$\begin{array}{r} 7 \\ 65\overline{)453} \\ -455 \end{array}$$

Since the estimate is too high, adjust by decreasing the number in the quotient.

Unlock the Problem

A new music group makes 6,127 copies of its first CD. The group sells 75 copies of the CD at each of its shows. How many shows does it take the group to sell all of the CDs?

Divide. 6,127 ÷ 75   **Estimate.** 6,300 ÷ 70 = 90

STEP 1 Use the estimate, 90. Try 9 tens.

- Is the estimate too high, too low, or correct?

_____

- Adjust the number in the quotient if needed.

_____

STEP 2 Estimate the next digit in the quotient. Divide the ones. Estimate: 140 ÷ 70 = 2. Try 2 ones.

- Is the estimate too high, too low, or correct?

_____

- Adjust the number in the quotient if needed.

So, it takes the group _____ shows to sell all of the CDs.

$$75\overline{)6,127}$$

Try This! When the difference is equal to or greater than the divisor, the estimate is too low.

Divide. 336 ÷ 48   Estimate. 300 ÷ 50 = 6

Use the estimate. Try 6 ones.

$$\overset{6}{48\overline{)336}}$$

Since _____ , the estimate is _____ .

336 ÷ 48 = _____

Adjust the estimated digit in the quotient if needed. Then divide. Try _____ .

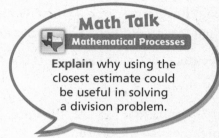

Math Talk

Mathematical Processes

Explain why using the closest estimate could be useful in solving a division problem.

Share and Show

Adjust the estimated digit in the quotient, if needed. Then divide.

 1. $\overset{4}{41\overline{)1,546}}$

2. $\overset{2}{16\overline{)416}}$

3. $\overset{9}{34\overline{)2,831}}$

Problem Solving

H.O.T. **Algebra** Write the unknown number for each ▪.

4. ▪ ÷ 33 = 11

5. 1,092 ÷ 52 = ▪

6. 429 ÷ ▪ = 33

▪ = _____

▪ = _____

▪ = _____

7. How do you know whether an estimated quotient is too low or too high? **Explain**.

_____

_____

_____

92

Name _____

8. Multi-Step A banquet hall serves 2,394 pounds of turkey during a 3-week period. If the same amount is served each day, how many pounds of turkey does the banquet hall serve each day?

(A) 50,274 pounds   (C) 342 pounds

(B) 798 pounds   (D) 114 pounds

a. What do you need to find? _____

_____

b. What information are you given? _____

_____

c. What other information will you use?

_____

_____

_____

d. Find how many days there are in 3 weeks.

There are _____ days in 3 weeks.

e. Divide to solve the problem.

f. Fill in the bubble for the correct answer choice.

9. **H.O.T.** **Multi-Step** Kainoa collects trading cards. He has 1,025 baseball cards, 713 basketball cards, and 836 football cards. He wants to put all of them in albums. Each page in the album holds 18 cards. How many pages will he need to hold all of his cards?

_____

10. The Box of Sox company packs 12 pairs of socks in a box. How many boxes will the company need to pack 1,020 pairs of socks?

_____

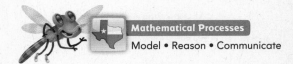

Daily Assessment Task

Fill in the bubble completely to show your answer.

11. **Apply** A ranch director would like to place a fence around some land he purchased for horses. He needs 992 feet of wire to fence the area. There are 45 feet of fence in each roll. How many rolls should he buy?

Ⓐ 25 rolls   Ⓒ 23 rolls

Ⓑ 22 rolls   Ⓓ 20 rolls

12. Sarah works part time at a zoo. She purchases food for the lions. The lions eat 1,330 pounds of food a year. The food comes in 22-pound bags. Which shows the closest estimate of how many bags of food Sarah orders each year?

Ⓐ $1,000 \div 20 = 50$ Ⓒ $1,200 \div 30 = 40$

Ⓑ $1,300 \div 20 = 65$ Ⓓ $1,400 \div 20 = 70$

13. **Multi-Step** Dylan traveled through Texas for the summer. He took 15 photos each day for 18 days. He placed the photos in a 30-page album. If each page has the same number of photos, how many photos are on each page?

Ⓐ 8

Ⓑ 12

Ⓒ 9

Ⓓ 15

 TEXAS Test Prep

14. Marcos mixes 624 ounces of lemonade. He wants to fill the 52 cups he has with equal amounts of lemonade. How much lemonade should he put in each cup?

Ⓐ 10 ounces

Ⓑ 12 ounces

Ⓒ 14 ounces

Ⓓ 13 ounces

Homework and Practice

Name _____

2.7 Adjust Quotients

Divide.

1. $3,234 \div 32$

2. $1,453 \div 16$

3. $6,305 \div 42$

4. $1,074 \div 21$

5. $4,893 \div 28$

6. $2,015 \div 15$

Write the unknown number for each **.**

7. ■ $\div 75 = 23$

8. $658 \div 47 =$ ■

9. $3,360 \div$ ■ $= 80$

■ = _____

■ = _____

■ = _____

Problem Solving

10. Kirsten wants to divide $762 \div 21$. She estimates that 2 is the first digit in the quotient. Is her estimate correct? **Explain**.

_____

_____

11. Ming has 4,173 songs on his MP3 player. He organizes the songs into 39 playlists with the same number of songs in each list. How many songs are in each playlist?

_____

_____

Fill in the bubble completely to show your answer.

12. Mr. Longo bakes 573 muffins to be sold at the school football game. He puts the muffins into boxes of 15. What is the greatest number of full boxes Mr. Longo will bring to the game?

(A) 35

(B) 38

(C) 41

(D) 39

13. **Multi-Step** A movie theater sold 4,494 tickets during a two-week period. If the same number of tickets were sold each day, how many tickets were sold on Wednesday and Thursday of one week?

(A) 600

(B) 642

(C) 321

(D) 806

14. Jenny wants to estimate the quotient for 6,253 ÷ 39. Which is the best estimate for the first digit in the quotient?

(A) 1

(B) 2

(C) 4

(D) 3

15. An art museum has 1,120 paintings. To display the paintings, the curator will divide the paintings equally among 16 rooms. How many paintings will be displayed in each room?

(A) 68

(B) 71

(C) 70

(D) 69

16. Factory workers pack 25 umbrellas in each box. If 1,300 umbrellas are shipped out, how many boxes were packed?

(A) 52

(B) 45

(C) 50

(D) 40

17. **Multi-Step** A store had 1,116 customers on Monday, 882 customers on Tuesday, and 1,194 customers on Wednesday. The store is open 14 hours each day. If the same number of customers arrived each hour during the three days, how many customers arrived each hour?

(A) 69

(B) 47

(C) 76

(D) 70

2.8 PROBLEM SOLVING • Division

TEKS Number and Operations—5.3.C
MATHEMATICAL PROCESSES
5.1.B, 5.1.E

 Essential Question How can the strategy *draw a diagram* help you solve a division problem?

🔑 Unlock the Problem

Sean and his crew operate a fishing charter company. They caught a blue marlin and an amberjack. The weight of the blue marlin was 12 times as great as the weight of the amberjack. The combined weight of both fish was 1,014 pounds. How much did each fish weigh?

Read

What do I need to find?

I need to find _____

_____.

What information am I given?

I know that they caught a total

of _____ pounds of fish and the weight of the blue marlin

was _____ times as great as the weight of the amberjack.

Plan

What is my plan or strategy?

I can use the strategy

_____

and then divide. I can draw and use a strip diagram to write the division problem that helps me find the weight of each fish.

Solve

I will draw one box to show the weight of the amberjack. Then I will draw a strip of 12 boxes of the same size to show the weight of the blue marlin. I can divide the total weight of the two fish by the total number of boxes.

amberjack [ ]

blue marlin [ ][ ][ ][ ][ ][ ][ ][ ][ ][ ][ ][ ] } 1,014 pounds

$$\begin{array}{r} 7 \\ 13\overline{)1,014} \\ -91 \\ \hline \\ - \\ \hline \end{array}$$

Write the quotient in each box. Multiply it by 12 to find the weight of the blue marlin.

So, the amberjack weighed _____ pounds and the

blue marlin weighed _____ pounds.

Try Another Problem

Jason, Murray, and Dana went fishing. Dana caught a red snapper. Jason caught a tuna with a weight 3 times as great as the weight of the red snapper. Murray caught a sailfish with a weight 12 times as great as the weight of the red snapper. If the combined weight of the three fish was 208 pounds, how much did the tuna weigh?

Read

What do I need to find?

What information am I given?

Plan

What is my plan or strategy?

Solve

So, the tuna weighed _____ pounds.

- How can you check if your answer is correct? _____

_____

_____

Math Talk

Mathematical Processes

Explain how you could use another strategy to solve this problem.

Share and Show

1. Paula caught a tarpon with a weight that was 10 times as great as the weight of a permit fish she caught. The total weight of the two fish was 132 pounds. How much did each fish weigh?

First, draw one box to represent the weight of the permit fish and ten boxes to represent the weight of the tarpon.

Next, divide the total weight of the two fish by the total number of boxes you drew. Place the quotient in each box.

Last, find the weight of each fish.

The permit fish weighed _____ pounds. The tarpon weighed

_____ pounds.

2. What if the weight of the tarpon was 11 times the weight of the permit fish, and the total weight of the two fish was 132 pounds? How much would each fish weigh?

permit fish: _____ pounds   tarpon: _____ pounds

Problem Solving Real World

3. **H.O.T.** **Multi-Step** The crew on a fishing boat caught four fish that weighed a total of 1,092 pounds. The tarpon weighed twice as much as the amberjack and the white marlin weighed twice as much as the tarpon. The weight of the tuna was 5 times the weight of the amberjack. How much did each fish weigh?

4. **H.O.T.** **Multi-Step** A fish market bought two swordfish at a rate of $13 per pound. The cost of the larger fish was 3 times as great as the cost of the smaller fish. The total cost of the two fish was $3,952. How much did each fish weigh?

Daily Assessment Task

Fill in the bubble completely to show your answer.

5. An ostrich at the zoo weighs 3 times as much as Mark's pet dog. Together, the ostrich and the dog weigh 448 pounds. How much does the ostrich weigh?

(A) 149 pounds   (C) 224 pounds

(B) 112 pounds   (D) 336 pounds

6. **Use Diagrams** A student drew this diagram to solve a word problem. Which statement matches what she drew?

Man

Cat

(A) A man weighs 12 times as much as a cat.

(B) A cat weighs 12 times as much as a man.

(C) A man weighs 13 times as much as a cat.

(D) A cat weighs 13 times as much as a man.

7. **Multi-Step** A juice factory uses 4,650 pounds of pears and apples a day. The factory uses 30 times as much apples than pears. How many pounds of pears and how many pounds of apples does the factory use each day?

(A) 93 lb pears and 4,557 lb apples

(B) 150 lb pears and 4,500 lb apples

(C) 155 lb pears and 4,495 lb apples

(D) 310 lb pears and 4,340 lb apples

 TEXAS Test Prep

8. **Apply** Captain James offers a deep-sea fishing tour. He charges $2,940 for a 14-hour trip. How much does each hour of the tour cost?

(A) $201   (C) $210

(B) $138   (D) $294

TEKS Number and Operations—5.3.C
MATHEMATICAL PROCESSES 5.1.B, 5.1.E
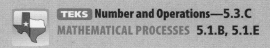

Name _____

2.8 PROBLEM SOLVING • Division

Eddie's Moving Company moved 3 boxes out of Mrs. Diaz's house. The box labeled "Kitchen" was 4 times heavier than the box labeled "Bedroom." The box labeled "Library" was 14 times heavier than the box marked "Bedroom." If the combined weight of the boxes was 817 pounds, how much did the box labeled "Kitchen" weigh?

1. What do I need to find?

_____

_____

_____

2. What information am I given?

_____

_____

_____

3. Draw a diagram.

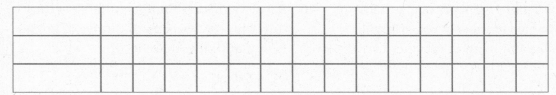

4. Solve.

_____ ÷ _____ = _____

I can multiply _____ by _____ to find the weight of the "Kitchen" box.

So, the box labeled "Kitchen" weighed _____ pounds.

Problem Solving Real World

5. An athlete ran 1,200 laps around a track over a two-month period. He ran 4 times the number of laps in the second month than he ran in the first month. How many laps did the athlete run the first month?

_____

6. The diagram below compares the weights of a boy and a fish. Tell what the diagram means.

Boy ▢▢▢▢▢▢▢▢▢▢▢

Fish ▢

_____

Fill in the bubble completely to show your answer.

7. Yani drew this diagram to solve a word problem. Which statement matches what she drew?

hamster ☐

duck ☐☐☐☐☐☐☐

Ⓐ A hamster weighs 7 times as much as a duck.

Ⓑ A duck weighs 7 times as much as a hamster.

Ⓒ A hamster weighs 6 times as much as a duck.

Ⓓ A duck weighs 6 times as much as a hamster.

8. An oak tree in Jake's yard is 13 times taller than a model tree that he is making for a performance set. Together, the oak tree and model tree are 112 feet tall. How tall is the model tree?

Ⓐ 8 feet

Ⓑ 14 feet

Ⓒ 26 feet

Ⓓ 96 feet

9. Lori's book has 6 times more pages than Sal's book. The combined number of pages for the two books is 532. How many pages does Lori's book have?

Ⓐ 76

Ⓑ 88

Ⓒ 456

Ⓓ 532

10. Raj drives his car 5 times farther than Gary drives his car. Together they drive 624 miles. How many miles does Raj drive?

Ⓐ 520 miles

Ⓑ 416 miles

Ⓒ 104 miles

Ⓓ 312 miles

11. **Multi-Step** The total number of books in the community's mobile library is 1,155. There are 20 times more nonfiction books than fiction books. How many fiction books and how many nonfiction books are in the mobile library?

Ⓐ 110 fiction and 1,045 nonfiction

Ⓑ 55 fiction and 1,100 nonfiction

Ⓒ 55 fiction and 1,045 nonfiction

Ⓓ 1,100 fiction and 55 nonfiction

12. **Multi-Step** Charlie's weight is 5 times as great as the weight of his little sister, Tali. If the total weight of the two children is 132 pounds, how much does each child weigh?

Ⓐ Tali: 22 pounds; Charlie: 110 pounds

Ⓑ Tali: 110 pounds; Charlie: 22 pounds

Ⓒ Tali: 44 pounds; Charlie: 88 pounds

Ⓓ Tali: 88 pounds; Charlie: 44 pounds

Name _____

 # Module 2 Assessment

Vocabulary

Vocabulary

- compatible numbers
- partial quotients
- place value

Choose the best term from the box.

1. You can use _____ to estimate quotients because they are easy to compute with mentally. (p. 53)

2. To decide where to place the first digit in the quotient, you can estimate or use _____. (p. 37)

Concepts and Skills

Estimate. Then find the product. TEKS 5.3.A, 5.3.B

3. Estimate: _____

$$576 \\ \times \quad 3$$

4. Estimate: _____

$$219 \\ \times \quad 6$$

5. Estimate: _____

$$72 \\ \times 37$$

6. Estimate: _____

$$359 \\ \times 18$$

7. Estimate: _____

$$804 \\ \times \quad 37$$

Use compatible numbers to estimate the quotient. TEKS 5.3.A

8. $522 \div 60$

9. $1,285 \div 32$

10. $6,285 \div 89$

_____   _____   _____

Divide. TEKS 5.3.C

11. $156 \div 13$

12. $318 \div 53$

13. $1,562 \div 34$

14. $4,024 \div 68$

_____   _____   _____   _____

Fill in the bubble completely to show your answer.

15. Dylan's dog weighs 12 times as much as his pet rabbit. The dog and rabbit weigh 104 pounds altogether. How much does Dylan's dog weigh? ↳ TEKS 5.3.C

Ⓐ 88 pounds

Ⓑ 96 pounds

Ⓒ 104 pounds

Ⓓ 8 pounds

16. Tickets for the basketball game cost $14 each. If the sale of the tickets brought in $2,212, how many tickets were sold? ↳ TEKS 5.3.C

Ⓐ 172

Ⓑ 158

Ⓒ 150

Ⓓ 168

17. Adele earns $194 every two weeks delivering newspapers. She spends $30 of each paycheck and saves the rest. If she is paid 26 times this year, how much will Adele save? ↳ TEKS 5.3.B

Ⓐ $3,244

Ⓑ $4,264

Ⓒ $772

Ⓓ $5,044

18. A local orange grower processes 2,330 oranges from his grove this year. The oranges are packaged in crates that each hold 96 oranges. All but one crate is full. How many oranges are in this last crate? Record your answer and fill in the bubbles on the grid. Be sure to use the correct place value. ↳ TEKS 5.3.C

⓪	⓪	⓪	·	⓪	⓪
①	①	①		①	①
②	②	②		②	②
③	③	③		③	③
④	④	④		④	④
⑤	⑤	⑤		⑤	⑤
⑥	⑥	⑥		⑥	⑥
⑦	⑦	⑦		⑦	⑦
⑧	⑧	⑧		⑧	⑧
⑨	⑨	⑨		⑨	⑨

Name _____

TEKS Number and Operations—5.3.E
MATHEMATICAL PROCESSES
5.1.F

Essential Question

How can patterns help you place the decimal point in a product?

Unlock the Problem

Cindy is combining equal-sized rectangles from different fabric patterns to make a postage-stamp quilt. Each rectangle has an area of 0.75 of a square inch. If she uses 1,000 rectangles to make the quilt, what will be the area of the quilt?

 Use the pattern to find the product.

$1 \times 0.75 = 0.75$

$10 \times 0.75 = 7.5$

$100 \times 0.75 = 75.$

$1,000 \times 0.75 = 750.$

The quilt will have an area of _____ square inches.

1. As you multiply by 10, 100, and 1,000, how does the position of the decimal point change in the product? _____

_____

Place value patterns can be used to find the product of a number and the decimals 0.1 and 0.01.

Example

Jorge is making a scale model of the Willis Tower in Chicago for a theater set. The height of the tower is 1,353 feet. If the model is $\frac{1}{100}$ of the actual size of the building, how tall is the model?

$1 \times 1,353 = 1,353$

$0.1 \times 1,353 = 135.3$

$0.01 \times 1,353 = $ [ ] $\leftarrow \frac{1}{100}$ of 1,353

- What fraction of the actual size of the building is the model?

_____

- Write the fraction as a decimal.

_____

Jorge's model of the Willis Tower is _____ feet tall.

2. As you multiply by 0.1 and 0.01, how does the position of the decimal point change in the product?

_____

Share and Show

Complete the pattern.

1. $1 \times \$17.04 = \$17.04$

  $10 \times \$17.04 = \$170.40$

  $100 \times \$17.04 = \$1,704$

  $1,000 \times \$17.04 = \underline{\hspace{2cm}}$

Think: The decimal point moves one place to the _____ for each equation.

Think: Money is expressed in hundredths. 170.4 = 170.40.

2. $1 \times 3.19 = \underline{\hspace{1.5cm}}$

  $10 \times 3.19 = \underline{\hspace{1.5cm}}$

  $100 \times 3.19 = \underline{\hspace{1.5cm}}$

  $1,000 \times 3.19 = \underline{\hspace{1.5cm}}$

☑ 3. $45.6 \times 1 = \underline{\hspace{1.5cm}}$

  $45.6 \times 10 = \underline{\hspace{1.5cm}}$

  $45.6 \times 100 = \underline{\hspace{1.5cm}}$

  $45.6 \times 1,000 = \underline{\hspace{1.5cm}}$

☑ 4. $1 \times 6,391 = \underline{\hspace{1.5cm}}$

  $0.1 \times 6,391 = \underline{\hspace{1.5cm}}$

  $0.01 \times 6,391 = \underline{\hspace{1.5cm}}$

Math Talk
Mathematical Processes

Explain how you know that when you multiply the product of 10×34.1 by 0.1, the result will be 34.1.

Problem Solving

Algebra Find the value of n.

5. $n \times \$3.25 = \$325.00$

  $n = \underline{\hspace{1.5cm}}$

6. $0.1 \times n = 89.5$

  $n = \underline{\hspace{1.5cm}}$

7. $1,000 \times n = 630$

  $n = \underline{\hspace{1.5cm}}$

8. Multi-Step A glacier in Alaska moved more than 29.9 meters a day. About how much farther would it move in 1,000 days than it would move in 100 days?

---

9. **H.O.T.** **Analyze** Three friends are selling items at an arts and crafts fair. Josey makes $45.75 selling jewelry. Mark makes 100 times as much as Josey makes by selling his custom furniture. Chance makes a tenth of the money Mark makes by selling paintings. How much money does each friend make?

Name

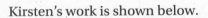

Problem Solving (Real World)

H.O.T. **What's the Error?**

10. Kirsten is making lanyards for a convention. She needs to make 1,000 lanyards and knows that 1 lanyard uses 1.75 feet of cord. How much cord will Kirsten need?

Kirsten's work is shown below.

$1 \times 1.75 = 1.75$

$10 \times 1.75 = 10.75$

$100 \times 1.75 = 100.75$

$1,000 \times 1.75 = 1,000.75$

Find and describe Kirsten's error.

Solve the problem using the correct pattern.

So, Kirsten needs _____ feet of cord to make 1,000 lanyards.

11. **Communicate** how Kirsten could have solved the problem without writing out the pattern needed.

_____

_____

Daily Assessment Task

Fill in the bubble completely to show your answer.

12. **Connect** When a number is multiplied by 1,000, the result is 320. When the number is multiplied by 100, the result is 32. What it the result when the number is multiplied by 10?

   (A) 3.2   (C) 16

   (B) 3,200   (D) 160

13. **Use Math Language** When a number is multiplied by 1,000, the result is 8,510. When the number is multiplied by 10, the result is 85.1. Which sentence follows the same pattern?

   (A) When multiplied by 100, the result is 8.51.

   (B) When multiplied by 100, the result is 851.

   (C) When multiplied by 1, the result is 85.1.

   (D) When multiplied by 1, the result is 851.

14. **Multi-Step** When a number is multiplied by 1,000 and then by 0.1, the result is 6,810. What is the original number?

   (A) 0.681

   (B) 681

   (C) 6.81

   (D) 68.1

 TEXAS Test Prep

15. A box of crackers costs $0.26 per ounce. If the box contains 10 ounces, what is the cost of the box of crackers?

   (A) $0.026

   (B) $2.60

   (C) $0.260

   (D) $26.00

TEKS **Number and Operations—5.3.E**
MATHEMATICAL PROCESSES 5.1.F

Name _____

3.1 Multiplication Patterns with Decimals

Find the value of *n*.

1. $n \times 43.50 = 435$

2. $394 \times n = 3.94$

3. $n \times 721 = 72.1$

n = _____

n = _____

n = _____

4. $n \times \$5.06 = \$506.00$

5. $0.074 \times n = 74$

6. $8{,}034 \times n = 80.34$

n = _____

n = _____

n = _____

Problem Solving

7. Jaden sells a painting for 10 times the original price. He sells the painting for $45.50. What was the original price of the painting?

_____

8. Marla thinks her dog might not be feeling well. He ate 0.1 times as much dog food on Wednesday as he ate on Tuesday. If her dog ate 6 cups of dog food on Tuesday, how much did he eat on Wednesday?

_____

Fill in the bubble completely to show your answer.

9. The camp counselors cut ribbons for an art project. They cut 1,000 pieces of ribbon. Each ribbon is 1.45 feet long. Which equation correctly shows the number of feet of ribbon cut for the project?

Ⓐ $1,000 \times 1.45 = 14.50$

Ⓑ $1,000 \times 1.45 = 145$

Ⓒ $1,000 \times 1.45 = 1,450$

Ⓓ $1,000 \times 1.45 = 14,500$

10. Marbles cost $0.50 per ounce. A box of marbles at the warehouse store contains 100 ounces of marbles. What is the cost of the box of marbles?

Ⓐ $5

Ⓑ $50

Ⓒ $500

Ⓓ $5,000

11. Which equation correctly shows the next product in the pattern?

$$1 \times 0.67 = 0.67$$
$$10 \times 0.67 = 6.7$$
$$100 \times 0.67 = 67$$

Ⓐ $1,000 \times 0.67 = 0.067$

Ⓑ $1,000 \times 0.67 = 67,000$

Ⓒ $1,000 \times 0.67 = 6,700$

Ⓓ $1,000 \times 0.67 = 670$

12. Bianca plants a tree at the park that is 0.3 meter tall. An oak tree nearby is 100 times taller. How tall is the oak tree?

Ⓐ 0.03 meter

Ⓑ 3 meters

Ⓒ 30 meters

Ⓓ 300 meters

13. **Multi-Step** Leo practices his violin 12.5 hours each week. He also practices singing for 3.5 hours each week. If he practices the same amount of time each week, how many hours does Leo practice in 10 weeks?

Ⓐ 125 hours

Ⓑ 160 hours

Ⓒ 16 hours

Ⓓ 1,600 hours

14. **Multi-Step** Greg ran 3 times as far as Jed. RJ ran 0.1 times as far as Greg. If Jed ran 25 yards, how far did Greg and RJ run?

Ⓐ Greg: 75 yards; RJ: 7.5 yards

Ⓑ Greg: 7.5 yards; RJ: 75 yards

Ⓒ Greg: 750 yards; RJ: 75 yards

Ⓓ Greg: 7.5 yards; RJ: 0.75 yards

3.2 Multiply Decimals and Whole Numbers

 **TEKS** Number and Operations—5.3.D
MATHEMATICAL PROCESSES
5.1.D, 5.1.E

? Essential Question

How can you use a model to multiply a whole number and a decimal?

Investigate

Materials ■ decimal models ■ color pencils

Giant tortoises move very slowly. They can travel a distance of about 0.17 mile in 1 hour. If a giant tortoise travels at the same speed, how far could it move in 4 hours?

A. Complete the statement to describe the problem.

I need to find how many total miles are in _____ groups

of _____.

- Write an expression to represent the problem. _____

B. Use the decimal model to find the answer.

- What does each small square in the decimal model represent?

_____

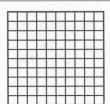

C. Shade a group of _____ squares to represent the distance a giant tortoise can move in 1 hour.

D. Use a different color to shade each additional

group of _____ squares until you

have _____ groups of _____ squares.

E. Record the total number of squares shaded. _____ squares

So, the giant tortoise can move _____ mile in 4 hours.

Math Talk
Mathematical Processes

Explain how the model helps you determine if your answer is reasonable.

Make Connections

You can use base-ten blocks to solve decimal multiplication problems. A quick picture is a way to record your work.

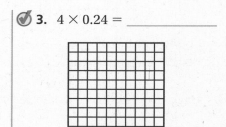

Find the product. 3×0.46

STEP 1
Make 3 groups of 4 tenths and 6 hundredths. Remember that a square or a flat is equal to 1. Draw a quick picture to record your work.

STEP 2 Combine the hundredths and rename.

There are _____ hundredths. I will rename _____

hundredths as _____. In your quick picture, cross out

the hundredths you renamed.

STEP 3 Combine the tenths and rename.

There are _____ tenths. I will rename _____ tenths as

_____. In your quick picture, cross out the tenths you

renamed.

STEP 4 Record the value shown by your completed quick picture.

So, $3 \times 0.46 =$ _____.

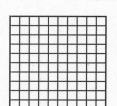

Share and Show

Math Talk
Mathematical Processes

Explain how renaming decimals is like renaming whole numbers.

Use the decimal model to find the product.

1. $5 \times 0.06 =$ _____

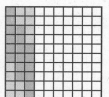

2. $2 \times 0.38 =$ _____

✓ 3. $4 \times 0.24 =$ _____

4. $3 \times 0.62 =$ _____

✓ 5. $4 \times 0.32 =$ _____

112

Name _____

Problem Solving Real World

Use the table for 6–8. Use quick pictures or base-ten blocks to help.

6. Each day a bobcat drinks about 3 times as much water as a Canada goose drinks. How much water does a bobcat drink in one day?

_____

7. **H.O.T.** **Multi-Step** River otters drink about 5 times as much water as a bald eagle drinks in a day. How much water does a river otter drink in three days?

_____

Water Consumption

Animal	Average Amount (liters per day)
Canada Goose	0.24
Cat	0.15
Mink	0.10
Opossum	0.30
Bald Eagle	0.16

8. **Write Math** ▶ **Explain** how you could use a quick picture to find the amount of water that a cat drinks in 5 days.

_____

_____

_____

_____

_____

_____

Write Math ▶ Show Your Work • • • •

9. **H.O.T.** **Compare** the product of 0.46 and 3 with each of the factors. Which number has the greatest value? **Explain** how this is different than multiplying two whole numbers.

_____

_____

_____

_____

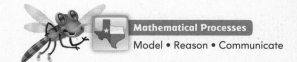
Daily Assessment Task

Fill in the bubble completely to show your answer.

10. **Representations** What multiplication expression does the model show?

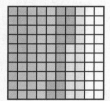

Ⓐ 5×0.4

Ⓒ 16×0.05

Ⓑ 5×0.6

Ⓓ 5×0.16

11. **Display** Which equation matches the model?

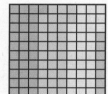 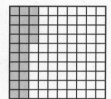

Ⓐ $4 \times 0.31 = 1.24$

Ⓒ $4 \times 0.39 = 1.24$

Ⓑ $4 \times 0.31 = 1.51$

Ⓓ $4 \times 0.39 = 1.56$

12. **Multi-Step Use Diagrams** Use a quick picture to multiply 3×0.16. Then multiply the result by 3 again. What is the final product?

Ⓐ 0.32

Ⓒ 1.44

Ⓑ 0.48

Ⓓ 1.24

 TEXAS Test Prep

13. Jared has a parakeet that weighs 1.44 ounces. Susie has a Senegal parrot that weighs 3 times as much as Jared's parakeet. How many ounces does Susie's parrot weigh?

Ⓐ 0.32 ounce

Ⓒ 4.32 ounces

Ⓑ 43.2 ounces

Ⓓ 0.43 ounce

114

Homework and Practice

Name _____

3.2 Multiply Decimals and Whole Numbers

Use the decimal model to find the product.

1. $4 \times 0.07 =$ _____

2. $3 \times 0.21 =$ _____

3. $4 \times 0.13 =$ _____

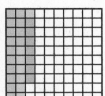

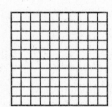

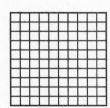

Find the product. Draw a quick picture.

4. $3 \times 0.38 =$ _____

5. $2 \times 0.41 =$ _____

Problem Solving Real World

6. Lars walks his dog 4 times farther than Michelle walks her dog. Michelle walks her dog 0.23 mile. How far does Lars walk his dog?

7. One day, Nat's dog drank 3 times as much water as his cat. If his cat drank 0.83 liter of water, how many liters did his dog drink?

_____ _____

Fill in the bubble completely to show your answer.

8. Which equation matches the model?

Ⓐ 5 × 0.18 = 0.9

Ⓑ 5 × 0.18 = 90

Ⓒ 5 × 0.18 = 9.0

Ⓓ 5 × 0.18 = 0.09

9. Sidney's bag of popcorn weighs 1.89 ounces. Sam's bag of popcorn weighs 4 times as much as Sidney's. What is the weight of Sam's bag of popcorn?

Ⓐ 0.756 ounce

Ⓑ 7.56 ounces

Ⓒ 75.6 ounces

Ⓓ 756 ounces

10. A beaker is filled with 0.23 liter of water. Leon fills another beaker with 3 times as much water. How much water is in Leon's beaker?

Ⓐ 0.96 liter

Ⓑ 0.84 liter

Ⓒ 0.69 liter

Ⓓ 0.47 liter

11. In a swimming race, Yvonne swam 0.18 mile. David swam 4 times as far as Yvonne. How far did David swim?

Ⓐ 2.2 miles

Ⓑ 0.22 mile

Ⓒ 7.2 miles

Ⓓ 0.72 mile

12. **Multi-Step** Carrie has 0.73 liters of juice in her pitcher. Sanji's pitcher has 2 times as much juice as Carrie's pitcher. Lee's pitcher has 4 times as much juice as Carrie's pitcher. Sanji and Lee pour all their juice into a large bowl. How much juice is in the bowl?

Ⓐ 1.46 liters

Ⓑ 4.38 liters

Ⓒ 2.92 liters

Ⓓ 5.11 liters

13. **Multi-Step** Justin and Hayden are playing a number game. Justin's number is the product of 4 × 0.06. Hayden's number 0.04 less than the product of Justin's number and 4. What is Hayden's number?

Ⓐ 0.92

Ⓑ 0.96

Ⓒ 0.60

Ⓓ 1.0

Name _____

 3.3 **Multiplication with Decimals and Whole Numbers**

 TEKS Number and Operations—5.3.E
Also, 5.3.A
MATHEMATICAL PROCESSES
5.1.A, 5.1.C

? Essential Question

How can you use properties and place value to multiply a decimal and a whole number?

🔑 Unlock the Problem

In 2010, the United States Mint released a newly designed Lincoln penny. A Lincoln penny has a mass of 2.5 grams. If there are 5 Lincoln pennies on a tray, what is the total mass of the pennies?

 Multiply. 5 × 2.5

Estimate the product. Round to the nearest whole number.

5 × _____ = _____

- How much mass does one penny have?

_____

- Use grouping language to describe what you are asked to find.

_____

🔑 One Way
Use the Distributive Property.

5 × 2.5 = 5 × (_____ + 0.5)

= (_____ × 2) + (5 × _____)

= _____ + _____

= _____

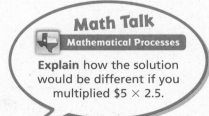
Math Talk
Mathematical Processes
Explain how the solution would be different if you multiplied $5 × 2.5.

🔑 Another Way
Show partial products.

STEP 1 Multiply the tenths by 5.

```
  2.5
×   5
```
← 5 × 5 tenths = 25 tenths, or 2 ones and 5 tenths

STEP 2 Multiply the ones by 5.

```
  2.5
×   5
  2.5
```
← 5 × 2 ones = 10 ones, or 1 ten

STEP 3 Add the partial products.

```
   2.5
 ×   5
   2.5
+ 10
```

So, 5 Lincoln pennies have a mass of _____ grams.

Example Use place value patterns.

Having a thickness of 1.35 millimeters, the dime is the thinnest coin produced by the United States Mint. If you stacked 8 dimes, what would be the total thickness of the stack?

Multiply. 8 × 1.35

STEP 1

Write the decimal factor as a whole number.

Think: 1.35 × 100 = 135

STEP 2

Multiply as with whole numbers.

STEP 3

Place the decimal point.

Think: 0.01 of 135 is 1.35. Find 0.01 of 1,080 and record the product.

$$
\begin{array}{r}
1.35 \\
\times\ \ 8 \\
\hline
?
\end{array}
\xrightarrow{\times\ 100}
\begin{array}{r}
135 \\
\times\ \ 8 \\
\hline
1,080
\end{array}
\xrightarrow{\times\ 0.01}
\begin{array}{r}
1.35 \\
\times\ \ 8 \\
\hline
\end{array}
$$

A stack of 15 dimes would have a thickness of _____ millimeters.

Share and Show

MATH BOARD

Place the decimal point in the product.

1.
$$
\begin{array}{r}
6.81 \\
\times\ \ 7 \\
\hline
4\,7\,6\,7
\end{array}
$$
Think: The place value of the decimal factor is hundredths.

2.
$$
\begin{array}{r}
3.7 \\
\times\ \ 2 \\
\hline
7\,4
\end{array}
$$

3.
$$
\begin{array}{r}
19.34 \\
\times\ \ 5 \\
\hline
9\,6\,7\,0
\end{array}
$$

Find the product.

4.
$$
\begin{array}{r}
6.32 \\
\times\ \ 3 \\
\hline
\end{array}
$$

✓ 5.
$$
\begin{array}{r}
4.5 \\
\times\ \ 8 \\
\hline
\end{array}
$$

6.
$$
\begin{array}{r}
40.7 \\
\times\ \ 5 \\
\hline
\end{array}
$$

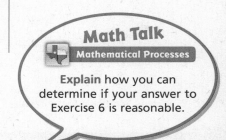

Math Talk

Mathematical Processes

Explain how you can determine if your answer to Exercise 6 is reasonable.

Name _____

Problem Solving

Practice: Copy and Solve Find the product.

7. 8 × 7.2

8. 3 × 1.45

9. 9 × 8.6

10. 6 × 0.79

11. 4 × 9.3

12. 7 × 0.81

13. 6 × 2.08

14. 5 × 23.66

15. **H.O.T.** **Write Math** ▶ Julie multiplies 6.27 by 7 and claims the product is 438.9. **Explain** without multiplying how you know Julie's answer is not correct. Find the correct answer.

_____

_____

_____

_____

Problem Solving

Use the table for 16–18.

16. Sari has a bag containing 6 half dollars. What is the mass of the half dollars in Sari's bag?

_____

Coin	Mass (in grams)
Nickel	5.00
Dime	2.27
Quarter	5.67
Half Dollar	11.34
Dollar	8.1

17. Felicia is running a game booth at a carnival. One of the games requires participants to guess the mass, in grams, of a bag of 9 dimes. What is the actual mass of the dimes in the bag?

_____

18. **H.O.T.** **Multi-Step** Chance has $2 in quarters. Blake has $5 in dollar coins. Whose coins have the greatest mass? **Explain**.

_____

_____

Daily Assessment Task

Fill in the bubble completely to show your answer.

19. **Apply** A hummingbird weighs 5.8 grams. If the hummingbird eats 8 times its body weight each day, how much does the bird eat in four days?

    (A) 23.2 grams

    (B) 46.4 grams

    (C) 185.6 grams

    (D) 464 grams

20. **Use Symbols** Which expression shows how to use the Distributive Property to find 5.17×9?

    (A) $5.17 + 9$

    (B) $9 \times (5.1) + 7$

    (C) $9 \times (5.1 + 7)$

    (D) $9 \times (5 + 0.17)$

21. **Multi-Step** The cost to park a car in a parking lot is $1.10 per hour. Maleek parked his car for 4 hours on Monday, 4 hours on Tuesday, and 4 hours on Wednesday. How much did he spend on parking in all?

    (A) $4.10

    (B) $4.40

    (C) $13.10

    (D) $13.20

 TEXAS Test Prep

22. Every day on his way to and from school, Milo walks a total of 3.65 miles. If he walks to school 5 days, how many miles will Milo have walked?

    (A) 1,825 miles

    (B) 18.25 miles

    (C) 182.5 miles

    (D) 1.825 miles

Name _____

3.3 Multiplication with Decimals and Whole Numbers

Find the product.

1. 4×7.12 **2.** 3×0.29 **3.** 8×2.19 **4.** 7×18.3

5. 5×9.29 **6.** 2×42.1 **7.** 7×0.34 **8.** 9×7.21

9. 4×5.2 **10.** 7×17.2 **11.** 4×3.92 **12.** 8×0.21

13. Logan multiplies 5.31 by 3 and says the product is 159.3. Explain why Logan's answer is not correct.

_____

_____

_____

Problem Solving

14. Minnie rides her bike 2.76 miles each day. How many miles will she bike in 7 days?

_____

15. Dominick buys a package of soup mix that is 1.38 ounces. How many ounces are 6 packages of soup mix?

_____

Fill in the bubble completely to show your answer.

16. Sandra uses 6.39 ounces of beans in a recipe. If she triples the recipe, how many ounces of beans will Sandra need?

Ⓐ 17.29 ounces

Ⓑ 18.83 ounces

Ⓒ 19.17 ounces

Ⓓ 20.19 ounces

17. Kip uses the Distributive Property to rewrite an expression.

$$(4 \times 3) + (4 \times 0.7)$$

What is the value of the expression?

Ⓐ 3.07

Ⓑ 11.7

Ⓒ 14.8

Ⓓ 29.6

18. Manny charges $1.25 for a cup of lemonade at the lemonade stand. He sells 9 cups. How much money does Manny collect?

Ⓐ $10.75

Ⓑ $11.00

Ⓒ $11.25

Ⓓ $11.75

19. Fabric costs $11.99 a yard. Leo buys 4 yards of red fabric and 3 yards of blue fabric. How much does Leo spend on fabric?

Ⓐ $47.96

Ⓑ $35.97

Ⓒ $77.33

Ⓓ $83.93

20. **Multi-Step** On the first day of summer, a rainstorm brought 2.29 inches of rain to the area. During the rest of the summer, there was 3 times as much rain as on the first day. What was the total number of inches of rainfall for the summer?

Ⓐ 6.29 inches

Ⓑ 5.67 inches

Ⓒ 6.87 inches

Ⓓ 9.16 inches

21. **Multi-Step** Nicky bought 14.2 pounds of coffee for the coffee shop. The shop usually uses 5 times that amount of coffee during one week. How much more coffee will Nicky need to purchase to get the right amount of coffee for the week?

Ⓐ 71 pounds

Ⓑ 56.8 pounds

Ⓒ 85.2 pounds

Ⓓ 50 pounds

3.4 Multiply Using Expanded Form

TEKS Number and Operations—5.3.D, 5.3.E
Also, 5.2.A
MATHEMATICAL PROCESSES
5.1.G

? Essential Question

How can you use expanded form and place value to multiply a decimal and a whole number?

Unlock the Problem Real World

The length of a day is the amount of time it takes a planet to make a complete rotation on its axis. On Jupiter, there are 9.8 Earth hours in a day. How many Earth hours are there in 46 days on Jupiter?

You can use a model and partial products to solve the problem.

One Way Use a model.

Multiply. 46 × 9.8

THINK	MODEL	RECORD

STEP 1

Rewrite the factors in expanded form, and label the model.

46 = _____ + _____

9.8 = _____ + _____

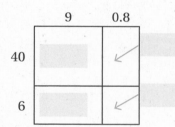

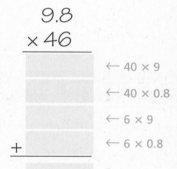

$$\begin{array}{r} 9.8 \\ \times 46 \\ \hline \end{array}$$

← 40 × 9

← 40 × 0.8

← 6 × 9

← 6 × 0.8

+ _____

STEP 2

Multiply to find the area of each section. The area of each section represents a partial product.

STEP 3

Add the partial products.

So, there are _____ Earth hours in 46 days on Jupiter.

---

1. What if you wanted to find the number of Earth hours in 125 days on Jupiter? How would your model change?

_____

_____

🔑 Another Way Use place value patterns.

A day on the planet Mercury lasts about 58.6 Earth days. How many Earth days are there in 14 days on Mercury?

Multiply. 14 × 58.6

STEP 1

Write the decimal factor as a whole number.

_____

STEP 2

Multiply as with whole numbers.

_____

STEP 3

Place the decimal point.

The decimal product is _____ of the whole number product.

So, there are _____ Earth days in 14 days on Mercury.

$$58.6 \xrightarrow{\times 10} 586 \xrightarrow{\times 0.1} 58.6$$

$$\begin{array}{r} 586 \\ \times\ 14 \\ \hline 2{,}344 \\ +\ 5{,}860 \\ \hline 8{,}204 \end{array}$$

$$\begin{array}{r} 58.6 \\ \times\ 14 \\ \hline \end{array}$$

$$\begin{array}{r} 58.6 \\ \times\ 14 \\ ? \end{array}$$

8,204 $\xrightarrow{\times 0.1}$

Math Talk

Mathematical Processes

What if you rewrite the problem as (10 + 4) × 58.6 and use the Distributive Property to solve? **Explain** how this is similar to your model using place value.

Share and Show

MATH BOARD

Draw a model to find the product.

1. 19 × 0.75 = _____

	0.7	0.05
10		
9		

✓ 2. 27 × 8.3 = _____

Find the product.

3. 18 × 8.7 = _____

4. 23 × 56.1 = _____

✓ 5. 47 × 5.92 = _____

Unlock the Problem

6. **H.O.T.** While researching facts on the planet Earth, Kate learned that a true Earth day is about 23.93 hours long. How many hours are in 2 weeks on Earth?

a. What are you being asked to find?

_____

_____

b. What information do you need to know to solve the problem?

_____

_____

_____

c. Write an expression to represent the problem to be solved. _____

d. Show the steps you used to solve the problem.

e. Complete the sentences.

On Earth, there are about _____,

hours in a day, _____ days in 1 week,

and _____ days in two weeks.

Since _____ × _____ =

_____ , there are about

_____ hours in 2 weeks on Earth.

7. **H.O.T.** **Multi-Step** A jacket costs $40 at the store. Max pays only 0.7 of the price because his father works at the store. Evan has a coupon for $10 off. **Explain** Who will pay the least for the jacket?

_____

_____

Daily Assessment Task

Fill in the bubble completely to show your answer.

8. In the rain forest, you find a beetle. You use beads to measure the beetle. It only measures 11 beads long. If the length of each bead is 12.8 mm, what is the length of this beetle?

   (A) 128 mm   (C) 157.7 mm

   (B) 140.8 mm   (D) 166.4 mm

9. **Use Math Language** Which would help you find the solution to 12×4.7?

   (A) Multiply 10 and 2 each by 4 and 0.7. Then add.

   (B) Multiply 4.7 by 1, and 4.7 by 2. Then add.

   (C) Multiply 1 by 4, and 2 by 0.7. Then add.

   (D) Multiply 1 and 0.2 each by 40 and 0.7. Then add.

10. **Multi-Step** Alonzo wanted to find the solution to 23×12.53. He made the area model shown below. Where did he go wrong in his calculations?

    $240 + 36 + 106 + 15.9 = 397.9$

	12	5.3
20	240	106
3	36	15.9

    (A) Alonzo is correct.

    (B) He used 20 and 3 in the area model.

    (C) He found the sum of the values in the area model incorrectly.

    (D) He used 5.3 in the area model instead of 0.53.

 TEXAS Test Prep

11. A car travels 56.7 miles in an hour. If it continues at the same speed, how far will the car travel in 12 hours?

    (A) 6,804 miles

    (B) 680.04 miles

    (C) 680.4 miles

    (D) 68.004 miles

TEKS Number and Operations—5.3.D, 5.3.E
Also, 5.2.A
MATHEMATICAL PROCESSES 5.1.G

3.4 Multiply Using Expanded Form

Draw a model to find the product.

1. $21 \times 0.64 =$ _____

	0.6	0.04
20		
1		

2. $16 \times 3.7 =$ _____

	3	0.7
10		
6		

Find the product.

3. $42 \times 7.2 =$ _____

4. $28 \times 3.17 =$ _____

5. $34 \times 0.41 =$ _____

Problem Solving (Real World)

6. Craig works at a restaurant for 21 hours in January. At this rate, how many hours will he work after 7.5 months?

7. Lori's dog eats 3.82 pounds of food in one week. How much food will the dog eat in 18 weeks?

_____   _____

Fill in the bubble completely to show your answer.

8. Amid needs 32.9 meters of fabric to make one tent. He has an order for 12 tents. How many meters of fabric does he need?

Ⓐ 367.2 meters

Ⓑ 394.8 meters

Ⓒ 288.3 meters

Ⓓ 416.9 meters

9. Angeline fills one water jug with 5.8 gallons of water. She needs to fill 17 water jugs for day camp. How many gallons of water does she need?

Ⓐ 114.2 gallons

Ⓑ 82.5 gallons

Ⓒ 98.6 gallons

Ⓓ 107.9 gallons

10. Corey rides his bike 17.4 miles in one hour. If he rides this distance every day, how far will he ride in 11 days?

Ⓐ 191.4 miles

Ⓑ 187.1 miles

Ⓒ 213.8 miles

Ⓓ 176.4 miles

11. Kavita's younger sister measures objects by using paper clips that are 16.2 mm long. Kavita's desk is 76 paper clips wide. What is the width of Kavita's desk?

Ⓐ 1,394.9 mm

Ⓑ 1,231.2 mm

Ⓒ 1,230.8 mm

Ⓓ 1,213.2 mm

12. **Multi-Step** Max makes an expanded form model to find the solution to 23×11.09. Which calculation reflects the numbers in his model?

Ⓐ 220 + 34 + 18 + .27

Ⓑ 220 + 22 + 1.8 + 2.7

Ⓒ 217 + 33 + 1.8 + .27

Ⓓ 220 + 33 + 1.8 + .27

13. **Multi-Step** Kim makes an expanded form model to find the solution to 18×14.39. The calculation shows the numbers in each box of the model. Which number in the calculation is incorrect?

$$140 + 112 + 3.09 + 3.12$$

Ⓐ 140

Ⓑ 112

Ⓒ 3.09

Ⓓ 3.12

3.5 PROBLEM SOLVING • Multiply Money

TEKS Number and Operations—5.3.D, 5.3.E, Also 5.10.D
MATHEMATICAL PROCESSES 5.1.B

? Essential Question

How can the strategy *draw a diagram* help you solve a decimal multiplication problem?

🔑 Unlock the Problem

A group of friends go to a local fair. Jayson spends $3.75. Maya spends 3 times as much as Jayson. Tia spends $5.25 more than Maya. How much does Tia spend?

Use the graphic organizer below to help you solve the problem.

Read

What do I need to find?

I need to find _____

_____

_____ .

What information am I given?

I need to use the amount spent by _____

to find the amount spent by _____ and

_____ at the fair.

Plan

What is my plan or strategy?

I can draw a diagram to show _____

_____

_____ .

Solve

The amount of money Maya and Tia spend depends on the amount Jayson spends. Draw a diagram to compare the amounts without calculating. Then, use the diagram to find the amount each person spends.

Jayson	$3.75

| Maya | ___ | ___ | ___ |

| Tia | ___ | ___ | ___ | $5.25 |

Jayson: $3.75

Maya: 3 × _____ = _____

Tia: _____ + $5.25 = _____

So, Tia spent _____ at the fair.

Julie's savings account has a balance of $57.85 in January. By March, her balance is 4 times as much as her January balance. Between March and November, Julie deposits a total of $78.45. If she does not withdraw any money from her account, what should Julie's balance be in November?

Read

What do I need to find?

What information am I given?

Plan

What is my plan or strategy?

Solve

So, Julie's savings account balance will be

_____ in November.

- How does the diagram help you determine if your answer is reasonable?

_____

_____

_____

Math Talk

Mathematical Processes

Describe a different diagram you could use to solve the problem.

Name _____

✓ 1. Manuel collects $45.18 for a fundraiser. Gerome collects $18.07 more than Manuel. Cindy collects 2 times as much as Gerome. How much money does Cindy collect for the fundraiser?

First, draw a diagram to show the amount Manuel collects.

Then, draw a diagram to show the amount Gerome collects.

Next, draw a diagram to show the amount Cindy collects.

Finally, find the amount each person collects.

Cindy collects _____ for the fundraiser.

✓ 2. **What if** Gerome collects $9.23 more than Manuel? If Cindy still collects 2 times as much as Gerome, how much money would Cindy collect?

_____

Problem Solving

3. **H.O.T.** **Multi-Step** It costs $5.15 to rent a kayak for 1 hour at a local state park. The price per hour stays the same for up to 5 hours of rental. After 5 hours, the cost decreases to $3.75 per hour. How much would it cost to rent a kayak for 6 hours?

_____

4. **H.O.T.** **Multi-Step** Jenn buys a pair of jeans for $24.99. Her friend Karen spends $3.50 more for the same pair of jeans. Vicki paid the same price as Karen for the jeans but bought 2 pairs. How much did Vicki spend?

_____

Write Math ▶ **Show Your Work** · · · ·

Daily Assessment Task

Fill in the bubble completely to show your answer.

5. **Apply** A recipe for chili calls for three types of beans. How much will the beans cost if black beans are $12.15, kidney beans are $16.27, and spicy refried beans are twice the cost of black beans?

Ⓐ $40.57

Ⓒ $54.69

Ⓑ $52.72

Ⓓ $60.96

6. **Use Math Language** Ada and Chen are cooking different chili recipes. Ada spent $21.88 on ingredients while Chen spent twice as much as Ada. What method could you use to find out how much Chen spent on ingredients?

Ⓐ Divide $21.88 by 2.

Ⓑ Add $21.88, $14.44, and $14.44.

Ⓒ Add $21.88, $21.88, and $21.88.

Ⓓ Multiply $21.88 by 2.

7. **Multi-Step** Marco spent $17.18 on tomatoes. Then he spent three times as much on peppers. How much did he spend on tomatoes and peppers?

Ⓐ $17.18

Ⓒ $57.81

Ⓑ $51.54

Ⓓ $68.72

 TEXAS Test Prep

8. At a bagel shop in town, each bagel costs $0.79. If Mr. Thomas buys a box of 8 bagels, how much will he pay for the bagels?

Ⓐ $6.32

Ⓑ $87.90

Ⓒ $63.20

Ⓓ $8.79

3.5 PROBLEM SOLVING • Multiply Money

1. Brandy buys 6 packs of party favors. The favors cost $3.49 per pack. She pays $1.26 in sales tax. How much does Brandy spend on the party favors?

_____

2. Hector sells his used books at a garage sale for $2.75 each. On Saturday, he sells 3 books. On Sunday, he sells 7 books. How much does Hector make selling his books?

_____

3. The original price for a case of paper is $12.88. The case of printer paper is on sale for 0.5 times the original price. How much will Alison spend on 5 cases of printer paper if she buys them on sale?

_____

4. Jordan has $14.56 in her wallet. Nico has three times as much money as Jordan in his wallet. Avery has $5.25 more than Nico. How much money does Avery have?

_____

5. In September, Ellen deposits $52.00 in her savings account. The next month, she deposits $22.50 more in her account. In November, Ellen deposits four times the amount she deposits in October. How much does Ellen deposit in her account in the three months?

_____

6. Leticia buys a magazine and rents 2 movies for her weekend entertainment. The price of a movie rental is $4.95. The magazine costs $5.99. How much does Leticia spend on her weekend entertainment?

_____

Problem Solving Real World

7. Sam and Justin each rent a bike for 4 hours. The rental price for 1 bike is $4.35 per hour. Then the boys decide to ride together on a tandem bike for another hour for $6.75. What is the total cost of the boys' bike rental?

_____

8. Kevan spends $19.99 at the mall. Amir spends $2.99 more than Kevan. Raul spends twice as much as Amir. How much does Raul spend?

_____

Fill in the bubble completely to show your answer.

9. Amelia spent $3.16 on peaches. Then she spent four times as much on raspberries. How much did she spend on peaches and raspberries?

   (A) $12.64

   (B) $15.80

   (C) $6.32

   (D) $8.50

10. Ryan buys 3 cans of tennis balls for $2.67 each. He buys 2 pairs of socks for $3.55 each. He pays with a $20 bill. How much change does Ryan get?

    (A) $2.64

    (B) $15.11

    (C) $13.78

    (D) $4.89

11. Sonya counts the coins in her coin purse. She has 7 quarters, 11 dimes, and 15 nickels. She has two more pennies than the number of quarters and dimes combined. What is the value of Sonya's coins?

    (A) $3.80

    (B) $3.65

    (C) $3.70

    (D) $3.95

12. Chef Michaels spends $24.46 on ingredients for a cake and $13.92 on ingredients for a pie. What method could you use to find out how much Chef Michaels spends on ingredients for the cake if he doubles the recipe?

    (A) Add $24.46 and $13.92.

    (B) Add $24.46, $24.46, and $13.92.

    (C) Multiply $24.46 by 2.

    (D) Divide $24.46 by 2.

13. **Multi-Step** At the farmer's market, heirloom tomatoes cost $5.99 a pound, beefsteak tomatoes cost $3.19 a pound, and cherry tomatoes cost $2.99 a pound. Joe bought 2 pounds of each type of tomato. How much did he spend on tomatoes?

    (A) $21.35

    (B) $12.17

    (C) $24.34

    (D) $18.16

14. **Multi-Step** Carnations cost $0.99 each, daisies cost $1.75 each, and lilies cost $2.26 each. How much would an arrangement cost that is made with 3 carnations, two more daisies than carnations, and twice as many lilies as daisies?

    (A) $34.32

    (B) $15.51

    (C) $25.28

    (D) $40.59

Decimal Multiplication

TEKS Number and Operations—5.3.D
MATHEMATICAL PROCESSES
5.1.D, 5.1.E.

? Essential Question

How can you use a model to multiply decimals?

Investigate

Materials ■ color pencils

The distance from Charlene's house to her school is 0.8 mile. Charlene rides her bike 7 tenths of the distance and walks the rest of the way. How far does Charlene ride her bike to school?

You can use a decimal square to multiply decimals.

Multiply. 0.7 × 0.8

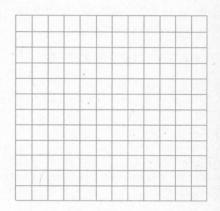

A. Draw a square with 10 equal columns.

  • What decimal value does each column represent? _____

B. Using a color pencil, shade columns on the grid to represent the distance to Charlene's school.

  • The distance to the school is 0.8 mile.

   How many columns did you shade? _____

C. Divide the square into 10 equal rows.

  • What decimal value does each row represent? _____

> **Math Idea**
> A decimal square can be used to make an area model.

D. Using a different color, shade rows that overlap the shaded columns to represent the distance to school that Charlene rides her bike.

  • What part of the distance to school does Charlene ride her bike? _____

  • How many rows of the shaded columns did you shade? _____

E. Count the number of squares that you shaded twice.

   There are _____ squares. Each square represents _____.

   Record the value of the squares as the product. 0.7 × 0.8 = _____

So, Charlene rides her bike for _____ mile.

Make Connections

You can use decimal squares to multiply decimals greater than 1.

Multiply. 0.3 × 1.4

STEP 1

Shade columns to represent 1.4.

How many tenths are in 1.4?

_____

_____

STEP 2

Shade rows that overlap the shaded columns to represent 0.3.

How many rows of the shaded

columns did you shade? _____

_____

STEP 3

Count the number of squares that you shaded twice. Record the product at the right.

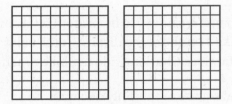

0.3 × 1.4 = _____

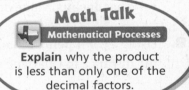

Math Talk

Mathematical Processes

Explain why the product is less than only one of the decimal factors.

Share and Show

Multiply. Use the decimal model.

1. 0.8 × 0.4 = _____

2. 0.1 × 0.7 = _____

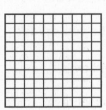

3. 0.4 × 1.6 = _____

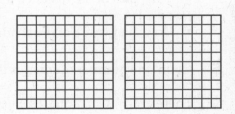

Name _____

H.O.T. Sense or Nonsense?

4. Use Diagrams Randy and Stacy used area models to find 0.3 of 0.5. Both Randy's and Stacy's models are shown below. Whose model makes sense? Whose model is nonsense? **Explain** your reasoning below each model. Then record the correct answer.

Randy's Area Model

Stacy's Area Model

$0.3 \times 0.5 =$ _____

5. **H.O.T.** **Multi-Step** A large bottle contains 1.2 liters of olive oil. A medium-sized bottle has 0.6 times the amount of olive oil as the large bottle. How much more olive oil does the large bottle contain than the medium-sized bottle ?

_____

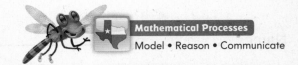

Daily Assessment Task

Fill in the bubble completely to show your answer.

6. **Representations** Farmer Green grows 0.9 tons of grain each year. Seven tenths of the grain grown is barley. Which model shows the amount of barley grown each year?

Ⓐ   Ⓒ

Ⓑ   Ⓓ

7. **Use Diagrams** What multiplication problem is modeled by the diagram?

Ⓐ $1.3 \times 0.3 = 1.03$

Ⓑ $0.7 \times 0.3 = 1.03$

Ⓒ $1.1 \times 0.3 = 0.3$

Ⓓ $0.3 \times 1.1 = 0.33$

8. **Multi-Step** An outdoor swimming race is 1.6 miles long. Simon swims 8 tenths of the course, and his friend Sheila swims 9 tenths of the course. How much farther did Sheila swim?

Ⓐ 0.16 mile   Ⓒ 0.1 mile

Ⓑ 0.72 mile   Ⓓ 0.2 mile

⭐ TEXAS Test Prep

9. Alex is 1.3 meters tall. His brother, Raul, is 0.6 times as tall as Alex. How tall is Raul?

Ⓐ 1.9 meters   Ⓒ 0.78 meter

Ⓑ 0.7 meter   Ⓓ 7.8 meters

138

Name _____

3.7 Multiply Decimals

? Essential Question

What strategies can you use to place a decimal point in a product?

Connect You can use what you have learned about patterns and place value to place the decimal point in the product when you multiply two decimals.

$1 \times 0.1 = 0.1$

$0.1 \times 0.1 = 0.01$

$0.01 \times 0.1 = 0.001$

Remember

Think about the pattern on the left. When a number is multiplied by a decimal, the decimal point moves one place to the left in the product for each decreasing place value being multiplied.

🔑 Unlock the Problem

A male leopard seal is measured and has a length of 2.8 meters. A male elephant seal is about 1.5 times as long. What length is the male elephant seal?

Multiply. 1.5×2.8

🔓 One Way Use place value.

STEP 1

Multiply as with whole numbers.

_____

STEP 2

Place the decimal point.

Think: Tenths are being multiplied by tenths. Use the pattern 0.1×0.1.

Place the decimal point so the value of the

decimal is _____.

So, the length of a male elephant seal is about _____ meters.

$$
\begin{array}{r}
28 \\
\times 15 \\
\hline
140 \\
+ 280 \\
\hline
420
\end{array}
$$

$28 \xrightarrow{\times 0.1} 2.8$ 1 place value

$\times 15 \xrightarrow{\times 0.1} \times 1.5$ 1 place value

         1 + 1, or 2 place values

$420 \xrightarrow{\times 0.01}$

- **What if** you multiplied 2.8 by 1.74? What would be the place value of the product? **Explain** your answer.

_____

🔑 Another Way Use estimation.

You can use an estimate to place the decimal point in a product.

Multiply. 7.8 × 3.12

STEP 1

Estimate by rounding each factor to the nearest whole number.

$$7.8 \quad \times \quad 3.12$$
$$\downarrow \qquad\qquad \downarrow$$
$$\underline{\quad\quad} \times \underline{\quad\quad} = \underline{\quad\quad}$$

312	3.12
× 78	× 7.8

STEP 2

Multiply as with whole numbers.

STEP 3

Use the estimate to place the decimal point.

Think: The product should be close to your estimate.

7.8 × 3.12 = _____

Share and Show

Place the decimal point in the product.

1.
    3.62
  × 1.4
  5 0 6 8
Think: A hundredth is being multiplied by a tenth. Use the pattern 0.01 × 0.1.

2.
  6.8
× 1.2
8 1 6
Estimate: 1 × 7 = _____

Find the product.

3.
  0.9
× 0.8

✓ 4.
  84.5
× 5.5

✓ 5.
  2.39
× 2.7

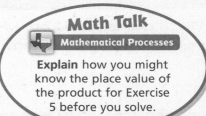

Math Talk
Mathematical Processes

Explain how you might know the place value of the product for Exercise 5 before you solve.

Name _____

Problem Solving

Practice: Copy and Solve Find the product.

6. 3.4×5.2

7. 0.9×2.46

8. 9.1×5.7

9. 4.8×6.01

10. 7.6×18.7

11. 1.5×9.34

12. 0.77×14.9

13. 3.3×58.14

14. **H.O.T.** **Write Math** ▶ In the multiplication problem 5.5×4.6, is the answer 25.3 or 25.30? **Explain** your reasoning.

_____

_____

Problem Solving Real World

Write Math ▶ **Show Your Work** · · · ·

15. **Analyze** Charlie has an adult Netherlands dwarf rabbit that weighs 1.2 kilograms. Cliff's adult Angora rabbit weighs 2.9 times as much as Charlie's rabbit. How much does Cliff's rabbit weigh?

_____

16. **Multi-Step** John has pet rabbits in an enclosure that has an area of 30.72 square feet. The enclosure Taylor is planning to build for his rabbits will be 2.2 times as large as John's. How many more square feet will Taylor's enclosure have than John's enclosure?

_____

17. **H.O.T.** A zoo is planning a new building for the penguin exhibit. First, they made a model that was 1.3 meters tall. Then, they made a more detailed model that was 1.5 times as tall as the first model. The building will be 2.5 times as tall as the height of the detailed model. What will be the height of the building?

_____

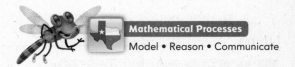
Daily Assessment Task

Fill in the bubble completely to show your answer.

18. Arnold is solving this multiplication problem: 8.12 × 4.7. Which of these estimates can Arnold use to help him determine where the decimal point belongs in the product?

    Ⓐ 80 × 40 = 3,200

    Ⓑ 8 × 5 = 40

    Ⓒ 800 × 4 = 3,200

    Ⓓ 800 × 5 = 4,000

19. Which multiplication problem will not give the same product as 5.5 × 4.44?

    Ⓐ 5.5 × 4.44

    Ⓑ 0.55 × 44.4

    Ⓒ 55 × 0.444

    Ⓓ 0.55 × 0.444

20. **Multi-Step** Gina bought 2.5 pounds of peaches that cost $1.38 per pound at the grocery store. Amy went to the local farmer's market and purchased 3.5 pounds of peaches at $0.98 per pound. Who spent more money, and how much more?

    Ⓐ Gina, $0.20   Ⓒ Amy, $0.20

    Ⓑ Gina, $0.02   Ⓓ Amy, $0.02

 TEXAS Test Prep

21. A vine in Mr. Jackson's garden was 3.6 feet long. When it is measured again, it is 2.1 times as long. How long is the vine?

    Ⓐ 7.5 feet   Ⓒ 5.7 feet

    Ⓑ 6.6 feet   Ⓓ 7.56 feet

144

Name _____

3.8 Zeros in the Product

❓ Essential Question

How do you know you have the correct number of decimal places in your product?

🗝 Unlock the Problem Real World

Connect When decimals are multiplied, the product may not have enough digits to place the decimal point. In these cases, you may need to write additional zeros.

Students are racing garden snails and measuring the distance the snails travel in 1 minute. Chris's snail travels a distance of 0.2 foot. Jamie's snail travels 0.4 times as far as Chris's snail. How far does Jamie's snail travel?

• Using the given information, describe what you are being asked to find.

_____

_____

_____

 Multiply. 0.4×0.2

STEP 1

Multiply as with whole numbers.

_____

STEP 2

Determine the position of the decimal point in the product.

Since tenths are being multiplied by tenths, the

product will show _____.

_____

STEP 3

Place the decimal point.

Are there enough digits in the product to place

the decimal point? _____

Write zeros, as needed, to the left of the whole number product to place the decimal point.

So, Jamie's snail travels a distance of _____ foot.

$$
\begin{array}{r}
2 \xrightarrow{\times 0.1} \\
\times 4 \xrightarrow{\times 0.1} \\
\hline
8 \xrightarrow{\times 0.01}
\end{array}
\qquad
\begin{array}{r}
0.2 \\
\times 0.4 \\
\hline
8
\end{array}
\quad
\begin{array}{l}
\text{1 place value} \\
\text{1 place value} \\
\text{1 + 1, or 2 place values}
\end{array}
$$

Math Talk
Mathematical Processes

Explain how you know when to write zeros in the product to place a decimal point.

🔓 **Example** Multiply money.

Multiply. $0.2 \times \$0.30$

STEP 1 Multiply as with whole numbers.

Think: The factors are 30 hundredths and 2 tenths.

What are the whole numbers you will multiply?

_____

_____

STEP 2 Determine the position of the decimal point in the product.

Since hundredths are being multiplied by tenths,

the product will show _____.

_____

STEP 3 Place the decimal point. Write zeros to the left of the whole number product as needed.

Since the problem involves dollars and cents, what place value should you use to show cents?

_____

So, $0.2 \times \$0.30$ is _____.

$$\$0.30$$
$$\times \quad 0.2$$

Share and Show

Write zeros in the product.

1. $\begin{array}{r} 0.05 \\ \times\ 0.7 \\ \hline 35 \end{array}$ **Think:** Hundredths are multiplied by tenths. What should be the place value of the product?

2. $\begin{array}{r} 0.2 \\ \times\ 0.3 \\ \hline 6 \end{array}$

3. $\begin{array}{r} 0.02 \\ \times\ 0.2 \\ \hline 4 \end{array}$

Find the product.

4. $\begin{array}{r} \$0.05 \\ \times\ 0.8 \\ \hline \end{array}$

☑ 5. $\begin{array}{r} 0.09 \\ \times\ 0.7 \\ \hline \end{array}$

☑ 6. $\begin{array}{r} 0.2 \\ \times\ 0.1 \\ \hline \end{array}$

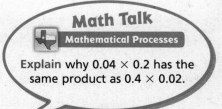

Math Talk
Mathematical Processes

Explain why 0.04×0.2 has the same product as 0.4×0.02.

Unlock the Problem

7. **H.O.T.** **Multi-Step** On an average day, a garden snail can travel about 0.05 mile. The snail travels 0.2 times as far as the average distance on Day 1. It travels 0.6 times as far as the average distance on Day 2. How far does it travel in two days?

(A) 0.01 mile   (C) 0.1 mile

(B) 0.03 mile   (D) 0.04 mile

a. What are you being asked to find? _____

b. What information will you use to solve the problem? _____

_____

_____

c. Which operations can you use to solve the problem? _____

_____

_____

d. Show how you will solve the problem.

e. Fill in the bubble for the correct answer choice above.

8. **H.O.T.** Michael multiplies 0.2 by a number. He records the product as 0.008. What number did Michael use?

_____

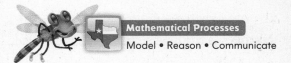

Daily Assessment Task

Fill in the bubble completely to show your answer.

9. **Apply** Newaye is making a salt solution. The instructions ask for 0.07 kilograms of salt to be added to every liter of water. How much salt should he use if he wants to make a solution with 0.5 liter of water?

   Ⓐ 0.35 kilogram

   Ⓑ 0.035 kilogram

   Ⓒ 0.305 kilogram

   Ⓓ 3.5 kilograms

10. Al buys raw peanuts for $0.40 for a pound. He roasts them and sells them in 0.2-pound bags. How much does a bag of peanuts cost Al?

   Ⓐ $8.00

   Ⓑ $0.80

   Ⓒ $0.08

   Ⓓ $0.008

11. **Multi-Step** Al finds a new supplier. He can buy raw peanuts for $0.30 for a pound. If he sells the peanuts in 0.2-pound bags for $2.50 a bag, how much profit is made on each bag?

   Ⓐ $2.44

   Ⓑ $2.04

   Ⓒ $1.90

   Ⓓ $0.60

 TEXAS Test Prep

12. **Apply** In a science experiment, Tania uses 0.8 ounce of water to create a reaction. She wants the next reaction to be 0.1 times the size of the previous reaction. How much water should she use?

   Ⓐ 0.08 ounce

   Ⓑ 0.9 ounce

   Ⓒ 0.8 ounce

   Ⓓ 0.09 ounce

150

3.8 Zeros in the Product

Write zeros in the product.

1.
```
    0.06
×   0.4
    ___
     24
```

2.
```
    0.3
×   0.3
    ___
      9
```

3.
```
    0.04
×   0.2
    ___
      8
```

4.
```
    0.05
×   0.9
    ___
     45
```

5.
```
    0.03
×   0.2
    ___
      6
```

6.
```
    0.9
×   0.1
    ___
      9
```

Find the product.

7.
```
   $0.04
×   0.5
```

8.
```
   $0.80
×   0.2
```

9.
```
    0.08
×   0.8
```

10.
```
    0.02
×   0.3
```

11.
```
    0.1
×   0.7
```

12.
```
   $0.60
×   0.5
```

Problem Solving

13. The distance from Mario's house to the park is 0.5 mile. His friend Kirk's house is 0.3 times as far from Mario's house as Mario's house is from the park. What is the distance from Mario's house to Kirk's house?

14. A scientist determines the mass of two specimens. Specimen A has a mass of 0.08 gram. Specimen B has a mass 0.9 times the mass of Specimen B. What is the mass of Specimen B?

_____

_____

Fill in the bubble completely to show your answer.

15. Joel makes a card for his dad. The length of the card is 0.7 foot. The width of the card is 0.4 times the length. What is the width of the card?

   (A) 0.11 foot

   (B) 0.74 foot

   (C) 0.28 foot

   (D) 0.21 foot

16. Carlos uses a ruler to measure the distances between cities on his map of the U.S. The first distance measures 0.6 meter. The second distance he measures is 0.1 times the first measurement. What is the second measurement?

   (A) 0.6 meter

   (B) 0.06 meter

   (C) 6 meters

   (D) 0.006 meter

17. The product is 0.016. One factor is 0.8. What is the other factor?

   (A) 0.02

   (B) 0.2

   (C) 2

   (D) 0.002

18. The mass of a vase is 0.3 kilogram. A flower has a mass that is 0.03 times as much as the vase. What is the mass of the flower?

   (A) 0.09 kilogram

   (B) 0.9 kilogram

   (C) 9.0 kilograms

   (D) 0.009 kilogram

Use the table for 19–21.

Ribbon Sale	
Fabric	**Price per yard**
Cotton	$0.20
Satin	$0.50
Silk	$0.40
Velvet	$0.90

19. Amanda buys 0.4 yard of cotton ribbon to wrap a package. How much does Amanda spend?

   (A) $0.80

   (B) $0.24

   (C) $0.08

   (D) $0.60

20. **Multi-Step** Li buys 0.8 yard of satin ribbon and 0.8 yard of velvet ribbon. How much more does she spend on the velvet ribbon?

   (A) $0.32   (B) $0.72

   (C) $0.40   (D) $0.12

21. **Multi-Step** Marta wants to buy 0.5 yard each of two types of ribbon. She wants to spend less than 40 cents. Which two types of ribbon can Marta buy?

   (A) Cotton and satin

   (B) Satin and silk

   (C) Silk and velvet

   (D) Cotton and velvet

Name _____

 Module 3 Assessment

Concepts and Skills

1. **Explain** how you can use a quick picture to find 3×2.7. ↳ TEKS 5.3.D

_____

_____

Use models or strategies to find the product. Show your work. ↳ TEKS 5.3.D, 5.3.E

2. $5 \times 0.89 =$ _____

3. $9 \times 2.35 =$ _____

4. $23 \times 8.6 =$ _____

5. $0.09 \times 0.7 =$ _____

6. $0.8 \times \$0.40 =$ _____

7. $0.75 \times \$2.60 =$ _____

Draw a diagram to solve. ↳ TEKS 5.3.D, 5.3.E

8. Julie spends $5.62 at the store. Micah spends 5 times as much as Julie. Jeremy spends $6.72 more than Micah. How much money does each person spend?

Julie: $5.62

Micah: _____

Jeremy: _____

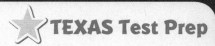

9. Sarah is cutting ribbons for a pep rally. The length of each ribbon needs to be 3.68 inches. If she needs 1,000 ribbons, what is the length of ribbon Sarah needs? ◆ TEKS 5.3.E

Ⓐ 368 inches

Ⓑ 36.8 inches

Ⓒ 3.68 inches

Ⓓ 3,680 inches

10. At Anne's Fabric Emporium, a yard of chiffon fabric costs $7.85. Lee plans to purchase 0.8 yard for a craft project. If Lee gives the cashier $10, how much change should he receive? ◆ TEKS 5.3.E

Ⓐ $6.28

Ⓑ $3.72

Ⓒ $7.05

Ⓓ $8.65

11. At the produce market, a pound of bananas costs $0.48 and a pound of oranges costs $0.80. Harry buys 2.75 pounds of bananas and 1.5 pounds of oranges. How much will Harry pay for the fruits? ◆ TEKS 5.3.E

Ⓐ $2.52

Ⓑ $1.32

Ⓒ $1.20

Ⓓ $4.23

12. Adam is carrying books to the classroom for his teacher. Each book weighs 3.85 pounds. If he carries 4 books, about how many pounds is Adam carrying? ◆ TEKS 5.3.A

Ⓐ 7.85 pounds

Ⓑ 13.2 pounds

Ⓒ 1.6 pounds

Ⓓ 16 pounds

Division Patterns with Decimals

ALGEBRA

TEKS Number and Operations—5.3.G

MATHEMATICAL PROCESSES
5.1.C, 5.1.D

Essential Question

How can patterns help you place the decimal point in a quotient?

Unlock the Problem Real World

The Healthy Wheat Bakery uses 560 pounds of flour to make 1,000 loaves of bread. Each loaf contains the same amount of flour. How many pounds of flour are used in each loaf of bread?

You can use place value patterns to help you find quotients. Dividing by 10, 100, or 1,000 is the same as multiplying by 0.1, 0.01, or 0.001.

- Underline the sentence that tells you what you are trying to find.
- Circle the numbers you need to use.

 Use place-value patterns.

Divide. 560 ÷ 1,000

Look for a pattern in these products and quotients.

560 × 1 = 560	560 ÷ 1 = 560
560 × 0.1 = 56.0	560 ÷ 10 = 56.0
560 × 0.01 = 5.60	560 ÷ 100 = 5.60
560 × 0.001 = 0.560	560 ÷ 1,000 = 0.560

So, _____ pound of flour is used in each loaf of bread.

1. As you divide by 10, 100, and 1,000, how does the position of the decimal point change in the quotients?

_____

Try This! Complete the pattern.

Ⓐ 32.6 ÷ 1 = _____

32.6 ÷ 10 = _____

32.6 ÷ 100 = _____

Ⓑ 150.2 ÷ 1 = _____

150.2 ÷ 10 = _____

150.2 ÷ 100 = _____

Math Talk

Mathematical Processes

Explain how you can determine where to place the decimal point in the quotient 47.3 ÷ 100.

Connect Dividing by 10 is the same as multiplying by 0.1 or finding $\frac{1}{10}$ of a number.

 **Example**

Liang used 25.5 pounds of tomatoes to make a large batch of salsa. He used one-tenth as many pounds of onions as pounds of tomatoes. He used one-hundredth as many pounds of green peppers as pounds of tomatoes. How many pounds of each ingredient did Liang use?

Tomatoes: 25.5 pounds

Onions: 25.5 pounds ÷ _____ | **Green Peppers:** 25.5 pounds ÷ _____

Think: 25.5 ÷ 1 = _____ | **Think:** _____ ÷ 1 = _____

25.5 ÷ 10 = _____ | _____ ÷ 10 = _____

_____ ÷ 100 = _____

So, Liang used 25.5 pounds of tomatoes, _____ pounds of onions,

and _____ pound of green peppers.

 Share and Show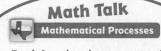

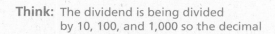

Math Talk
Mathematical Processes

Explain what happens to the value of a number when you divide by 10, 100, or 1,000.

Complete the pattern.

1. 456 ÷ 1 = 456

456 ÷ 10 = 45.6

456 ÷ 100 = 4.56

456 ÷ 1,000 = _____

Think: The dividend is being divided by 10, 100, and 1,000 so the decimal

point will move to the _____ one place for each equation.

2. 1,225 ÷ 1 = _____

1,225 ÷ 10 = _____

1,225 ÷ 100 = _____

1,225 ÷ 1,000 = _____

3. 605 ÷ 1 = _____

605 ÷ 10 = _____

605 ÷ 100 = _____

605 ÷ 1,000 = _____

4. 74.3 ÷ 1 = _____

74.3 ÷ 10 = _____

74.3 ÷ 100 = _____

Name _____

Problem Solving

Algebra Find the value of n.

5. $268 \div n = 0.268$

6. $n \div 100 = 0.123$

7. $n \div 10 = 4.6$

$n = $ _____

$n = $ _____

$n = $ _____

8. **Write Math** ▸ **Explain** how you know that the quotient $47.3 \div 10$ is equal to the product 47.3×0.1.

_____

_____

_____

Problem Solving Real World

Use the table to solve 9–11.

9. **Multi-Step** About how much more cornmeal than flour does each muffin contain?

_____

10. **H.O.T.** If each muffin contains the same amount of sugar, how many kilograms of sugar, to the nearest thousandth, are in each corn muffin?

Math on the Spot

_____

11. **H.O.T.** **Multi-Step** The bakery decides to make only 100 corn muffins on Tuesday. How many kilograms of sugar will be needed?

_____

Dry Ingredients for 1,000 Corn Muffins	
Ingredient	**Number of Kilograms**
Cornmeal	150
Flour	110
Sugar	66.7
Baking powder	10
Salt	4.17

Daily Assessment Task

Fill in the bubble completely to show your answer.

12. Orange crayons are usually made in batches of 100. If it takes 22 pounds of wax to make 100 orange crayons, then how much wax will you need to make one orange crayon?

Ⓐ 0.22 pound   Ⓒ 2 pounds

Ⓑ 22 pounds   Ⓓ 0.022 pound

13. **Use Symbols** A famous barbecue restaurant in Texas makes 1,000 pounds of barbecue pork each week. The owner has a catering order that requires 100 pounds of barbecue pork. The owner uses 44 pounds of sauce for every 1,000 pounds of barbecue pork. Which equation shows the amount of sauce needed for the catering order?

Ⓐ $44 \div 1 = 44$ pounds

Ⓑ $44 \div 10 = 4.4$ pounds

Ⓒ $44 \div 100 = 0.44$ pound

Ⓓ $44 \div 1,000 = 0.044$ pound

14. **Multi-Step** Loretta is trying to build the largest taco in the world. She uses 2,000 pounds of ground beef, one-tenth as many pounds of cheese, one-hundredth as many pounds of lettuce, and one-thousandth as many pounds of hot sauce. How many pounds of lettuce and cheese does she use?

Ⓐ 2,020 pounds   Ⓒ 2,200 pounds

Ⓑ 220 pounds   Ⓓ 20 pounds

⭐ TEXAS Test Prep

15. **Apply** Ella used 37.2 pounds of apples to make applesauce. She used one-tenth as many pounds of sugar as pounds of apples. How many pounds of sugar did Ella use?

Ⓐ 0.372 pound

Ⓑ 3.72 pounds

Ⓒ 372 pounds

Ⓓ 0.0372 pound

Homework and Practice

Name _____

4.1 Division Patterns with Decimals

Find the value of *n*.

1. $456 \div n = 4.56$

n = _____

2. $n \div 100 = 0.982$

n = _____

3. $n \div 10 = 32.7$

n = _____

4. $32 \div 1{,}000 = n$

n = _____

5. $1{,}672 \div n = 1.672$

n = _____

6. $24 \div 100 = n$

n = _____

7. $9{,}871 \div n = 987.1$

n = _____

8. $n \div 10 = 5.69$

n = _____

9. $n \div 1{,}000 = 0.823$

n = _____

 Problem Solving Real World

10. Mr. Baker drives 24.5 miles to his cousin's house. He drives one-tenth as many miles to his nephew's house. How many miles does Mr. Baker drive to his nephew's house?

_____

11. Elena sews sequins on a skirt for the dance recital. She sews 100 sequins end-to-end along the length of the skirt. The skirt is 50 centimeters long. What is the length of one sequin?

_____

Fill in the bubble completely to show your answer.

12. An online bookstore ships boxes with a copy of the new bestseller in each box. The total weight of the shipment is 1,200 pounds. If each box weighs 1.2 pounds, how many boxes are shipped?

    Ⓐ 10

    Ⓑ 10,000

    Ⓒ 1,000

    Ⓓ 100

13. A car dealership uses 1,350 gallons of gasoline to fill the tanks of 100 of their compact cars. How much gas does each tank hold?

    Ⓐ 13.5 gallons

    Ⓑ 1.35 gallons

    Ⓒ 135 gallons

    Ⓓ 0.135 gallon

Violet sells homemade granola at the Saturday market. Her recipe makes 10 large bags of granola or 100 snack-size bags. Use Violet's recipe at the right for 14–16.

14. Which equation shows the number of grams of almonds in one large bag?

    Ⓐ 750.2 ÷ 1 = 750.2 grams

    Ⓑ 750.2 ÷ 10 = 75.02 grams

    Ⓒ 750.2 ÷ 100 = 7.502 grams

    Ⓓ 750.2 ÷ 1,000 = 0.7502 gram

Bulk Granola Recipe	
Ingredient	Number of Grams
Oats	3000
Almonds	750.2
Sunflower seeds	450.5
Dried fruit	1,000

15. **Multi-Step** What is the total number of grams of oats and sunflower seeds in one large bag?

    Ⓐ 345.05 grams

    Ⓑ 750.5 grams

    Ⓒ 45.05 grams

    Ⓓ 120.07 grams

16. **Multi-Step** How many grams of sunflower seeds are in two snack-size servings of granola?

    Ⓐ 4.505 grams   Ⓒ 91 grams

    Ⓑ 45.05 grams   Ⓓ 9.01 grams

4.2 Divide Decimals by Whole Numbers

TEKS Number and Operations—5.3.F
MATHEMATICAL PROCESSES
5.1.C, 5.1.G

? Essential Question

How can you use a model to divide a decimal by a whole number?

Investigate

Materials ■ decimal models ■ color pencils

Angela has enough wood to make a picture frame with a perimeter of 2.4 meters. She wants the frame to be a square. What will be the length of each side of the frame?

A. Shade decimal models to show 2.4.

B. You need to share your model among _____ equal groups.

C. Since 2 wholes cannot be shared among 4 groups without regrouping, cut your model apart to show the tenths.

There are _____ tenths in 2.4.

Share the tenths equally among the 4 groups.

There are _____ ones and _____ tenths in each group.

Write a decimal for the amount in each group. _____

D. Use your model to complete the number sentence.

2.4 ÷ 4 = _____

So, the length of each side of the frame will be _____ meter.

Draw Conclusions

1. You can also use area models to represent division. Shade the area model below and circle groups to show 2.4 ÷ 4.

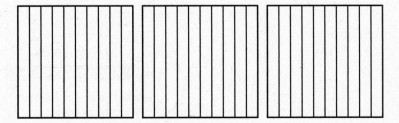

Math Talk
Mathematical Processes

What other manipulatives or models could you use to solve this problem?

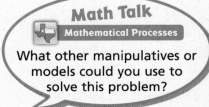

Make Connections

You can also use base-ten blocks to model division of a decimal by a whole number.

Materials ■ base-ten blocks

Kyle has a roll of ribbon 3.21 yards long. He cuts the ribbon into 3 equal lengths. How long is each piece of ribbon?

Divide. 3.21 ÷ 3

STEP 1

Use base-ten blocks to show 3.21.

Remember that a flat represents one, a long represents one tenth, and a small cube represents one hundredth.

There are _____ one(s), _____ tenth(s), and

_____ hundredth(s).

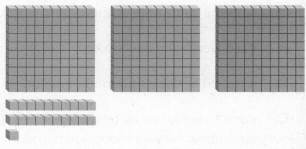

STEP 2 Share the ones.

Share an equal number of ones among 3 groups.

There is _____ one(s) shared in each group and _____ one(s) left over.

STEP 3 Share the tenths.

Two tenths cannot be shared among 3 groups without regrouping. Regroup the tenths by replacing them with hundredths.

There are _____ tenth(s) shared in each group and

_____ tenth(s) left over.

There are now _____ hundredth(s).

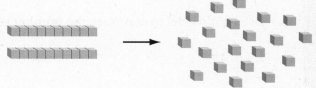

STEP 4 Share the hundredths.

Share the 21 hundredths equally among the 3 groups.

There are _____ hundredth(s) shared in each group

and _____ hundredth(s) left over.

So, each piece of ribbon is _____ yards long.

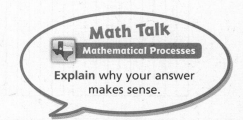

Math Talk

Mathematical Processes

Explain why your answer makes sense.

Name _____

Use the model to complete the number sentence.

1. $1.6 \div 4 =$ _____

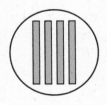
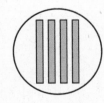

2. $3.42 \div 3 =$ _____

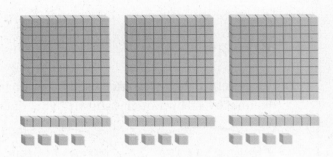

Problem Solving Real World

3. **H.O.T.** **What's the Error?** Aida is making banners from a roll of paper that is 4.05 meters long. She will cut the paper into 3 equal lengths. She uses base-ten blocks to model how long each piece will be. Describe Aida's error.

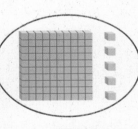
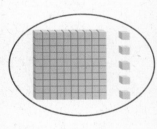

_____

_____

_____

_____

4. **Multi-Step** Sam can ride his bike 4.5 kilometers in 9 minutes, and Amanda can ride her bike 3.6 kilometers in 6 minutes. Which rider might go farther in 1 minute?

_____

5. **H.O.T.** **Explain** how you can use inverse operations to find $1.8 \div 3$.

_____

_____

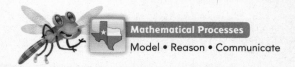

Daily Assessment Task

Fill in the bubble completely to show your answer.

6. **Multi-Step** Yesterday, a bamboo plant was 12.62 yards tall. Today, the bamboo had grown by 0.34 yard. Bryson chopped the bamboo into 6 equal pieces. How long was each piece?

Ⓐ 21.6 yd

Ⓒ 2.16 yd

Ⓑ 0.216 yd

Ⓓ 216 yd

7. **Representations** Terrance used base-ten blocks to help him divide a decimal by 4. His model is shown. What division problem did he model?

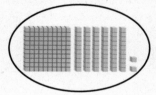 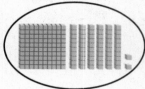 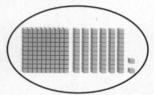 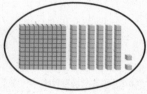

Ⓐ 1.26 ÷ 4

Ⓑ 1.62 ÷ 4

Ⓒ 6.48 ÷ 4

Ⓓ 6.84 ÷ 4

8. **Multi-Step** Marvyn worked for 3 days. He earned $87.20 each day. He uses his earnings to buy four chairs. If he has no money left over, what is the cost of each chair?

Ⓐ $65.40

Ⓒ $116.27

Ⓑ $261.60

Ⓓ $21.80

⭐ TEXAS Test Prep

9. A bag of oranges costs $7.65. Five friends want to share the bag. How much will each friend pay?

Ⓐ $38.25

Ⓒ $2.00

Ⓑ $1.53

Ⓓ $1.13

Name _____

4.2 Divide Decimals by Whole Numbers

Use the model to complete the number sentence.

1. $1.5 \div 3 =$ _____

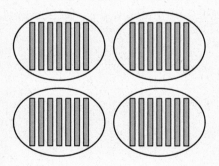

2. $2.48 \div 4 =$ _____

3. $2.8 \div 4 =$ _____

4. $3.54 \div 3 =$ _____

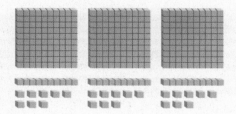

5. Explain how you can use the whole number expression $248 \div 4$ to check that your answer to Exercise 2 is reasonable.

_____

_____

Problem Solving

6. Mrs. Tillman builds furniture. She saws a maple board that is 4.56 meters long into 4 equal lengths. She saws an oak board that is 3.69 meters long into 3 equal lengths. Which is longer, a piece of oak or a piece of maple? **Explain**.

_____

_____

7. Drew has a video game with five different challenges. He sets the timer to play his game for 10.75 minutes. He spends the same amount of time playing each challenge. How long does Drew play the fifth challenge?

_____

_____

Fill in the bubble completely to show your answer.

8. Karina places concrete blocks along one side of her garden. The length of the border is 3.6 meters. If she uses 9 concrete blocks, what is the length of 1 block?

   (A) 0.3 meter

   (B) 0.9 meter

   (C) 0.04 meter

   (D) 0.4 meter

9. Max used base-ten blocks to solve the division problem 12.15 ÷ 3. Which set of blocks shows the quotient for 12.15 ÷ 3?

   (A) 4 ones, 5 tenths, 0 hundredths

   (B) 4 ones, 0 tenths, 5 hundredths

   (C) 0 ones, 4 tenths, 5 hundredths

   (D) 5 ones, 0 tenths, 4 hundredths

10. The base-ten blocks pictured below show Carter's solution to a division expression.

    Which expression did Carter solve?

    (A) 2.84 ÷ 4

    (B) 0.71 ÷ 4

    (C) 2.48 ÷ 4

    (D) 7.1 ÷ 4

11. Mr. Jefferson gives his two children $5.46 to spend at the garage sale. If they split the money evenly, how much will each child have to spend?

    (A) $1.82

    (B) $1.23

    (C) $2.23

    (D) $2.73

12. **Multi-Step** Mrs. Gonzales decorates the perimeter of her rectangular bulletin board with ribbon. She cuts a ribbon 3.72 yards long in half to decorate the top and the bottom. She cuts a ribbon 2.6 yards long in half to decorate the two sides. How much shorter is one side ribbon than the top ribbon?

    (A) 0.56 yard

    (B) 0.5 yard

    (C) 0.66 yard

    (D) 0.6 yard

13. **Multi-Step** Tamika bought 6 fish at the pet store for a total of $7.26. If two of the fish together cost $4.10, and each of the other four fish had the same cost, how much was each remaining fish?

    (A) $1.21

    (B) $2.05

    (C) $0.79

    (D) $3.16

4.3 Estimate Quotients

? Essential Question   How can you estimate decimal quotients?

🗝 Unlock the Problem Real World

Carmen likes to ski. The ski resort where she goes to ski got 3.2 feet of snow during a 5-day period. The *average* daily snowfall for a given number of days is the quotient of the total amount of snow and the number of days. Estimate the average daily snowfall.

You can estimate decimal quotients by using compatible numbers. When choosing compatible numbers, you can look at the whole-number part of a decimal dividend or rename the decimal dividend as tenths or hundredths.

🔑 Estimate. 3.2 ÷ 5

Carly and her friend Marco each find an estimate. Since the divisor is greater than the dividend, they both first rename 3.2 as tenths.

3.2 is _____ tenths.

CARLY'S ESTIMATE	**MARCO'S ESTIMATE**
30 tenths is close to 32 tenths and divides easily by 5. Use a basic fact to find 30 tenths ÷ 5.	35 tenths is close to 32 tenths and divides easily by 5. Use a basic fact to find 35 tenths ÷ 5.
30 tenths ÷ 5 is _____ tenths or _____.	35 tenths ÷ 5 is _____ tenths or _____.
So, the average daily snowfall is about	So, the average daily snowfall is about
_____ foot.	_____ foot.

1. Whose estimate do you think is closer to the exact quotient?

   Explain your reasoning. _____

   _____

2. **Explain** how you would rename the dividend in 29.7 ÷ 40 to choose compatible numbers and estimate the quotient.

   _____

   _____

Estimate with 2-Digit Divisors

When you estimate quotients with compatible numbers, the number you use for the dividend can be greater than the dividend or less than the dividend.

🔑 Example

A group of 31 students is going to visit the museum. The total cost for the tickets is $76.15. About how much money will each student need to pay for a ticket?

Estimate. $76.15 ÷ 31

Ⓐ Use a whole number greater than the dividend.

Use 30 for the divisor. Then find a number close to and greater than $76.15 that divides easily by 30.

$76.15 ÷ 31
  ↓   ↓
 $90 ÷ 30 = $ _____

So, each student will pay about $ _____ for a ticket.

_____

Ⓑ Use a whole number less than the dividend.

Use 30 for the divisor. Then find a number close to and less than $76.15 that divides easily by 30.

$76.15 ÷ 31
  ↓   ↓
 $60 ÷ 30 = $ _____

So, each student will pay about $ _____ for a ticket.

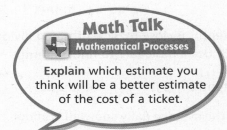

Math Talk
Mathematical Processes

Explain which estimate you think will be a better estimate of the cost of a ticket.

Share and Show

Use compatible numbers to estimate the quotient.

1. 28.8 ÷ 9

   _____ ÷ _____ = _____

2. 393.5 ÷ 41

   _____ ÷ _____ = _____

Estimate the quotient.

3. 161.7 ÷ 7

✓ 4. $17.90 ÷ 9

✓ 5. 145.4 ÷ 21

Problem Solving

6. **Write Math** ▶ **Explain** why you might want to find an estimate for a quotient.

_____

_____

7. **H.O.T.** **What's the Error?** During a 3-hour storm, it snowed 2.5 inches. Jacob said that it snowed an average of about 8 inches per hour.

_____

_____

Problem Solving

Use the table to solve 8–10.

8. Estimate the average daily snowfall for Alaska's greatest 7-day snowfall.

_____

9. **Multi-Step** How does the estimate of the average daily snowfall for Wyoming's greatest 7-day snowfall compare to the estimate of the average daily snowfall for South Dakota's greatest 7-day snowfall?

_____

_____

Greatest 7-Day Snowfall	
State	**Amount (in inches)**
Alaska	186.9
Wyoming	84.5
South Dakota	112.7

10. **H.O.T.** The greatest monthly snowfall total in Alaska is 297.9 inches. This happened in February, 1953. Compare the daily average snowfall for February, 1953, with the average daily snowfall for Alaska's greatest 7-day snowfall. Use estimation.

_____

_____

Daily Assessment Task

Fill in the bubble completely to show your answer.

11. You are participating in a remote control car race. It takes 215.78 seconds for your car to complete five laps. Which is the best estimate of the average time it takes to complete each lap?

   (A) 22 seconds   (C) 30 seconds

   (B) 44 seconds   (D) 55 seconds

12. **Communicate** Jake buys 12 books at the bookstore for $92.08. Each book costs the same amount. Jake uses 84 to estimate the cost of each book, and then also uses 96 to estimate. Why does he choose these numbers?

   (A) 92.08 falls between 84 and 96, and both whole numbers are divisible by 92.08.

   (B) 84 and 96 are even numbers.

   (C) 92.08 falls between 84 and 96, and both whole numbers are divisible by 12.

   (D) 92.08 does not fall between 84 and 96.

13. **Multi-Step** Last week, Alaina ran 12 miles in 131.25 minutes. The next week, Alaina ran 12 miles in 119.5 minutes. About how much faster did she run each mile in the second week?

   (A) 0 minutes

   (B) 1 minute

   (C) 3 minutes

   (D) 5 minutes

⭐ TEXAS Test Prep

14. A plant grew 23.8 inches over 8 weeks. Which is the best estimate of the average number of inches the plant grew each week?

   (A) 0.2 inch   (C) 0.3 inch

   (B) 2 inches   (D) 3 inches

170

4.3 Estimate Quotients

Use compatible numbers to estimate the quotient.

1. $78.8 \div 8$

2. $646.1 \div 34$

_____ ÷ _____ = _____

_____ ÷ _____ = _____

Estimate the quotient.

3. $434.2 \div 62$

4. $\$14.60 \div 5$

5. $35.6 \div 6$

6. $\$82.15 \div 23$

7. $63.2 \div 18$

8. $227.5 \div 21$

9. $36.9 \div 9$

10. $143.2 \div 7$

11. $\$9.65 \div 5$

Problem Solving Real World

12. Gino opens a savings account and deposits about the same amount each month for 5 months. At the end of 5 months he has deposited $33.55. About how much did Gino deposit each month?

13. Thunderstorms brought a total of 5.8 inches of rain to the first week of spring. Estimate the average daily rainfall for the first week of spring.

_____

_____

Fill in the bubble completely to show your answer.

14. Aaron gives an estimate of 2 for the quotient in a division problem. His teacher says his estimate is reasonable. If the divisor is 4, which number could be the dividend in Aaron's problem?

Ⓐ 80.4

Ⓑ 8.24

Ⓒ 0.84

Ⓓ 2.84

15. Natalie buys 4 pieces of wood to build a square pen for her rabbit. She decides the perimeter will be 6.96 meters. Which wood length should she buy to build each side of the pen so that she has enough wood, but has the least amount of wood left over?

Ⓐ 1 meter

Ⓑ 2 meters

Ⓒ 2.5 meters

Ⓓ 3 meters

16. It takes the printer in Reba's office 240.42 seconds to print out six reports. About how long does it take to print out each report?

Ⓐ 50–51 seconds

Ⓑ 24–25 seconds

Ⓒ 40–41 seconds

Ⓓ 30–31 seconds

17. Ross and Lydia estimate the quotient for $387.5 \div 73$. Ross uses a whole number greater than the dividend. Which equation shows how Lydia uses compatible numbers to get a closer estimate?

Ⓐ $400 \div 80 = 5$

Ⓑ $450 \div 75 = 6$

Ⓒ $360 \div 60 = 6$

Ⓓ $375 \div 75 = 5$

18. **Multi-Step** Mr. Williams owns an orchard. He has 211.9 pounds of grapefruits and 169.6 pounds of oranges to sell. He divides the fruit evenly into 8 shipments. About how many pounds are in each shipment?

Ⓐ 50 pounds

Ⓑ 30 pounds

Ⓒ 400 pounds

Ⓓ 20 pounds

19. **Multi-Step** Cara has $25. She buys a shirt for $13.68. She buys a hat that is half the cost of the shirt. Which is the best estimate for the amount of money Cara should expect to have left?

Ⓐ $4

Ⓑ $3

Ⓒ $6

Ⓓ $7

4.4 Division of Decimals by Whole Numbers

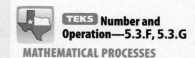

TEKS Number and Operation—5.3.F, 5.3.G
MATHEMATICAL PROCESSES
5.1.E, 5.1.F

 Essential Question

How can you divide decimals by whole numbers?

Unlock the Problem

In a swimming relay, each swimmer swims an equal part of the total distance. Brianna and 3 other swimmers won a relay in 5.68 minutes. What is the average time each girl swam?

● How many swimmers are part of the relay team?

_____

 Divide. 5.68 ÷ 4

MODEL

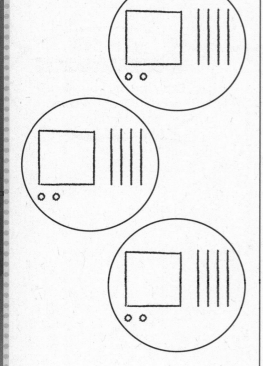

THINK AND RECORD

STEP 1 Share the ones.

$$4)\overline{5.68} \quad \begin{array}{c} 1 \\ -4 \end{array}$$

Divide. 5 ones ÷ 4

Multiply. 4 × 1 one(s)

Subtract. 5 ones − 4 ones

Check. _____ one(s) cannot be shared among 4 groups without regrouping.

STEP 2 Share the tenths.

$$4)\overline{5.68} \quad \begin{array}{c} 1 \\ -4 \downarrow \end{array}$$

Divide. _____ tenths ÷ 4

Multiply. 4 × _____ tenths

Subtract. _____ tenths − _____ tenths

Check. _____ tenth(s) cannot be shared among 4 groups.

STEP 3 Share the hundredths.

$$4)\overline{5.68} \quad \begin{array}{c} 1 \\ -4 \downarrow \\ 16 \\ -16 \downarrow \end{array}$$

Divide. 8 hundredths ÷ 4

Multiply. 4 × _____ hundredths

Subtract. _____ hundredths − _____ hundredths

Check. _____ hundredth(s) cannot be shared among 4 groups.

Place the decimal point in the quotient to separate the ones and the tenths.

So, each girl swam an average of _____ minutes.

When decimals are divided, the dividend may not have enough digits for you to complete the division. In these cases, you write zeros to the right of the last digit. Writing zeros to the right of the last digit does not change the value of the decimal.

 Example Divide. 45.8 ÷ 4

STEP 1

Share the tens, ones, and tenths.

4)45.8

_____ tenths cannot be shared among 4 groups without regrouping.

STEP 2

Write a zero in the dividend to show regrouping tenths as hundredths and continue dividing.

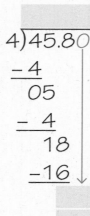

$$4\overline{)45.80}$$
$$-4$$
$$05$$
$$-4$$
$$18$$
$$-16$$

Divide.

_____ hundredths ÷ 4

Math Talk

Mathematical Processes

Explain how you would model 45.8 ÷ 4 using base-ten blocks.

Share and Show

Write the quotient with the decimal point placed correctly.

1. 4.92 ÷ 2 = 246 _____

2. 24.18 ÷ 3 = 806 _____

Divide.

3. 5)8.65

 4. 3)2.52

 5. 8)97.2

Name _____

Problem Solving

Practice: Copy and Solve Divide.

6. $3\overline{)\$7.71}$

7. $5\overline{)16.2}$

8. $3\overline{)2.31}$

9. $7\overline{)15.61}$

10. $9\overline{)88.2}$

11. $4\overline{)32.6}$

H.O.T. **Algebra** Write the unknown number for each ■.

12. ■ $\div 5 = 1.21$

13. $46.8 \div 4 =$ ■

14. $10.85 \div$ ■ $= 1.55$

■ = _____

■ = _____

■ = _____

15. **Write Math** ▶ **Analyze** How is $81.9 \div 9$ similar to $819 \div 9$? How is it different?

_____

_____

Problem Solving Real World

16. **Multi-Step** The standard width of 8 lanes in swimming pools used for competitions is 21.92 meters. The standard width of 9 lanes is 21.96 meters. How much wider is each lane when there are 8 lanes than when there are 9 lanes?

_____

17. **H.O.T.** **Multi-Step** Mei runs 80.85 miles in 3 weeks. If she runs 5 days each week, what is the average distance she runs each day?

_____

18. **Multi-Step** Rob buys 6 tickets to the basketball game. He pays $8.50 for parking. His total cost is $40.54. What is the cost of each ticket?

_____

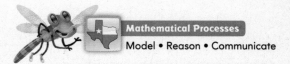

Daily Assessment Task

Fill in the bubble completely to show your answer.

19. In 1849, a gold miner had 4 ounces of gold to sell. The store owner offered him $67.68 for the gold. How much will the store owner pay for each ounce of gold?

   (A) $11.28

   (B) $15.76

   (C) $16.92

   (D) $23.64

20. **Use Symbols** A grocery store sells 6 ears of corn for $3.54. Which of the following shows how to find the amount of money that each ear of corn costs at the grocery store?

   (A) $3.54 × 6

   (B) 6 ÷ $3.54

   (C) 6 − $3.54

   (D) $3.54 ÷ 6

21. **Multi-Step** The school in town is building a track around its football stadium. The principal must decide whether to build a track with 6 lanes or 7 lanes. A 6-lane track will be 28.68 feet wide, and a 7-lane track will be 28.98 feet wide. If all lanes are of equal width in each track, how much wider will the lanes be in a 6-lane track than in a 7-lane track?

   (A) 4.78 feet

   (B) 0.64 foot

   (C) 0.50 foot

   (D) 4.14 feet

⭐ TEXAS Test Prep

22. A marathon is 26.2 miles long. Sue wants to run a marathon in 4 hours. What is the average number of miles she must run each hour?

   (A) 6.5 miles

   (B) 6.55 miles

   (C) 0.65 mile

   (D) 0.655 mile

TEKS Number and Operations—5.3.F, 5.3.G
MATHEMATICAL PROCESSES 5.1.F

Name _____

4.4 Division of Decimals by Whole Numbers

Divide.

1. $4\overline{)4.24}$

2. $5\overline{)3.25}$

3. $9\overline{)201.6}$

4. $3\overline{)1.35}$

5. $7\overline{)117.6}$

6. $9\overline{)\$25.11}$

7. $6\overline{)3.66}$

8. $3\overline{)28.8}$

9. $6\overline{)\$2.52}$

Write the unknown number for each ■.

10. ■ ÷ 9 = 3.4

11. 84.8 ÷ ■ = 10.6

12. 30.87 ÷ 7 = ■

■ = _____

■ = _____

■ = _____

Problem Solving

13. Abby and her 7 friends had lunch at the neighborhood burger barn. The bill was $47.60. If they shared the cost of the lunch equally, how much did each person pay?

14. Dion practiced the long jump. He jumped 3.05 meters, 2.74 meters, and 3.3 meters. What was the average length of Dion's jumps?

_____

_____

Fill in the bubble completely to show your answer.

15. An artist uses 49.4 centimeters of decorative molding to make a square picture frame. How long is each side of the frame?

- Ⓐ 12.35 centimeters
- Ⓑ 24.7 centimeters
- Ⓒ 12.2 centimeters
- Ⓓ 11.1 centimeters

16. A box of 8 snack bars costs $24.72. A single snack bar costs $3.47. What is the savings on each snack bar if you buy a box of 8 snack bars?

- Ⓐ $0.56
- Ⓑ $0.38
- Ⓒ $0.43
- Ⓓ $0.25

17. Jeremy saves $2.75 each week. How many weeks will it take him to save enough money to buy a model kit that costs $13.75?

- Ⓐ 3 weeks
- Ⓑ 4 weeks
- Ⓒ 5 weeks
- Ⓓ 6 weeks

18. Ari divides by 6 and gets a quotient of 9.3. What is the dividend in Ari's division problem?

- Ⓐ 3.3
- Ⓑ 1.55
- Ⓒ 55.8
- Ⓓ 54.8

19. Multi-Step Sam's van travels 208.8 miles on 9 gallons of gasoline. Hasan's small car travels 234.4 miles on 8 gallons of gasoline. What is the difference between the vehicles in the gallons of gasoline consumption per mile?

- Ⓐ 29.3 miles per gallon
- Ⓑ 23.2 miles per gallon
- Ⓒ 3.2 miles per gallon
- Ⓓ 6.1 miles per gallon

20. Multi-Step Seven students bought a ticket to the science museum. They paid a total of $40.25. Six students bought a ticket to the art museum. The total cost was $31.50. What is the difference in price between a ticket to the science museum and a ticket to the art museum?

- Ⓐ $0.50
- Ⓑ $1.00
- Ⓒ $8.75
- Ⓓ $1.25

Name _____

 4.5 **2-Digit Divisors**

TEKS Number and
Operations—5.3.G
Also 5.3.A
MATHEMATICAL PROCESSES
5.1.B

 Essential Question

How can you divide a decimal by a 2-digit whole number?

Unlock the Problem Real World

The annual rainfall in Greensville is 4.32 inches. What is the **average** monthly rainfall in Greensville?

One Way Use place value.

Divide. 4.32 ÷ 12

STEP 1 Share the ones.

$$\begin{array}{r} 0 \\ 12\overline{)4.32} \\ -0 \end{array}$$

4 ones cannot be shared among 12 groups without regrouping.

Place a zero to show there are no ones.

STEP 2 Share the tenths.

$$\begin{array}{r} 0 \\ 12\overline{)4.32} \\ -0\downarrow \\ \hline - \end{array}$$

Divide. _____ tenths ÷ 12

Multiply. 12 × _____ tenths

Subtract. _____ tenths − _____ tenths

Check. _____ tenths cannot be shared among 12 groups.

STEP 3 Share the hundredths.

$$\begin{array}{r} 0 \\ 12\overline{)4.32} \\ -0 \\ \hline 43 \\ -36\downarrow \\ \hline - \end{array}$$

Divide. _____ hundredths ÷ 12

Multiply. 12 × _____ hundredths

Subtract. _____ hundredths − _____ hundredths

Check. _____ hundredths cannot be shared among 12 groups.

Place the decimal point in the quotient to separate the ones and the tenths.

So, the average monthly rainfall in Greenville is _____ inch.

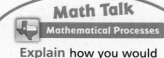
Math Talk
Mathematical Processes

Explain how you would model 10.32 ÷ 12 using base-ten blocks.

Another Way Use an estimate.

Divide as you would with whole numbers.

Divide. $40.89 ÷ 47

- Estimate the quotient. 4,000 hundredths ÷ 50 = 80 hundredths, or $0.80

$$\begin{array}{r} \$\,\rule{1.2cm}{0pt} \\ 47\overline{)\$40.89} \end{array}$$

- Divide the tenths.

- Divide the hundredths. When the remainder is zero and there are no more digits in the dividend, the division is complete.

- Use your estimate to place the decimal point. Place a zero to show there are no ones.

So, $40.89 ÷ 47 is _____.

- **Explain** how you used the estimate to place the decimal point in the quotient.

_____

_____

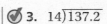 **Share and Show**   MATH BOARD

Divide.

1. 18)4.68

   Estimate the quotient.

   40 tenths ÷ 20 = _____

2. 23)52.9

3. 14)137.2

4. 42)$31.50

Problem Solving

5. **H.O.T.** **Representations** Make a model to find 11.16 ÷ 18. Describe your model.

_____

_____

_____

6. **Write Math** ▶ **What's the Error?** Darla divided 812.5 by 50. She says the quotient is 1.625. Describe Darla's error.

_____

_____

_____

Problem Solving *Real World*

7. Jin makes trail mix with apricots and walnuts. A package of dried apricots weighs 25.5 ounces. Jin divides the apricots equally among 34 bags of trail mix. How many ounces of apricots are in each bag?

**Write Math** ▶
Show Your Work

_____

8. **H.O.T.** **Analyze** A large box of cereal weighs 17 ounces and costs $5.95. A small box of the same cereal weighs 10 ounces and costs $3.90. Which has a greater cost per ounce?

_____

_____

9. **H.O.T.** **Multi-Step** Maya trains 5 days each week for a triathlon. In 5 weeks she logs 24.6 miles in the pool, 445.45 miles on the bike, and 167.45 miles running. On average, how many miles did Maya cover each day?

_____

_____

Daily Assessment Task

Fill in the bubble completely to show your answer.

10. A scientist conducting a dig spent $37.95 on 23 packets of hand wipes for her team of volunteers. What was the price of each packet?

    (A) $16.50   (C) $1.60

    (B) $16.05   (D) $1.65

11. Calvin needs to buy carpet to cover the floor of a rectangular room with an area of 170.8 square feet. Calvin measures the room's length to be 14 feet. He then divides the room's area by its length to find the room's width. How many decimal places will the quotient have?

    (A) 0   (C) 2

    (B) 1   (D) 3

12. **Multi-Step** Farmer Lee grows tomatoes and squash. He harvests 49.92 kilograms of tomatoes and 65.92 kilograms of squash. He distributes the tomatoes and squash into 32 farm share baskets. How many more kilograms of squash than tomatoes does each basket contain?

    (A) 2.06 kilograms

    (B) 0.5 kilogram

    (C) 1.56 kilograms

    (D) 3.62 kilograms

 TEXAS Test Prep

13. Jasmine uses 14.24 pounds of fruit for 16 servings of fruit salad. If each serving contains the same amount of fruit, how much fruit is in each serving?

    (A) 0.089 pound

    (B) 1.76 pounds

    (C) 0.89 pound

    (D) 17.6 pounds

Homework and Practice

Name _____

4.5 2-Digit Divisors

Divide.

1. $16\overline{)6.08}$

2. $21\overline{)94.5}$

3. $15\overline{)7.35}$

4. $21\overline{)\$13.65}$

5. $15\overline{)137.1}$

6. $13\overline{)111.8}$

7. $26\overline{)\$85.28}$

8. $18\overline{)349.2}$

9. $35\overline{)23.45}$

10. $90\overline{)\$10.80}$

11. $54\overline{)44.28}$

12. $12\overline{)32.4}$

Problem Solving

13. Carla's car travels 412.5 miles on a tank of gas. The tank holds 15 gallons of gas. How many miles can Carla go on each gallon?

14. Muffins cost $35.40 for a dozen or $18.72 for a half dozen. Which is the better buy? Explain.

_____

_____

_____

_____

Fill in the bubble completely to show your answer.

15. Anita pays $20.70 to copy an 18 page report. What is the cost for each page?

   (A) $1.05

   (B) $1.03

   (C) $1.15

   (D) $1.10

16. A florist sells a dozen roses for $29.88. What is the cost of one rose?

   (A) $2.41

   (B) $2.49

   (C) $2.40

   (D) $2.08

17. Cameron has a stack of 13 identical books that is 30.55 centimeters tall. He divides the total height by the number of books to find the width of one book. How many decimal places will the quotient have?

   (A) 3

   (B) 2

   (C) 1

   (D) 0

18. Kiera makes 188.6 ounces of punch for a pool party. She has 23 guests attending the party. How many ounces of punch does she make for each guest?

   (A) 8.2 ounces

   (B) 9.4 ounces

   (C) 8.1 ounces

   (D) 7.2 ounces

19. **Multi-Step** Last year, Mr. Henderson paid a total of $98.40 for phone service and $79.20 for garbage pickup. What was his average cost per month for phone service and garbage pickup?

   (A) $8.20

   (B) $6.60

   (C) $1.48

   (D) $14.80

20. **Multi-Step** Isabel worked 20 hours last week and earned $145.80. Nan worked 15 hours last week and earned $112.50. How much more does Nan earn per hour?

   (A) $2.22

   (B) $3.30

   (C) $0.39

   (D) $0.21

Name _____

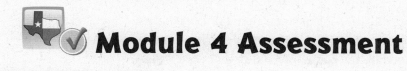 **Module 4 Assessment**

Concepts and Skills

1. **Explain** how the position of the decimal point changes in a quotient as you divide a number by 10, 100, and 1,000. TEKS 5.3.G

_____

2. **Explain** how you can use base-ten blocks to find 2.16 ÷ 3. TEKS 5.3.F

_____

_____

_____

_____

Complete the pattern. TEKS 5.3.G

3. 223 ÷ 1 = _____

   223 ÷ 10 = _____

   223 ÷ 100 = _____

   223 ÷ 1,000 = _____

4. 61 ÷ 1 = _____

   61 ÷ 10 = _____

   61 ÷ 100 = _____

   61 ÷ 1,000 = _____

5. 57.4 ÷ 1 = _____

   57.4 ÷ 10 = _____

   57.4 ÷ 100 = _____

Estimate the quotient. TEKS 5.3.A

6. 31.9 ÷ 4

7. 6.1 ÷ 8

8. 492.6 ÷ 48

Use models or strategies to divide. TEKS 5.3.F, 5.3.G

9. $5\overline{)4.35}$

10. $8\overline{)9.92}$

11. $61\overline{)207.4}$

12. The Westside Bakery uses 440 pounds of sugar to make 1,000 cakes. Each cake contains the same amount of sugar. How many pounds of sugar does the bakery need if they bake only 100 cakes? ⬩ TEKS 5.3.G

Ⓐ 4.4 pounds

Ⓑ 0.44 pound

Ⓒ 0.044 pound

Ⓓ 44 pounds

13. Fourteen boxes of candles were sold for $91.00. Each box contains 5 candles. What is the cost of 1 candle? ⬩ TEKS 5.3.G

Ⓐ $1.30

Ⓑ $6.50

Ⓒ $13.00

Ⓓ $0.65

14. Jason has a piece of wire that is 62.4 inches long. He cuts the wire into 3 equal pieces. Which is the best estimate of the length of each piece of wire? ⬩ TEKS 5.3.A

Ⓐ 30 inches

Ⓑ 3 inches

Ⓒ 20 inches

Ⓓ 2 inches

15. Elizabeth uses 33.75 ounces of granola for 15 servings of trail mix. If each serving contains the same amount of granola, how much granola is in each serving? ⬩ TEKS 5.3.G

Ⓐ 18.75 ounces

Ⓑ 2.25 ounces

Ⓒ 0.225 ounce

Ⓓ 33.9 ounces

Name _____

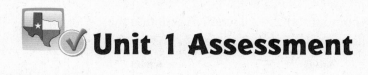 **Unit 1 Assessment**

Vocabulary

Choose the best term from the box.

1. The _____ states that changing the grouping of factors does not change the product. (p. 5)

2. Addition and subtraction are _____. (p. 41)

Concepts and Skills

Compare. Write <, >, or =. ⬇ TEKS 5.2.B

3. 6.35 ◯ 0.695

4. 0.02 ◯ 0.020

5. 0.132 ◯ 0.2

Estimate. Then solve. ⬇ TEKS 5.3.A, 5.3.B, 5.3.C

6. Estimate: _____

$$\begin{array}{r} 365 \\ \times\ 24 \\ \hline \end{array}$$

7. Estimate: _____

$616 \div 22$

8. Estimate: _____

$5{,}184 \div 18$

Use models or strategies to find the product. Show your work. ⬇ TEKS 5.3.D, 5.3.E

9. 0.05×1.32

10. 23×5.28

11. 4.2×14.85

Use models or strategies to find the quotient. Show your work. ⬇ TEKS 5.3.F, 5.3.G

12. $3.6 \div 4$

13. $16.24 \div 29$

14. $96.72 \div 62$

15. Kaya's score in the gymnastics competition is 15.4 when rounded to the nearest tenth. Which of the following is her actual score? 🪝TEKS 5.2.C

(A) 15.333

(B) 15.496

(C) 15.395

(D) 15.349

16. A bakery uses 1,750 kilograms of flour to make 1,000 loaves of bread. How much flour is needed to make 10 loaves? 🪝TEKS 5.3.G

(A) 17.5 kilograms

(B) 175,000 kilograms

(C) 1.75 kilograms

(D) 175 kilograms

17. Maxine paints a mural that is 4.65 meters long. The width of the mural is 0.8 times the length. Maxine increases the width by another 0.5 meters. How wide is the mural? 🪝TEKS 5.3.E, 5.3.K

(A) 3.77 meters

(B) 37.2 meters

(C) 4.22 meters

(D) 3.72 meters

18. Juan uses the model below to solve a problem. Which of the following equations matches Juan's model? 🪝TEKS 5.3.F

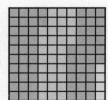 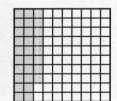

(A) $0.4 \times 32 = 12.8$

(B) $1.28 \div 4 = 0.32$

(C) $0.32 \div 4 = 0.08$

(D) $0.32 + 4 = 4.32$

19. The price of a shirt is $26.50. The matching shorts are 0.9 times the price of the shirt. If Li wants to buy the shirt and the shorts, how much money will he need? 👆 TEKS 5.3.E, 5.3.K

Ⓐ $238.50

Ⓑ $35.50

Ⓒ $23.85

Ⓓ $50.35

20. Ali's times for the four laps of the race are: 15.36 seconds, 15.95 seconds, 17.83 seconds, and 18.25 seconds. About how long did Ali take to complete the whole race? 👆 TEKS 5.3.A

Ⓐ 47 seconds

Ⓑ 18 seconds

Ⓒ 15 seconds

Ⓓ 67 seconds

21. Goran wants to build a square picture frame with sides that are 5.25 inches long. Natalie wants to build a square sandbox and needs 11 times the amount of wood that Goran needs to build his frame. They have 4 pieces of wood that are each 65.5 inches long. How much wood will they have left over after making the frame and sandbox?
👆 TEKS 5.3.E, 5.3.K

Ⓐ 10 inches

Ⓑ 2.5 inches

Ⓒ 7.75 inches

Ⓓ Not here

22. Mustafa buys 6 cans of beans. Each can contains 12.6 ounces of beans. Mustafa uses 0.7 of the beans in a stew and the rest of the beans for tacos. How many ounces does he use for the tacos? 👆 TEKS 5.3.E, 5.3.K

Ⓐ 21 ounces

Ⓑ 75.60 ounces

Ⓒ 52.92 ounces

Ⓓ 22.68 ounces

23. The scale at a butcher shop shows the weight of the meat as 5.363 pounds. The butcher rounds the weight to the nearest hundredth. Which of the following shows the new number in expanded form? TEKS 5.2.A, 5.2.C

Ⓐ $5 + 0.3 + 0.06 + 0.003$

Ⓑ $5 + 0.3 + 0.07$

Ⓒ $5 + 0.3 + 0.06$

Ⓓ $5 + 3 + 6 + 3$

24. The table shows the times recorded by the top 3 swimmers in the 100 meter race. What is the value of the digit 6 in the fastest recorded time? TEKS 5.2.A, 5.2.B

Ⓐ 0.06

Ⓑ 0.006

Ⓒ 0.6

Ⓓ 6

Swimming Times

Alia	51.695 seconds
Robin	51.563 seconds
Anna	51.536 seconds

25. Tickets to the school play cost $3.65 for children and $5.65 for adults. Sonal buys tickets for 3 children and 2 adults. How much money should she get back if she gives the cashier $50? TEKS 5.3.E, 5.3.K

Ⓐ $39.05

Ⓑ $27.75

Ⓒ $26

Ⓓ $38.70

26. The prices for different beverages and snacks at a snack stand in a park are shown in the table. Emily spent $8.11 on park snacks for her friends and herself. Make a list of the items she may have purchased. Justify the amount spent. TEKS 5.3.K

Park Snacks	
Item	**Price**
Fruit Juice	$0.89
Iced Tea	$1.29
Lemonade	$1.78
Pretzel	$2.50
Popcorn	$1.25

_____

_____

_____

_____

Number and Operations: Fractions

Name _____

▶ **Part of a Whole** **Write a fraction to name the shaded part.**

1.

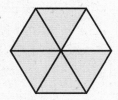

number of shaded parts _____

number of total parts _____

fraction _____

2.

number of shaded parts _____

number of total parts _____

fraction _____

▶ **Add and Subtract Fractions**

Write the sum or difference in simplest form.

3. $\frac{3}{6} + \frac{1}{6} =$ _____   4. $\frac{4}{10} + \frac{1}{10} =$ _____   5. $\frac{7}{8} - \frac{3}{8} =$ _____   6. $\frac{9}{12} - \frac{2}{12} =$ _____

▶ **Equivalent Fractions**

Write an equivalent fractions.

7. $\frac{3}{4}$ _____   8. $\frac{9}{15}$ _____   9. $\frac{24}{40}$ _____   10. $\frac{5}{7}$ _____

Vocabulary Builder

▶ **Visualize It** ••••••••••••••••••••••••••••••••

Use the ✓words to complete the H-diagram.

Add and Subtract Fractions with equal	Add and Subtract Fractions with unequal

▶ **Understand Vocabulary** ••••••••••••••••••••••

Draw a line to match the word with its definition.

1. common multiple
   • a number that is made up of a whole number and a fraction

2. benchmark
   • a number that is a multiple of two or more numbers

3. simplest form
   • a common multiple of two or more denominators

4. mixed number
   • the form of a fraction in which the numerator and denominator have only 1 as their common factor

5. common denominator
   • a familiar number used as a point of reference

6. equivalent fractions
   • fractions that name the same amount or part

GO DIGITAL
• Interactive Student Edition
• Multimedia *eGlossary*

Name _____

Reading To get the right answer to a mathematics problem, you need to make sure you understand the question.

Problem 1

Three friends ordered a pizza with 8 slices. Jeanette ate $\frac{2}{8}$ of the pizza. Marissa ate $\frac{4}{8}$ of the pizza. Ariel ate the rest. How many slices of Pizza did Ariel eat?

A. 1 slice

B. 2 slices

C. 4 slices

D. 6 slices

Writing Now it's your turn. Answer Problem 2. Then write about how you solved the problem, step by step.

Problem 2

The Perez family ordered a large pizza for dinner. A large pizza is divided into 8 slices. Marco ate $\frac{3}{8}$ of the pizza. Ramon ate 1 slice more than Marco. Emilio ate the rest. How much of the pizza did Emilio eat?

A. $\frac{1}{8}$ of the pizza

B. $\frac{2}{8}$ of the pizza

C. $\frac{4}{8}$ of the pizza

D. $\frac{5}{8}$ of the pizza

Thinking Through the Problem

Understand the question You want to know how many slices Ariel ate. Will your answer be a fraction or whole number?

Plan Find out what fraction of the pizza Ariel ate. Look at the numerator to tell how many pizza slices Ariel ate.

Solve Follow your plan. Write the answer to the problem.

Look Back Use fraction strips to check your answer.

The correct answer is **B**.

Think
I always check to see if I answered the question that was asked.

_____

_____

_____

Action Fractions

Object of the Game Practice comparing fractions.

Materials
- Number/Symbol Cards: 2 sets labeled 1, 2, 3, 4, 6, 8

Number of Players 2

Set Up
Give each player 2 sets of number cards. Players shuffle their cards and place them face down in a stack.

How to Play

1 One player shuffles and deals all cards facedown. Players stack their cards.

2 Players take 3 cards from the top of their stacks. Using 2 of the 3 cards, each player makes a fraction whose numerator is less than or equal to its denominator. The unused card is returned to the bottom of the player's stack.

3 Players compare the fractions. The player with the greater fraction earns 1 point. If the fractions are equivalent, each player earns 1 point.

4 Repeat Steps 2 and 3. The player with more points after all the cards have been used is the winner.

1	2	3
4	6	8

5.1 Addition with Unequal Denominators

TEKS Number and Operations—5.3.H, 5.3.K
MATHEMATICAL PROCESSES
5.1.C

? Essential Question

How can you use models to add fractions that have unequal denominators?

Investigate

Hilary is using red fabric to make a tote bag. She uses one piece that is $\frac{1}{2}$ yard long. She uses another piece that is $\frac{1}{4}$ yard long. How much red fabric does she use?

Materials ▪ fraction strips ▪ MathBoard

A. Find $\frac{1}{2} + \frac{1}{4}$. Place a $\frac{1}{2}$ strip and a $\frac{1}{4}$ strip under the 1-whole strip on your MathBoard.

B. Find fraction strips, all with the same denominator, that are equivalent to $\frac{1}{2}$ and $\frac{1}{4}$ and fit exactly under the sum $\frac{1}{2} + \frac{1}{4}$. Record the addends, using equal denominators.

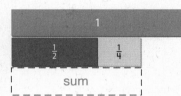

C. Record the sum in simplest form. $\frac{1}{2} + \frac{1}{4} =$ _____

So, Hilary uses _____ yard of fabric.

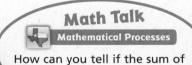

Math Talk
Mathematical Processes

How can you tell if the sum of the fractions is less than 1?

Draw Conclusions

1. **Describe** how you would determine what fraction strips, all with the same denominator, would fit exactly under $\frac{1}{2} + \frac{1}{3}$. What are they?

_____

_____

2. **H.O.T.** **Explain** the difference between finding fraction strips with the same denominator for $\frac{1}{2} + \frac{1}{3}$ and $\frac{1}{2} + \frac{1}{4}$.

_____

_____

Make Connections

Sometimes, the sum of two fractions is greater than 1. When adding fractions with unequal denominators, you can use the 1-whole strip to help determine if a sum is greater than 1 or less than 1.

Use fraction strips to solve. $\frac{3}{5} + \frac{1}{2}$

STEP 1

Work with another student. Place three $\frac{1}{5}$ fraction strips under the 1-whole strip on your MathBoard. Then place a $\frac{1}{2}$ fraction strip beside the three $\frac{1}{5}$ strips.

STEP 2

Find fraction strips, all with the same denominator, that are equivalent to $\frac{3}{5}$ and $\frac{1}{2}$. Place the fraction strips under the sum. At the right, draw a picture of the model and write the equivalent fractions.

$\frac{3}{5} = $ _____ $\frac{1}{2} = $ _____

STEP 3

Add the fractions with equal denominators. Use the 1-whole strip to rename the sum in simplest form.

Think: How many fraction strips with the same denominator are equal to 1 whole?

$\frac{3}{5} + \frac{1}{2} = $ _____ $+$ _____

$ = $ _____ , *or* _____

Math Talk
Mathematical Processes

In what step did you find out that the answer is greater than 1? Explain.

Share and Show

Use fraction strips to find the sum. Write your answer in simplest form.

1.

$\frac{1}{2} + \frac{3}{8} = $ _____ $+$ _____ $= $ _____

2.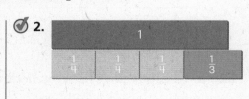

$\frac{3}{4} + \frac{1}{3} = $ _____ $+$ _____ $= $ _____

Name _____

Use fraction strips to find the sum. Write your answer in simplest form.

3. $\frac{2}{5} + \frac{3}{10} =$ _____

4. $\frac{1}{4} + \frac{1}{12} =$ _____

5. $\frac{1}{2} + \frac{3}{10} =$ _____

Problem Solving Real World

6. **H.O.T.** **Multi-Step** Maya makes trail mix by combining $\frac{1}{3}$ cup of mixed nuts, $\frac{1}{4}$ cup of dried fruit, and $\frac{1}{6}$ cup of chocolate morsels. What is the total amount of ingredients in her trail mix?

_____

7. **H.O.T.** **Pose a Problem** Write a new problem using different amounts for ingredients Maya used. Each amount should be a fraction with a denominator of 2, 3, or 4.

Write Math ▶ **Show Your Work** · · ·

_____

_____

_____

8. **Use Diagrams** Solve the problem you wrote. Draw a picture of the fractions strips you use to solve your problem.

_____

9. **Explain** why you chose the amounts you did for your problem.

_____

_____

_____

10. **Write Math** ▶ **Explain** how using fraction strips with equal denominators makes it possible to add fractions with unequal denominators.

_____

_____

_____

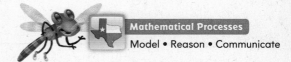

Daily Assessment Task

Fill in the bubble completely to show your answer.

11. In a garden, bluebonnets occupy $\frac{7}{10}$ of the garden. After winter, the bluebonnets spread to cover another $\frac{1}{5}$ of the garden. What fraction of the garden is now covered in bluebonnets?

  Ⓐ $\frac{1}{5}$ Ⓒ $\frac{8}{10}$

  Ⓑ $\frac{1}{2}$ Ⓓ $\frac{9}{10}$

12. Ling is using fraction strips to add $\frac{2}{3}$ and $\frac{7}{12}$. The sum is one whole, plus how many twelfths?

  Ⓐ 1

  Ⓑ 2

  Ⓒ 3

  Ⓓ 4

13. **Multi-Step** Juan uses $\frac{1}{5}$ liter to water a small plant, and he uses $\frac{1}{2}$ liter to water a large plant. Now he has $\frac{2}{10}$ liter left in the pitcher. How much water did Juan have in the beginning?

  Ⓐ $\frac{3}{5}$ L

  Ⓑ $\frac{9}{10}$ L

  Ⓒ $\frac{1}{10}$ L

  Ⓓ $\frac{3}{10}$ L

 TEXAS Test Prep

14. Wilhelm is making a pie. He uses $\frac{1}{2}$ cup of blueberries and $\frac{2}{3}$ cup of raspberries. What is the total amount of berries in Wilhelm's pie?

  Ⓐ $\frac{3}{5}$ cup

  Ⓑ $\frac{2}{6}$ cup

  Ⓒ $\frac{7}{6}$ cups

  Ⓓ $\frac{3}{6}$ cup

198

TEKS Number and Operations—5.3.H, 5.3.K
MATHEMATICAL PROCESSES 5.1.C

Name _____

5.1 Addition with Unequal Denominators

Use fraction strips to find the sum. Write your answer in simplest form.

1.

1

$\frac{1}{3}$	$\frac{1}{6}$

2.

1

$\frac{1}{3}$	$\frac{1}{3}$	$\frac{1}{4}$	$\frac{1}{4}$	$\frac{1}{4}$

$\frac{1}{3} + \frac{1}{6} =$ _____ + _____ = _____

$\frac{2}{3} + \frac{3}{4} =$ _____ + _____ = _____

3. $\frac{1}{6} + \frac{3}{4} =$ _____

4. $\frac{5}{6} + \frac{1}{2} =$ _____

5. $\frac{1}{2} + \frac{2}{5} =$ _____

6. $\frac{1}{4} + \frac{2}{3} =$ _____

7. $\frac{1}{3} + \frac{5}{6} =$ _____

8. $\frac{3}{5} + \frac{3}{10} =$ _____

9. $\frac{1}{8} + \frac{3}{4} =$ _____

10. $\frac{7}{10} + \frac{1}{2} =$ _____

11. $\frac{5}{6} + \frac{1}{12} =$ _____

Problem Solving

12. Cooper is grating cheese for the family taco dinner. He grates $\frac{1}{2}$ cup of cheddar cheese and $\frac{3}{4}$ cup of monterey jack cheese. How much cheese does Cooper grate?

13. Jasmine has to mix $\frac{3}{4}$ cup of flour and $\frac{3}{8}$ cup of cornmeal. She has a container that holds 1 cup. Can Jasmine mix the flour and cornmeal in the container? **Explain.**

_____

_____

_____

_____

Fill in the bubble completely to show your answer.

14. Julio spent $\frac{1}{10}$ of his weekly allowance on a set of markers and $\frac{2}{5}$ of it on a book. What fraction of Julio's allowance is this altogether?

   Ⓐ $\frac{1}{2}$

   Ⓑ $\frac{3}{10}$

   Ⓒ $\frac{3}{5}$

   Ⓓ $\frac{1}{5}$

15. Kate is using fraction strips to add $\frac{4}{10}$ and $\frac{4}{5}$. She uses one whole strip to represent the sum. How many fifths strips does she need to complete the sum?

   Ⓐ 1

   Ⓑ 2

   Ⓒ 5

   Ⓓ 8

16. Which fraction correctly completes the equation?

$$\frac{6}{8} + \frac{\blacksquare}{\blacksquare} = 1$$

   Ⓐ $\frac{1}{2}$

   Ⓑ $\frac{1}{8}$

   Ⓒ $\frac{3}{8}$

   Ⓓ $\frac{1}{4}$

17. An apple was cut into 8 equal-size pieces. Stacy ate $\frac{1}{4}$ of the apple. Tony ate $\frac{3}{8}$ of the apple. What part of the apple did Stacy and Tony eat in all?

   Ⓐ $\frac{1}{2}$

   Ⓑ $\frac{5}{8}$

   Ⓒ $\frac{3}{4}$

   Ⓓ $\frac{1}{4}$

18. **Multi-Step** Last weekend, Beatrice walked her poodle $\frac{2}{3}$ mile on Saturday and $\frac{5}{6}$ mile on Sunday. Fiona walked her beagle $\frac{1}{3}$ mile on Saturday and $\frac{1}{2}$ mile on Sunday. How much farther did the poodle walk last weekend than the beagle?

   Ⓐ $\frac{1}{2}$ mile

   Ⓑ $1\frac{1}{3}$ miles

   Ⓒ $\frac{2}{3}$ mile

   Ⓓ $1\frac{1}{2}$ miles

19. **Multi-Step** Rick worked in his garden on Friday. He pulled weeds for $\frac{5}{6}$ hour, planted seeds for $\frac{1}{2}$ hour, and watered for $\frac{1}{6}$ hour. How much time did Rick spend working in his garden on Friday?

   Ⓐ $\frac{1}{2}$ hour

   Ⓑ 1 hour

   Ⓒ $1\frac{1}{3}$ hours

   Ⓓ $1\frac{1}{2}$ hours

5.2 Subtraction with Unequal Denominators

TEKS Number and Operations—5.3.H, 5.3.K
MATHEMATICAL PROCESSES
5.1.C

? **Essential Question**

How can you use models to subtract fractions that have unequal denominators?

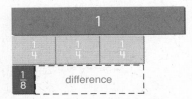

Investigate

Mario fills a hummingbird feeder with $\frac{3}{4}$ cup of sugar water on Friday. On Monday, Mario sees that $\frac{1}{8}$ cup of sugar water is left. How much sugar water did the hummingbirds drink?

Materials ■ fraction strips ■ MathBoard

A. Find $\frac{3}{4} - \frac{1}{8}$. Place three $\frac{1}{4}$ strips under the 1-whole strip on your MathBoard. Then place a $\frac{1}{8}$ strip under the $\frac{1}{4}$ strips.

B. Find fraction strips all with the same denominator that fit exactly under the difference $\frac{3}{4} - \frac{1}{8}$.

1

$\frac{1}{4}$	$\frac{1}{4}$	$\frac{1}{4}$

| $\frac{1}{8}$ | difference |

C. Record the difference. $\frac{3}{4} - \frac{1}{8} =$ _____

So, the hummingbirds drank _____ cup of sugar water.

Math Talk
Mathematical Processes

How can you tell if the difference of the fractions is less than 1? **Explain.**

Draw Conclusions

1. **Describe** how you determined what fraction strips, all with the same denominator, would fit exactly under the difference. What are they?

_____

_____

2. **H.O.T.** **Explain** whether you could have used fraction strips with any other denominator to find the difference. If so, what is the denominator?

_____

Make Connections

Sometimes you can use different sets of same-denominator fraction strips to find the difference. All of the answers will be correct.

Solve. $\frac{2}{3} - \frac{1}{6}$

A Find fraction strips, all with the same denominator, that fit exactly under the difference $\frac{2}{3} - \frac{1}{6}$.

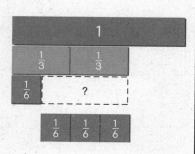

$\frac{2}{3} - \frac{1}{6} = \frac{3}{6}$

B Find another set of fraction strips, all with the same denominator, that fit exactly under the difference $\frac{2}{3} - \frac{1}{6}$. Draw the fraction strips you used.

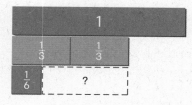

$\frac{2}{3} - \frac{1}{6} = $ _____

C Find other fraction strips, all with the same denominator, that fit exactly under the difference $\frac{2}{3} - \frac{1}{6}$. Draw the fraction strips you used.

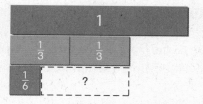

$\frac{2}{3} - \frac{1}{6} = $ _____

While each answer appears different, all of the answers can be simplified to _____ .

Math Talk
Mathematical Processes

Which other fraction strips with the same denominator could fit exactly in the difference of $\frac{2}{3} - \frac{1}{6}$?

Share and Show

MATH BOARD

Use fraction strips to find the difference. Write your answer in simplest form.

1.

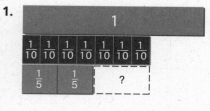

$\frac{7}{10} - \frac{2}{5} = $ _____

2.

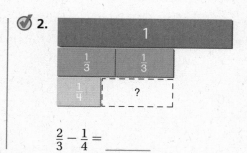

$\frac{2}{3} - \frac{1}{4} = $ _____

Use fraction strips to find the difference. Write your answer in simplest form.

3. $\frac{3}{4} - \frac{1}{3} = $ _____

4. $\frac{5}{6} - \frac{1}{2} = $ _____

5. $\frac{3}{4} - \frac{7}{12} = $ _____

202

Name _____

6. **H.O.T.** **Multi-Step** The picture at the right shows how much pizza was left over from lunch. Jason eats $\frac{1}{4}$ of the whole pizza for dinner. Which subtraction sentence represents the amount of pizza that is remaining after dinner?

(A) $1 - \frac{1}{4} = \frac{3}{4}$ (C) $\frac{3}{8} - \frac{1}{4} = \frac{2}{8}$

(B) $\frac{5}{8} - \frac{1}{4} = \frac{3}{8}$ (D) $1 - \frac{3}{8} = \frac{5}{8}$

a. What problem are you being asked to solve? _____

_____

b. How will you use the diagram to solve the problem? _____

_____

_____

c. Jason eats $\frac{1}{4}$ of the whole pizza. How many slices does he eat? _____

d. Redraw the diagram of the pizza. Shade the sections of pizza that are remaining after Jason eats his dinner.

e. Write a fraction to represent the amount of pizza that is remaining.

_____

f. Fill in the bubble for the correct answer choice above.

7. **H.O.T.** **Explain** how a model for $\frac{3}{5} - \frac{1}{2}$ is different from a model for $\frac{3}{5} - \frac{3}{10}$.

_____

_____

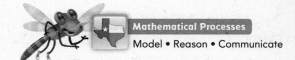
Daily Assessment Task

Fill in the bubble completely to show your answer.

8. You are making cranberry lemonade for the Tastiest Beverage contest. You use $\frac{3}{10}$ liter cranberry juice and $\frac{1}{2}$ liter lemonade. You drink $\frac{1}{10}$ liter, just to be sure that it tastes delicious! How much cranberry lemonade do you have left?

(A) $\frac{7}{10}$ liter

(C) $\frac{3}{11}$ liter

(B) $\frac{9}{10}$ liter

(D) $\frac{3}{10}$ liter

9. **Use Diagrams** Calvin used fraction strips correctly to model the difference of $\frac{7}{12} - \frac{1}{3}$. Which of these describes his model?

(A) seven $\frac{1}{12}$ strips, one $\frac{1}{3}$ strip, two $\frac{1}{4}$ strips

(B) seven $\frac{1}{12}$ strips, one $\frac{1}{3}$ strip, one $\frac{1}{2}$ strip

(C) seven $\frac{1}{12}$ strips, two $\frac{1}{6}$ strips, one $\frac{1}{8}$ strip

(D) seven $\frac{1}{12}$ strips, one $\frac{1}{3}$ strip, one $\frac{1}{4}$ strip

10. **Multi-Step** Bethany made her Apple Surprise drink by mixing $\frac{1}{8}$ pint lemon juice, $\frac{1}{8}$ pint grape juice, and $\frac{4}{8}$ pint apple juice. She then drank $\frac{1}{4}$ pint of the mixture. How much Apple Surprise was left?

(A) $\frac{1}{2}$ pint

(C) $\frac{1}{4}$ pint

(B) $\frac{1}{8}$ pint

(D) $\frac{3}{8}$ pint

TEXAS Test Prep

11. The diagram shows what Tina had left from a yard of fabric. She now uses $\frac{2}{3}$ yard of fabric for a project. How much of the original yard of fabric does Tina have left after the project?

(A) $\frac{1}{2}$ yard

(B) $\frac{2}{3}$ yard

(C) $\frac{1}{3}$ yard

(D) $\frac{1}{6}$ yard

204

5.2 Subtraction with Unequal Denominators

Use fraction strips to find the difference. Write your answer in simplest form.

1.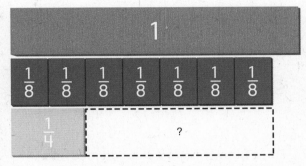

$$\frac{7}{8} - \frac{1}{4} = \underline{\hspace{1cm}}$$

2.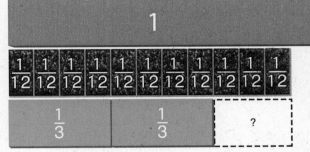

$$\frac{11}{12} - \frac{2}{3} = \underline{\hspace{1cm}}$$

3. $\frac{1}{2} - \frac{1}{3} = \underline{\hspace{1cm}}$

4. $\frac{9}{10} - \frac{2}{5} = \underline{\hspace{1cm}}$

5. $\frac{11}{12} - \frac{3}{4} = \underline{\hspace{1cm}}$

6. $\frac{5}{6} - \frac{1}{3} = \underline{\hspace{1cm}}$

7. $\frac{2}{3} - \frac{1}{12} = \underline{\hspace{1cm}}$

8. $\frac{3}{4} - \frac{5}{12} = \underline{\hspace{1cm}}$

9. $\frac{9}{10} - \frac{1}{2} = \underline{\hspace{1cm}}$

10. $\frac{5}{8} - \frac{1}{2} = \underline{\hspace{1cm}}$

11. $\frac{3}{4} - \frac{2}{3} = \underline{\hspace{1cm}}$

Problem Solving Real World

12. Annette is making a fruit drink that calls for $\frac{3}{4}$ cup of fresh lemon juice. She has $\frac{1}{2}$ cup of lemon juice. How much more lemon juice does Annette need?

13. Ramon needs to walk $\frac{3}{4}$ mile to the bus stop. He has walked $\frac{3}{8}$ mile so far. How much farther does Ramon need to walk to get to the bus stop?

_____

_____

Fill in the bubble completely to show your answer.

14. Matt spent $\frac{1}{3}$ of the money in his pocket on a movie ticket. He spent $\frac{1}{4}$ of the money on a snack. What fraction of his money is left?

Ⓐ $\frac{7}{12}$

Ⓑ $\frac{5}{12}$

Ⓒ $\frac{1}{12}$

Ⓓ $\frac{1}{6}$

15. Jabar used fraction strips to model the difference of $\frac{7}{12} - \frac{1}{6}$. Which represents the difference?

Ⓐ seven $\frac{1}{12}$ strips

Ⓑ one $\frac{1}{12}$ strip

Ⓒ two $\frac{1}{12}$ strips

Ⓓ five $\frac{1}{12}$ strips

16. Which fraction correctly completes the equation?

$$\frac{3}{4} - \underline{\quad\quad} = \frac{1}{8}$$

Ⓐ $\frac{7}{8}$

Ⓑ $\frac{1}{2}$

Ⓒ $\frac{5}{8}$

Ⓓ $\frac{1}{4}$

17. Three friends share a pizza divided into eighths. If each person eats one slice, how many more slices must be eaten so that $\frac{1}{2}$ of the pizza remains?

Ⓐ 1

Ⓑ 2

Ⓒ 3

Ⓓ 4

18. **Multi-Step** Sara and Jon each ordered a medium pizza. Sara ate $\frac{3}{8}$ of her pizza for lunch and $\frac{1}{4}$ for a snack. Jon ate $\frac{1}{2}$ of his pizza for lunch and $\frac{1}{4}$ for a snack. How much more pizza did Jon eat?

Ⓐ $\frac{1}{8}$

Ⓑ $\frac{1}{4}$

Ⓒ $\frac{1}{2}$

Ⓓ $\frac{1}{3}$

19. **Multi-Step** On field day, $\frac{1}{10}$ of the students in Mrs. Brown's class competed in jumping events, $\frac{3}{5}$ of the students competed in running events, and $\frac{1}{10}$ competed in throwing events. What part of Mrs. Brown's class did not compete in jumping, running, or throwing events?

Ⓐ $\frac{1}{5}$

Ⓑ $\frac{7}{10}$

Ⓒ $\frac{2}{5}$

Ⓓ $\frac{4}{5}$

5.3 Estimate Fraction Sums and Differences

TEKS Number and Operations—5.3.A
MATHEMATICAL PROCESSES
5.1.D, 5.1.E

 Essential Question How can you make reasonable estimates of fraction sums and differences?

Unlock the Problem

Kimberly will be riding her bike to school this year. The distance from her house to the end of the street is $\frac{1}{6}$ mile. The distance from the end of the street to the school is $\frac{3}{8}$ mile. About how far is Kimberly's house from school?

You can use benchmarks to find reasonable estimates by rounding fractions to 0, $\frac{1}{2}$, or 1.

One Way Use a number line.

Estimate. $\frac{1}{6} + \frac{3}{8}$

STEP 1 Place a point at $\frac{1}{6}$ on the number line.

The fraction is between _____ and _____.

The fraction $\frac{1}{6}$ is closer to the benchmark _____.

Round to _____.

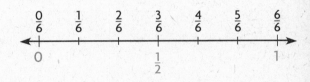

STEP 2 Place a point at $\frac{3}{8}$ on the number line.

The fraction is between _____ and _____.

The fraction $\frac{3}{8}$ is closer to the benchmark _____.

Round to _____.

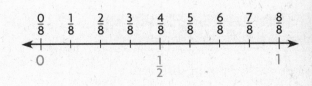

STEP 3 Add the rounded fractions.

$$\frac{1}{6} \rightarrow \boxed{}$$

$$+\frac{3}{8} \rightarrow +\boxed{}$$

$$\overline{} \quad \overline{\boxed{}}$$

So, Kimberly's house is about _____ mile from the school.

Another Way Use mental math.

You can compare the numerator and the denominator to round a fraction and find a reasonable estimate.

Estimate. $\frac{9}{10} - \frac{5}{8}$

STEP 1 Round $\frac{9}{10}$. **Think:** The numerator is about the same as the denominator.

Round the fraction $\frac{9}{10}$ to _____.

STEP 2 Round $\frac{5}{8}$. **Think:** The numerator is about half the denominator.

Round the fraction $\frac{5}{8}$ to _____.

STEP 3 Subtract.

$$\frac{9}{10} \rightarrow$$

$$-\frac{5}{8} \rightarrow -$$

So, $\frac{9}{10} - \frac{5}{8}$ is about _____.

> **Remember**
> A fraction with the same numerator and denominator, such as $\frac{2}{2}$, $\frac{5}{5}$, $\frac{12}{12}$, or $\frac{96}{96}$, is equal to 1.

> **Math Talk**
> Mathematical Processes
> **Explain** another way you could use benchmarks to estimate $\frac{9}{10} - \frac{5}{8}$.

Share and Show

Estimate the sum or difference.

1. $\frac{5}{6} + \frac{3}{8}$

   a. Round $\frac{5}{6}$ to its closest benchmark. _____

   b. Round $\frac{3}{8}$ to its closest benchmark. _____

   c. Add to find the estimate. _____ + _____ = _____

2. $\frac{5}{9} - \frac{3}{8}$

3. $\frac{5}{6} + \frac{2}{5}$

4. $\frac{9}{10} - \frac{1}{9}$

Name _____

5. How do you know whether your estimate for $\frac{9}{10} + 3\frac{6}{7}$ would be greater than or less than the actual sum? **Explain**.

_____

_____

6. **Write Math** ▶ Nick estimated that $\frac{5}{8} + \frac{4}{7}$ is about 2. **Explain** how you know his estimate is not reasonable.

_____

_____

Problem Solving (Real World)

7. Lisa and Valerie are picnicking in Trough Creek State Park in Pennsylvania. Lisa has brought a salad that she made with $\frac{3}{4}$ cup of strawberries, $\frac{7}{8}$ cup of peaches, and $\frac{1}{6}$ cup of blueberries. About how many total cups of fruit are in the salad?

_____

8. **H.O.T.** Multi-Step At Trace State Park in Mississippi, there is a 40-mile mountain bike trail. Tommy rode $\frac{1}{2}$ of the trail on Saturday and $\frac{1}{5}$ of the trail on Sunday. He estimates that he rode more than 22 miles over the two days. Is Tommy's estimate reasonable?

_____

_____

9. **H.O.T.** **Explain** how you know that $\frac{5}{8} + \frac{6}{10}$ is greater than 1.

_____

_____

_____

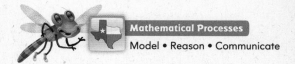

Daily Assessment Task

Fill in the bubble completely to show your answer.

10. Mia uses $\frac{1}{5}$ of a bag of gravel in the morning and $\frac{11}{12}$ of a bag in the afternoon. About how much gravel does she use in one day?

    Ⓐ 0 bags

    Ⓑ $\frac{1}{2}$ of a bag

    Ⓒ 1 bag

    Ⓓ $2\frac{1}{2}$ bags

11. **Evaluate Reasonableness** Hector and Veronica are going hiking. They made a trail mix that has $\frac{2}{3}$ cup of almonds, $\frac{7}{8}$ cup of peanuts, and $\frac{4}{5}$ cup of raisins in it. Hector estimates that they made about 3 cups of trail mix. Is the estimate greater than or less than the actual sum? How do you know?

    Ⓐ The estimate is greater because each fraction is rounded up to a benchmark.

    Ⓑ The estimate is less because each fraction is rounded down to a benchmark.

    Ⓒ The estimate is greater because they really made more than 3 cups.

    Ⓓ The estimate is less because each fraction is rounded up to a benchmark.

12. **Multi-Step** Amanda picked $\frac{3}{5}$ pound of blueberries at her local farm yesterday. She used $\frac{3}{8}$ pound of blueberries. Today she picked $\frac{4}{5}$ pound of blueberries. About how many pounds of blueberries does Amanda have now?

    Ⓐ $\frac{1}{5}$ lb

    Ⓑ $\frac{1}{2}$ lb

    Ⓒ 1 lb

    Ⓓ $1\frac{1}{2}$ lbs

 TEXAS Test Prep

13. Jake added $\frac{1}{8}$ cup of sunflower seeds and $\frac{4}{5}$ cup of banana chips to his sundae. Which is the best estimate of the total amount of toppings Jake added to his sundae?

    Ⓐ about 2 cups

    Ⓑ about 1 cup

    Ⓒ about $1\frac{1}{2}$ cups

    Ⓓ about $\frac{1}{2}$ cup

5.3 Estimate Fraction Sums and Differences

Estimate the sum or difference.

1. $\frac{3}{8} + \frac{4}{5}$

2. $\frac{9}{10} - \frac{3}{8}$

3. $\frac{5}{8} + \frac{2}{5}$

4. $\frac{6}{7} + \frac{3}{5}$

5. $\frac{3}{8} - \frac{1}{6}$

6. $\frac{7}{12} + \frac{1}{7}$

7. $\frac{4}{9} - \frac{5}{8}$

8. $\frac{1}{9} + \frac{5}{6}$

9. $\frac{7}{8} + \frac{4}{7}$

10. $\frac{1}{5} + \frac{3}{8}$

11. $\frac{7}{9} - \frac{2}{6}$

12. $\frac{9}{10} - \frac{7}{8}$

13. Explain how you can estimate the sum of $\frac{4}{5}$ and $\frac{1}{6}$.

_____

_____

_____

Problem Solving

14. Jena uses $\frac{7}{8}$ cup of raisins for muffins and $\frac{5}{8}$ cup of raisins for a bowl of oatmeal. Does Jena need more than or less than 1 cup of raisins to make muffins and oatmeal? **Explain**.

_____

_____

15. A group of students ate $\frac{5}{12}$ of a cheese pizza, $\frac{7}{8}$ of a pepperoni pizza, and $\frac{5}{8}$ of a veggie pizza. About how many pizzas were eaten?

_____

Fill in the bubble completely to show your answer.

16. On Saturday, the scouts hiked $\frac{4}{5}$ mile up the mountain. On Sunday, they hiked $\frac{1}{4}$ mile up the mountain. About how far did the scouts hike up the mountain in all?

(A) $\frac{1}{2}$ mile

(B) 1 mile

(C) $1\frac{1}{2}$ miles

(D) 2 miles

17. Which of the following best describes the difference for $\frac{11}{12} - \frac{7}{10}$?

(A) less than $\frac{1}{2}$

(B) greater than $\frac{1}{2}$

(C) greater than 1

(D) greater than $1\frac{1}{2}$

18. Which sum is greatest? Use estimation to decide.

(A) $\frac{2}{7} + \frac{3}{8}$

(B) $\frac{1}{10} + \frac{3}{8}$

(C) $\frac{1}{6} + \frac{1}{8}$

(D) $\frac{2}{9} + \frac{1}{8}$

19. Which statement is not correct? Use estimation to decide.

(A) $\frac{2}{3} + \frac{5}{9} > \frac{4}{8} + \frac{7}{12}$

(B) $\frac{3}{4} + \frac{5}{12} < \frac{5}{12} + \frac{3}{10}$

(C) $\frac{2}{9} + \frac{2}{5} < \frac{5}{6} + \frac{1}{10}$

(D) $\frac{5}{9} + \frac{9}{10} > \frac{5}{12} + \frac{2}{3}$

20. Multi-Step Michaela has $\frac{11}{12}$ yard of orange fabric and $\frac{7}{8}$ yard of green fabric. She uses $\frac{1}{2}$ yard of each color for her sewing project. About how much fabric does Michaela have left if she combines the two colors?

(A) 1 yard

(B) $\frac{1}{2}$ yard

(C) $1\frac{1}{2}$ yards

(D) 2 yards

21. Multi-Step Dustin buys $\frac{9}{10}$ yard of striped fabric. He uses $\frac{3}{8}$ yard. He buys $\frac{7}{8}$ yard more. About how much fabric does Dustin have now?

(A) 1 yard

(B) $\frac{1}{2}$ yard

(C) $1\frac{1}{2}$ yards

(D) 2 yards

Name _____

 5.4 # Common Denominators and Equivalent Fractions

TEKS **Number and Operations—5.3**
MATHEMATICAL PROCESSES
5.1.F

? Essential Question

How can you rewrite a pair of fractions so that they have a common denominator?

🔑 Unlock the Problem

Sarah planted two 1-acre gardens. One had 3 sections of flowers and the other had 4 sections of flowers. She plans to divide both gardens into more sections so that they have the same number of equal-sized sections. How many sections will each garden have?

You can use a **common denominator** or a common multiple of two or more denominators to write fractions that name the same part of a whole.

 Find the common denominator.

THINK

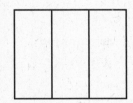 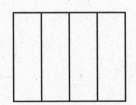

Divide each $\frac{1}{3}$ into fourths and divide each $\frac{1}{4}$ into thirds, each of the wholes will be divided into the same size parts, twelfths.

So, both gardens will have _____ sections.

RECORD

- Multiply the denominators to find a common denominator.

  A common denominator of $\frac{1}{3}$ and $\frac{1}{4}$ is _____.

- Write $\frac{1}{3}$ and $\frac{1}{4}$ as equivalent fractions using the common denominator.

  $\frac{1}{3} = \boxed{}$ $\frac{1}{4} = \boxed{}$

 Find the least common denominator of $\frac{3}{4}$ and $\frac{1}{6}$.

- List nonzero multiples of the denominators. Find the least common multiple.

  Multiples of 4: _____

  Multiples of 6: _____

  So, the least common denominator

  of $\frac{3}{4}$ and $\frac{1}{6}$ is _____.

- Use the least common denominator to write equivalent fractions.

  $\frac{3}{4} = \frac{?}{12} = \frac{3 \times 3}{4 \times 3} = \frac{}{}$

  $\frac{1}{6} = \frac{?}{12} = \frac{1 \times }{6 \times } = \frac{}{}$

  $\frac{3}{4}$ can be rewritten as _____ and $\frac{1}{6}$ can be

  rewritten as _____.

1. Find a common denominator of $\frac{1}{6}$ and $\frac{1}{9}$. Rewrite the pair of fractions using the common denominator.

   - Multiply the denominators.
     A common denominator of $\frac{1}{6}$ and $\frac{1}{9}$ is _____.
   - Rewrite the pair of fractions using the common denominator.

   $$\frac{1}{6} = \frac{}{} \qquad \frac{1}{9} = \frac{}{}$$

Math Talk
Mathematical Processes

Explain two methods for finding a common denominator of two fractions.

Use a common denominator to write an equivalent fraction for each fraction.

2. $\frac{1}{3}, \frac{1}{5}$ common denominator: _____

   _____

3. $\frac{2}{3}, \frac{5}{9}$ common denominator: _____

   _____

4. $\frac{2}{9}, \frac{1}{15}$ common denominator: _____

   _____

Use the least common denominator to write an equivalent fraction for each fraction.

5. $\frac{1}{4}, \frac{3}{8}$ least common denominator: _____

   _____

6. $\frac{11}{12}, \frac{5}{8}$ least common denominator: _____

   _____

7. $\frac{4}{5}, \frac{1}{6}$ least common denominator: _____

   _____

Problem Solving

Practice: Copy and Solve Use the least common denominator to write an equivalent fraction for each fraction.

8. $\frac{1}{6}, \frac{4}{9}$

9. $\frac{7}{9}, \frac{8}{27}$

10. $\frac{7}{10}, \frac{3}{8}$

11. $\frac{1}{3}, \frac{5}{11}$

H.O.T. **Algebra** Write the unknown number for each ■.

12. $\frac{1}{5}, \frac{1}{8}$ least common denominator: ■

    ■ = _____

13. $\frac{2}{5}, \frac{1}{■}$ least common denominator: 15

    ■ = _____

14. $\frac{3}{■}, \frac{5}{6}$ least common denominator: 42

    ■ = _____

15. What does a common denominator of two fractions represent? **Explain.**

_____

_____

Name _____

16. Katie made two pies for the bake sale. One was cut into three equal
slices and the other into 5 equal slices. She will continue to cut the pies
so each one has the same number of equal-sized slices. What is the least
number of equal-sized slices each pie could have?

a. What information are you given? _____

_____

b. What problem are you being asked to solve? _____

_____

c. When Katie cuts the pies more, can she cut each pie the same number
of times and have all the slices the same size? **Explain.**

_____

_____

d. Use the diagram to show the steps you use to
solve the problem.

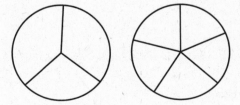

e. Complete the sentences.

The least common denominator of

$\frac{1}{3}$ and $\frac{1}{5}$ is _____.

Katie can cut each piece of the first pie

into _____ and each piece of the

second pie into _____.
That means that Katie can cut each pie into

pieces that are _____ of the whole pie.

17. **H.O.T.** **Multi-Step** Arnold had three pieces of different color
string all the same length. Arnold cut the blue string into 2 equal lengths.
He cut the red string into 3 equal-size lengths, and the green string into
6 equal-size lengths. He needs to cut the string so each color has the
same number of equal-size lengths. What is the least number of
equal-sized lengths each color string could have?

_____

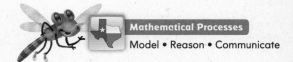
Daily Assessment Task

Fill in the bubble completely to show your answer.

18. **Reasoning** Magara entered the fractions $\frac{1}{4}$ and $\frac{7}{\blacksquare}$ into a computer program. The computer used the least common denominator to rename the fractions as $\frac{5}{20}$ and $\frac{14}{20}$. What is the unknown denominator?

(A) 20   (C) 12

(B) 8   (D) 10

19. Alejandro wants to use the least common denominator to write equivalent fractions for $\frac{3}{7}$ and $\frac{4}{5}$. He rewrites the fractions as $\frac{15}{35}$ and $\frac{20}{35}$. How should he change his answer?

(A) The numerators are correct, but the denominators should be 7.

(B) $\frac{20}{35}$ is correct, but $\frac{15}{35}$ should be $\frac{21}{25}$.

(C) $\frac{15}{35}$ is correct, but $\frac{20}{35}$ should be $\frac{28}{35}$.

(D) The denominators are correct, but both numerators should be 12.

20. **Multi-Step** Aiesha and her mom are cutting two sandwiches into smaller bite-size pieces. They cut the first sandwich in four equal-sized pieces. They cut the second sandwich into six equal-sized pieces. However, they want an equal number of pieces from each sandwich. What is the least number of pieces they could cut from each sandwich?

(A) 4   (C) 10

(B) 6   (D) 12

 TEXAS Test Prep

21. Which fractions use the least common denominator and are equivalent to $\frac{5}{8}$ and $\frac{7}{10}$?

(A) $\frac{10}{40}$ and $\frac{14}{40}$

(B) $\frac{25}{80}$ and $\frac{21}{80}$

(C) $\frac{25}{40}$ and $\frac{28}{40}$

(D) $\frac{50}{80}$ and $\frac{56}{80}$

216

Homework and Practice

Name _____

5.4 Common Denominators and Equivalent Fractions

Use the least common denominator to write an equivalent fraction for each fraction.

1. $\frac{1}{10}, \frac{1}{5}$ _____

2. $\frac{1}{3}, \frac{2}{9}$ _____

3. $\frac{1}{6}, \frac{2}{4}$ _____

4. $\frac{2}{3}, \frac{1}{2}$ _____

5. $\frac{3}{4}, \frac{3}{8}$ _____

6. $\frac{11}{12}, \frac{1}{6}$ _____

7. $\frac{1}{2}, \frac{2}{5}$ _____

8. $\frac{5}{7}, \frac{3}{5}$ _____

9. $\frac{1}{4}, \frac{3}{16}$ _____

10. $\frac{2}{5}, \frac{3}{4}$ _____

11. $\frac{2}{15}, \frac{5}{6}$ _____

12. $\frac{7}{8}, \frac{1}{2}$ _____

Write the unknown number for each ■.

13. $\frac{2}{3}, \frac{1}{6}$ least common denominator: ■

    ■ = _____

14. $\frac{1}{8}, \frac{2}{■}$ least common denominator: 24

    ■ = _____

15. $\frac{1}{■}, \frac{2}{7}$ least common denominator: 21

    ■ = _____

Problem Solving Real World

16. Daria bought two same-sized posterboards. She cut the posterboards into equal-sized pieces to make placemats for her dinner guests. She cut the first posterboard into 5 pieces and the second posterboard into 2 pieces. She will continue to cut the pieces of posterboard so that each one is divided into the same number of equal-sized pieces. What is the least number of equal-sized pieces each posterboard could have?

    _____

17. A recipe for homemade goop calls for $\frac{1}{4}$ cup of cornstarch and $\frac{1}{8}$ cup of glue. Find the least common denominator of the fractions used in the recipe.

    _____

Fill in the bubble completely to show your answer.

18. How can you find the least common denominator for $\frac{1}{8}$ and $\frac{2}{9}$?

    (A) Multiply 8 and 9.

    (B) Add 8 and 9.

    (C) Multiply each number by 2.

    (D) Add 2 to 8 and 1 to 9.

19. If the least common denominator for $\frac{1}{\blacksquare}$ and $\frac{5}{12}$ is 12, which of the following could not be the unknown denominator?

    (A) 2

    (B) 3

    (C) 4

    (D) 5

20. Which fractions use the least common denominator and are equivalent to $\frac{3}{10}$ and $\frac{1}{6}$?

    (A) $\frac{18}{60}$ and $\frac{10}{60}$

    (B) $\frac{30}{60}$ and $\frac{10}{60}$

    (C) $\frac{10}{30}$ and $\frac{18}{30}$

    (D) $\frac{5}{30}$ and $\frac{9}{30}$

21. Lindsay writes two fractions with a least common denominator of 36. Which fractions does Lindsay write?

    (A) $\frac{2}{3}, \frac{5}{12}$

    (B) $\frac{2}{9}, \frac{1}{12}$

    (C) $\frac{3}{8}, \frac{7}{72}$

    (D) $\frac{1}{8}, \frac{5}{36}$

22. **Multi-Step** An archeologist marks off two equal-sized sites for excavation. She uses a grid system to divide each square site into sections. One square has 8 sections. The other square has 6 sections. She plans to divide both squares into more sections so that they have the same number of equal-sized sections. How many sections will each square have?

    (A) 14

    (B) 8

    (C) 24

    (D) 36

23. **Multi-Step** Mr. Nickelson tells the class that they double the least common denominator for $\frac{1}{2}$, $\frac{3}{5}$, and $\frac{9}{15}$ to find the number of the day. Which number is the number of the day?

    (A) 30

    (B) 15

    (C) 60

    (D) 32

Name _____

TEKS **Number and Operations—5.3.K**

MATHEMATICAL PROCESSES **5.1.C**

? **Essential Question**

How can you use a common denominator to add and subtract fractions with unequal denominators?

Connect You can use what you have learned about common denominators to add or subtract fractions with unequal denominators.

 Unlock the Problem Real World

Malia bought shell beads and glass beads to weave into designs in her baskets. She bought $\frac{1}{4}$ pound of shell beads and $\frac{3}{8}$ pound of glass beads. How many pounds of beads did she buy?

- Underline the question you need to answer.
- Draw a circle around the information you will use.

🔑 **Add.** $\frac{1}{4} + \frac{3}{8}$ **Write your answer in simplest form.**

One Way

Find a common denominator by multiplying the denominators.

$4 \times 8 =$ _____ ← common denominator

Use the common denominator to write equivalent fractions with equal denominators. Then add, and write your answer in simplest form.

$$\frac{1}{4} = \frac{1 \times }{4 \times } =$$

$$+ \frac{3}{8} = + \frac{3 \times }{8 \times } = +$$

$$=$$

Another Way

Find the least common denominator.

The least common denominator

of $\frac{1}{4}$ and $\frac{3}{8}$ is _____.

$$\frac{1}{4} = \frac{1 \times }{4 \times } =$$

$$+ \frac{3}{8} \qquad +$$

So, Malia bought _____ pound of beads.

1. Explain how you know whether your answer is reasonable. _____

_____

🔑 Example

When subtracting two fractions with unequal denominators, follow the same steps you follow when adding two fractions. However, instead of adding the fractions, subtract.

Subtract. $\frac{9}{10} - \frac{2}{5}$ **Write your answer in simplest form.**

$$\frac{9}{10} =$$

$$-\frac{2}{5} =$$

Describe the steps you took to solve the problem.

_____

_____

_____

_____

2. Explain how you know whether your answer is reasonable.

_____

_____

Share and Show

Find the sum or difference. Write your answer in simplest form.

1. $\frac{5}{12} + \frac{1}{3}$

2. $\frac{2}{5} + \frac{3}{7}$

✅ **3.** $\frac{1}{6} + \frac{3}{4}$

4. $\frac{3}{4} - \frac{1}{8}$

5. $\frac{1}{4} - \frac{1}{7}$

✅ **6.** $\frac{9}{10} - \frac{1}{4}$

Math Talk
Mathematical Processes

Explain why it is important to check your answer for reasonableness.

Name _____

Practice: Copy and Solve Find the sum or difference. Write your answer in simplest form.

7. $\frac{1}{3} + \frac{4}{18}$

8. $\frac{3}{5} + \frac{1}{3}$

9. $\frac{3}{10} + \frac{1}{6}$

10. $\frac{1}{2} + \frac{4}{9}$

11. $\frac{1}{2} - \frac{3}{8}$

12. $\frac{5}{7} - \frac{2}{3}$

13. $\frac{4}{9} - \frac{1}{6}$

14. $\frac{11}{12} - \frac{7}{15}$

 Algebra Find the unknown number.

15. $\frac{9}{10} - \blacksquare = \frac{1}{5}$

16. $\frac{5}{12} + \blacksquare = \frac{1}{2}$

$\blacksquare = $ _____

$\blacksquare = $ _____

Problem Solving *Real World*

Use the picture for 17–18.

17. Sara is making a key chain using the bead design shown. What fraction of the beads in her design are either blue or red?

_____

18. 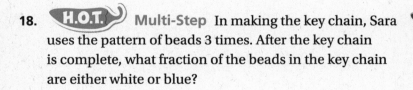 **Multi-Step** In making the key chain, Sara uses the pattern of beads 3 times. After the key chain is complete, what fraction of the beads in the key chain are either white or blue?

_____

19. **Write Math** ▶ Jamie had $\frac{4}{5}$ of a spool of twine. He then used $\frac{1}{2}$ of a spool of twine to make friendship knots. He claims to have $\frac{3}{10}$ of the original spool of twine left over. **Explain** how you know whether Jamie's claim is reasonable.

Write Math ▶ **Show Your Work** • • • • • • •

_____

_____

_____

_____

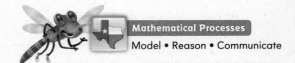

Daily Assessment Task

Fill in the bubble completely to show your answer.

20. **Apply** Students are voting for a new school mascot. So far, the results show that $\frac{3}{10}$ of the students voted for "Fightin' Titan," $\frac{1}{2}$ of the students voted for "Nifty Knight," and the rest of the students have not voted yet. What fraction of the student population has not voted yet?

(A) $\frac{3}{10}$　　　　(C) $\frac{2}{5}$

(B) $\frac{1}{5}$　　　　(D) $\frac{4}{5}$

21. Tina spent $\frac{3}{5}$ of her paycheck on a trip to the beach. She spent $\frac{3}{8}$ of her paycheck on new clothes for the trip. What fraction of her paycheck did Tina spend on the trip and clothes together?

(A) $\frac{9}{40}$

(B) $\frac{3}{4}$

(C) $\frac{7}{8}$

(D) $\frac{39}{40}$

22. **Multi-Step** On Friday, $\frac{1}{6}$ of band practice was spent trying on uniforms. The band spent $\frac{1}{4}$ of practice on marching. What fraction of practice time was left for playing music?

(A) $\frac{5}{12}$　　　　(C) $\frac{1}{2}$

(B) $\frac{7}{12}$　　　　(D) $\frac{1}{4}$

⭐ TEXAS Test Prep

23. Which equation represents the fraction of beads that are green or yellow?

(A) $\frac{1}{2} + \frac{1}{4} = \frac{3}{4}$

(B) $\frac{1}{4} + \frac{1}{8} = \frac{3}{8}$

(C) $\frac{1}{2} + \frac{1}{8} = \frac{5}{8}$

(D) $\frac{3}{4} + \frac{2}{8} = 1$

Homework and Practice

Name _____

5.5 Add and Subtract Fractions

Find the sum or difference. Write your answer in simplest form.

1. $\frac{1}{5} + \frac{1}{2}$ _____

2. $\frac{2}{3} + \frac{1}{6}$ _____

3. $\frac{1}{4} + \frac{2}{3}$ _____

4. $\frac{3}{4} + \frac{1}{8}$ _____

5. $\frac{2}{9} + \frac{1}{3}$ _____

6. $\frac{1}{2} + \frac{2}{6}$ _____

7. $\frac{3}{10} + \frac{1}{3}$ _____

8. $\frac{4}{18} + \frac{2}{6}$ _____

9. $\frac{6}{12} - \frac{1}{3}$ _____

10. $\frac{3}{4} - \frac{1}{6}$ _____

11. $\frac{5}{7} - \frac{1}{2}$ _____

12. $\frac{8}{9} - \frac{2}{3}$ _____

13. $\frac{5}{9} - \frac{1}{6}$ _____

14. $\frac{2}{3} - \frac{1}{4}$ _____

15. $\frac{7}{14} - \frac{2}{7}$ _____

16. $\frac{5}{6} - \frac{3}{4}$ _____

Find the unknown number.

17. $\frac{7}{12} - \blacksquare = \frac{1}{6}$

    $\blacksquare =$ _____

18. $\frac{5}{18} + \blacksquare = \frac{1}{2}$

    $\blacksquare =$ _____

19. $\frac{7}{10} - \blacksquare = \frac{2}{5}$

    $\blacksquare =$ _____

20. $\blacksquare + \frac{1}{9} = \frac{1}{3}$

    $\blacksquare =$ _____

Problem Solving

21. There are 12 students in the pep squad. Three students are wearing white shirts. Six students are wearing blue shirts. What fraction of the students in the pep squad are wearing either white or blue shirts?

    _____

22. Tiffany ran $\frac{5}{6}$ mile. Shayne ran $\frac{3}{4}$ mile. Who ran farther? How much farther?

    _____

Fill in the bubble completely to show your answer.

23. Mr. Benson spent $\frac{2}{5}$ of the monthly budget on rent and $\frac{3}{10}$ of the budget on food. What fraction of Mr. Benson's budget was spent on rent and food?

(A) $\frac{1}{3}$

(B) $\frac{3}{10}$

(C) $\frac{7}{10}$

(D) $\frac{1}{2}$

24. The Ortega family made $\frac{15}{16}$ pound of confetti for the annual Fiesta celebration in San Antonio. They used $\frac{1}{4}$ pound to make confetti filled eggs. How much confetti is left to use next year?

(A) $\frac{11}{16}$ pound

(B) $\frac{9}{16}$ pound

(C) $\frac{4}{5}$ pound

(D) $\frac{3}{4}$ pound

Use the recipe for 25–26.

25. If Rory measures the lemon juice and the vanilla extract into one spoon before adding them to the blender, how much liquid will be in the spoon?

(A) $\frac{5}{8}$ teaspoon

(B) $\frac{1}{5}$ teaspoon

(C) $\frac{1}{4}$ teaspoon

(D) $\frac{3}{8}$ teaspoon

Berry Smoothie

2 cups strawberries

1 cup blueberries

$\frac{1}{4}$ cup milk

1 Tbsp sugar

$\frac{1}{2}$ tsp lemon juice

$\frac{1}{8}$ tsp vanilla extract

26. **Multi-Step** Rory has $\frac{5}{8}$ cup of milk. How much milk does she have left after she doubles the recipe for the smoothie?

(A) $\frac{3}{8}$ cup

(B) $\frac{1}{8}$ cup

(C) $\frac{3}{4}$ cup

(D) $\frac{1}{2}$ cup

27. **Multi-Step** Tom has $\frac{7}{8}$ cup of olive oil. He uses $\frac{1}{2}$ cup to make salad dressing and $\frac{1}{4}$ cup to make tomato sauce. How much olive oil does Tom have left?

(A) $\frac{5}{4}$ cups

(B) $\frac{5}{8}$ cup

(C) $\frac{3}{8}$ cup

(D) $\frac{1}{8}$ cup

5.6 Add and Subtract Mixed Numbers

TEKS Number and Operations—5.3.K
MATHEMATICAL PROCESSES
5.1.A

? Essential Question

How can you add and subtract mixed numbers with unequal denominators?

🔑 Unlock the Problem

Denise mixed $1\frac{4}{5}$ ounces of blue paint with $2\frac{1}{10}$ ounces of yellow paint. How many ounces of paint did Denise mix?

- What operation should you use to solve the problem?

_____

- Do the fractions have the same denominator?

_____

🔑 **Add.** $1\frac{4}{5} + 2\frac{1}{10}$

To find the sum of mixed numbers with unequal denominators, you can use a common denominator.

STEP 1 Estimate the sum.

_____

_____

STEP 2 Find a common denominator. Use the common denominator to write equivalent fractions with equal denominators.

_____

STEP 3 Add the fractions. Then add the whole numbers. Write the answer in simplest form.

$$1\frac{4}{5} = \boxed{}$$
$$+\,2\frac{1}{10} = +\boxed{}$$

So, Denise mixed _____ ounces of paint.

Math Talk
Mathematical Processes

Did you use the least common denominator? **Explain.**

1. **Explain** how you know whether your answer is reasonable. _____

_____

_____

2. What other common denominator could you have used? _____

_____

🔑 Example

Subtract. $4\frac{5}{6} - 2\frac{3}{4}$

You can also use a common denominator to find the difference of mixed numbers with unequal denominators.

STEP 1 Estimate the difference. _____

STEP 2 Find a common denominator. Use the common denominator to write equivalent fractions with equal denominators.

_____

STEP 3 Subtract the fractions. Subtract the whole numbers. Write the answer in simplest form.

$$4\frac{5}{6} = $$

$$-2\frac{3}{4} = - $$

_____

3. **Explain** how you know whether your answer is reasonable. _____

_____

_____

Share and Show 🖊 MATH BOARD

1. Use a common denominator to write equivalent fractions with equal denominators and then find the sum. Write your answer in simplest form.

$$7\frac{2}{5} = $$

$$+4\frac{3}{4} = + $$

_____

Find the sum. Write your answer in simplest form.

2. $2\frac{3}{4} + 3\frac{3}{10}$

✓ 3. $5\frac{3}{4} + 1\frac{1}{3}$

✓ 4. $3\frac{4}{5} + 2\frac{3}{10}$

Name _____

Problem Solving

Practice: Copy and Solve Find the sum or difference. Write your answer in simplest form.

5. $1\frac{5}{12} + 4\frac{1}{6}$ **6.** $8\frac{1}{2} + 6\frac{3}{5}$ **7.** $2\frac{1}{6} + 4\frac{5}{9}$ **8.** $3\frac{5}{8} + \frac{5}{12}$

9. $3\frac{2}{3} - 1\frac{1}{6}$ **10.** $5\frac{6}{7} - 1\frac{2}{3}$ **11.** $2\frac{7}{8} - \frac{1}{2}$ **12.** $4\frac{7}{12} - 1\frac{2}{9}$

13. Communicate Why do you need to write equivalent fractions with common denominators to add $4\frac{5}{6}$ and $\frac{11}{8}$? **Explain**.

_____

_____

Problem Solving

Use the table to solve 14–15.

14. **H.O.T.** **Multi-Step** Gavin needs to make 2 batches of Mango paint. **Explain** how you could find the total amount of paint Gavin mixed.

_____

_____

_____

15. **H.O.T.** Gavin mixes the amount of red from one shade of paint with the amount of yellow from a different shade of paint. He mixes the batch so he will have the greatest possible amount of paint. What amounts of red and yellow from which shades are used in the mixture? **Explain** your answer.

Paint Gavin Uses (in ounces)		
Red	Yellow	Shade
$2\frac{5}{8}$	$3\frac{1}{4}$	Sunrise Orange
$3\frac{9}{10}$	$2\frac{3}{8}$	Tangerine
$5\frac{5}{6}$	$5\frac{5}{6}$	Mango

_____

_____

_____

Daily Assessment Task

Fill in the bubble completely to show your answer.

16. Dr. Whether-or-Not collects two hailstones during a storm in California. One hailstone weighs $2\frac{3}{8}$ pounds, and the other hailstone weighs $1\frac{3}{10}$ pounds. How much heavier is the larger hailstone than the smaller hailstone?

(A) $\frac{3}{40}$ pounds

(C) $1\frac{27}{40}$ pounds

(B) $1\frac{3}{40}$ pounds

(D) $3\frac{27}{40}$ pounds

17. **Apply** Jason is making a fruit salad. He mixes in $3\frac{1}{4}$ cups of orange melon and $2\frac{2}{3}$ cups of green melon. How many cups of melon does Jason put in the fruit salad?

(A) $5\frac{1}{4}$ cups

(C) $5\frac{7}{12}$ cups

(B) $5\frac{1}{3}$ cups

(D) $5\frac{11}{12}$ cups

18. **Multi-Step** Dakota makes a salad dressing by combining $6\frac{1}{3}$ fluid ounces of oil and $2\frac{3}{8}$ fluid ounces of vinegar in a jar. She then pours $2\frac{1}{4}$ fluid ounces of the dressing onto her salad. How much dressing remains in the jar?

(A) $6\frac{1}{8}$ fluid ounces

(B) $6\frac{3}{8}$ fluid ounces

(C) $6\frac{11}{24}$ fluid ounces

(D) $6\frac{17}{24}$ fluid ounces

⭐ TEXAS Test Prep

19. Yolanda walked $3\frac{6}{10}$ miles. Then she walked $4\frac{1}{2}$ more miles. How many miles did Yolanda walk?

(A) $7\frac{1}{10}$ miles

(B) $8\frac{7}{10}$ miles

(C) $8\frac{1}{10}$ miles

(D) $7\frac{7}{10}$ miles

Homework and Practice

Name _____

5.6 Add and Subtract Mixed Numbers

Find the sum or difference. Write your answer in simplest form.

1. $1\frac{1}{4} + 2\frac{2}{3}$ _____

2. $3\frac{3}{4} + 4\frac{5}{12}$ _____

3. $1\frac{1}{3} + 2\frac{1}{6}$ _____

4. $4\frac{1}{2} + 3\frac{4}{5}$ _____

5. $5\frac{5}{6} + 4\frac{2}{9}$ _____

6. $7\frac{1}{4} + 3\frac{2}{5}$ _____

7. $3\frac{2}{7} + 8\frac{1}{3}$ _____

8. $4\frac{3}{7} + 3\frac{1}{2}$ _____

9. $2\frac{4}{5} - 1\frac{1}{2}$ _____

10. $5\frac{3}{8} - 1\frac{1}{4}$ _____

11. $4\frac{1}{3} - 3\frac{1}{6}$ _____

12. $6\frac{5}{6} - 5\frac{7}{9}$ _____

13. $4\frac{1}{3} - 2\frac{1}{4}$ _____

14. $3\frac{1}{4} - 1\frac{1}{6}$ _____

15. $6\frac{3}{4} - 2\frac{5}{16}$ _____

16. $7\frac{3}{5} - 2\frac{1}{4}$ _____

17. Use two mixed numbers to write an equation with a sum of $4\frac{1}{4}$.

_____

Problem Solving

18. Lucas says his twin baby brothers have a total weight of $15\frac{1}{8}$ pounds. Jackson weighs $6\frac{1}{4}$ pounds, and Jeremy weighs $8\frac{7}{8}$ pounds. Explain how you can use estimation to tell if the total weight is reasonable.

_____

_____

19. The gas tank in Rebecca's old car held $14\frac{1}{5}$ gallons. The gas tank in Rebecca's new car holds $18\frac{1}{2}$ gallons. How many more gallons will the tank in Rebecca's new car hold than her old car?

_____

Fill in the bubble completely to show your answer.

Use the table for 20–21.

Four students made paper chains to decorate the community center. The table at the right shows the lengths of the paper chains.

Length of Paper Chains

Student	Length (in feet)
Skye	$8\frac{1}{12}$
Ioana	$7\frac{1}{2}$
Gabrielle	$5\frac{3}{4}$
Oksana	$9\frac{5}{6}$

20. If Ioana attaches her chain to the end of Gabrielle's chain, what will be the length of the combined chain?

Ⓐ $13\frac{3}{4}$ feet

Ⓑ $13\frac{1}{4}$ feet

Ⓒ $12\frac{1}{4}$ feet

Ⓓ $12\frac{1}{2}$ feet

21. How much longer is Oksana's chain than Gabrielle's chain?

Ⓐ $15\frac{7}{12}$ feet

Ⓑ $14\frac{1}{12}$ feet

Ⓒ $4\frac{1}{4}$ feet

Ⓓ $4\frac{1}{12}$ feet

22. Mia hiked $2\frac{1}{2}$ miles farther than Jacob. Which could be the two distances each person hiked?

Ⓐ Mia: $2\frac{1}{2}$ miles; Jacob: $1\frac{1}{4}$ miles

Ⓑ Mia: $2\frac{1}{2}$ miles; Jacob: $7\frac{1}{2}$ miles

Ⓒ Mia: $3\frac{2}{5}$ miles; Jacob: $5\frac{9}{10}$ miles

Ⓓ Mia: $5\frac{9}{10}$ miles; Jacob: $3\frac{2}{5}$ miles

23. **Multi-Step** Mr. Carter owned a ranch with $7\frac{1}{4}$ acres. Last year, he bought $3\frac{1}{5}$ acres of land from his neighbor. Then he sold $2\frac{1}{4}$ acres. How many acres does Mr. Carter own now?

Ⓐ $10\frac{9}{20}$ acres

Ⓑ $8\frac{1}{5}$ acres

Ⓒ $12\frac{7}{10}$ acres

Ⓓ $6\frac{3}{10}$ acres

24. **Multi-Step** This week, Maddie worked $2\frac{1}{2}$ hours on Monday, $2\frac{2}{3}$ hours on Tuesday, and $3\frac{1}{4}$ hours on Wednesday. How many more hours will Maddie need to work this week to make her goal of $10\frac{1}{2}$ hours a week?

Ⓐ $2\frac{1}{12}$ hours

Ⓑ $8\frac{5}{12}$ hours

Ⓒ $18\frac{11}{12}$ hours

Ⓓ $5\frac{1}{3}$ hours

5.7 Subtraction with Renaming

TEKS **Number and Operations—5.3.K**

MATHEMATICAL PROCESSES
5.1.G

? Essential Question How can you use renaming to find the difference of two mixed numbers?

? Unlock the Problem

To practice for a race, Kara is running $2\frac{1}{2}$ miles. When she reaches the end of her street, she knows that she has already run $1\frac{5}{6}$ miles. How many miles does Kara have left to run?

- Underline the sentence that tells you what you need to find.
- What operation should you use to solve the problem?

_____

🔓 One Way Rename the first mixed number.

Subtract. $2\frac{1}{2} - 1\frac{5}{6}$

STEP 1 Estimate the difference. _____

STEP 2 Find a common denominator. Use the common denominator to write equivalent fractions with like denominators.

STEP 3 Rename $2\frac{6}{12}$ as a mixed number with a fraction greater than 1.

   Think: $2\frac{6}{12} = 1 + 1 + \frac{6}{12} = 1 + \frac{12}{12} + \frac{6}{12} = 1\frac{18}{12}$

   $2\frac{6}{12} =$ _____

$$2\frac{1}{2} = 2\frac{6}{12} = \boxed{}$$
$$-1\frac{5}{6} = -1\frac{10}{12} = -1\frac{10}{12}$$
$$\boxed{} = \boxed{}$$

STEP 4 Find the difference of the fractions. Then find the difference of the whole numbers. Write the answer in simplest form. Check to make sure your answer is reasonable.

So, Kara has _____ mile left to run.

🔑 Another Way Rename both mixed numbers as fractions greater than 1.

Subtract. $2\frac{1}{2} - 1\frac{5}{6}$

STEP 1 Write equivalent fractions, using a common denominator.

A common denominator of $\frac{1}{2}$ and $\frac{5}{6}$ is 6.

$2\frac{1}{2} \longrightarrow$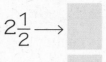

$1\frac{5}{6} \longrightarrow$

STEP 2 Rename both mixed numbers as fractions greater than 1.

$2\frac{3}{6} =$ ☐ **Think:** $\frac{6}{6} + \frac{6}{6} + \frac{3}{6}$

$1\frac{5}{6} =$ ☐ **Think:** $\frac{6}{6} + \frac{5}{6}$

STEP 3 Find the difference of the fractions. Then write the answer in simplest form.

☐ $-$ ☐ $=$ ☐

$=$ ☐

$2\frac{1}{2} - 1\frac{5}{6} =$ _____

Share and Show

 MATH BOARD

Estimate. Then find the difference and write it in simplest form.

✓ 1. Estimate: _____

$1\frac{3}{4} - \frac{7}{8}$

✓ 2. Estimate: _____

$12\frac{1}{9} - 7\frac{1}{3}$

Math Talk
Mathematical Processes

Explain the strategy you could use to solve $3\frac{1}{9} - 2\frac{1}{3}$.

Name _____

Problem Solving

Practice: Copy and Solve Find the difference and write it in simplest form.

3. $11\frac{1}{9} - 3\frac{2}{3}$

4. $6 - 3\frac{1}{2}$

5. $4\frac{3}{8} - 3\frac{1}{2}$

6. $9\frac{1}{6} - 3\frac{5}{8}$

7. Communicate Why is it important to write equivalent fractions before renaming? **Explain.**

_____

_____

Problem Solving Real World

A roller coaster has 3 trains with 8 rows per train. Riders stand in rows of 4, for a total of 32 riders per train. The operators of the coaster recorded the number of riders on each train during a run. On the first train, the operators reported that $7\frac{1}{4}$ rows were filled. On the second train, all 8 rows were filled, and on the third train, $5\frac{1}{2}$ rows were filled.

Use the summary to solve.

8. Evaluate How many more rows were filled on the first train than on the third train?

_____

_____

9. **H.O.T.** **Multi-Step** How many rows were empty on the first train? How many additional riders would it take to fill the empty rows? **Explain** your answer.

_____

_____

10. **H.O.T.** **Multi-Step** How many rows were empty on the third train? How many additional riders would it take to fill the empty rows? **Explain** your answer.

_____

_____

_____

Daily Assessment Task

Fill in the bubble completely to show your answer.

11. You plan to enter a song writing contest. Your song must be exactly $3\frac{1}{2}$ minutes long. You have a song that lasts for $4\frac{1}{5}$ minutes. How many minutes do you need to cut from the song?

   Ⓐ $1\frac{3}{10}$ Ⓒ $\frac{3}{10}$

   Ⓑ $\frac{7}{10}$ Ⓓ $1\frac{7}{10}$

12. Harris and Ji are spending a weekend camping. Their campsite is $6\frac{1}{4}$ kilometers from the main park road. They can take an ATV for the first $4\frac{7}{10}$ kilometers, but they must walk the rest of the way. How far do Harris and Ji need to walk to get to their campsite?

   Ⓐ $1\frac{11}{20}$ km

   Ⓑ $1\frac{19}{20}$ km

   Ⓒ $2\frac{9}{20}$ km

   Ⓓ $2\frac{19}{20}$ km

13. **Multi-Step** Three commercials are played in a row between songs on the radio. The three commercials fill exactly 3 minutes of time. If the first commercial uses $1\frac{1}{6}$ minutes, and the second uses $\frac{3}{5}$ minute, how long is the third commercial?

   Ⓐ $\frac{23}{30}$ minute

   Ⓑ $1\frac{23}{30}$ minutes

   Ⓒ $1\frac{7}{30}$ minutes

   Ⓓ $2\frac{7}{30}$ minutes

⭐ TEXAS Test Prep

14. Coach Lopes filled a water cooler with $4\frac{1}{2}$ gallons of water before a game. At the end of the game, $1\frac{3}{4}$ gallons of water were left over. How many gallons of water did the team drink during the game?

   Ⓐ $3\frac{1}{4}$ gallons   Ⓒ $2\frac{3}{4}$ gallons

   Ⓑ $2\frac{1}{2}$ gallons   Ⓓ $\frac{3}{4}$ gallon

Homework and Practice

Name _____

5.7 Subtraction with Renaming

Find the difference and write it in simplest form.

1. $5\frac{1}{2} - 1\frac{2}{3}$ _____

2. $4\frac{2}{9} - 3\frac{1}{3}$ _____

3. $8 - 3\frac{2}{7}$ _____

4. $7\frac{2}{5} - 2\frac{1}{2}$ _____

5. $4\frac{2}{3} - 2\frac{5}{6}$ _____

6. $8\frac{3}{10} - 5\frac{3}{5}$ _____

7. $4\frac{1}{8} - 1\frac{1}{2}$ _____

8. $6\frac{5}{12} - 5\frac{3}{4}$ _____

9. $12\frac{1}{6} - 4\frac{3}{8}$ _____

10. $9\frac{1}{6} - 3\frac{4}{5}$ _____

11. $13\frac{3}{5} - 4\frac{3}{4}$ _____

12. $6\frac{3}{8} - 2\frac{5}{9}$ _____

13. $2\frac{1}{3} - 1\frac{5}{6}$ _____

14. $5 - 2\frac{1}{2}$ _____

15. $1\frac{1}{10} - \frac{1}{2}$ _____

16. $7\frac{1}{4} - 1\frac{3}{8}$ _____

17. Tell how you know when you need to use renaming when subtracting mixed numbers.

_____

_____

_____

Problem Solving

18. Chef Rossi makes $7\frac{5}{8}$ gallons of soup for the soup kitchen. She needs to fill a large container with a capacity of $9\frac{1}{2}$ gallons. How many more gallons of soup does Chef Rossi need to make?

19. Derek made a rope swing with a length of $5\frac{3}{4}$ feet. Nick's rope swing is $6\frac{1}{8}$ feet long. How much longer is Nick's swing than Derek's swing?

_____

_____

Fill in the bubble completely to show your answer.

Use the table for 20–21.

20. Sasha and Lee are looking at the park's list of hiking trails in order to choose a hike. How much farther will they have to hike if they choose Lake Trail instead of Woodland Trail?

Ⓐ $4\frac{1}{3}$ miles

Ⓑ $2\frac{2}{3}$ miles

Ⓒ $2\frac{1}{2}$ miles

Ⓓ $1\frac{1}{2}$ miles

Hiking Trails	
Name	**Length (in miles)**
Woodland Trail	$2\frac{5}{6}$
Meadow Trail	$3\frac{1}{2}$
Lake Trail	$4\frac{1}{3}$
Sunset Trail	$1\frac{3}{4}$

21. Lee and Sasha have hiked $\frac{7}{8}$ mile on Meadow Trail. How much farther do they need to hike to get to the end of the trail?

Ⓐ $2\frac{5}{8}$ miles

Ⓑ 4 miles

Ⓒ $4\frac{3}{8}$ miles

Ⓓ $\frac{3}{8}$ mile

22. Mario renames the mixed numbers to fractions greater than 1 to find $4\frac{1}{2} - 2\frac{2}{3}$. Which fractions should Mario use to find the difference?

Ⓐ $\frac{27}{6}, \frac{16}{6}$

Ⓑ $\frac{24}{6}, \frac{12}{6}$

Ⓒ $\frac{27}{5}, \frac{16}{5}$

Ⓓ $\frac{7}{6}, \frac{8}{6}$

23. **Multi-Step** Ian's mother drives $8\frac{1}{5}$ miles to work each day. His father drives $9\frac{1}{2}$ miles round-trip between home and work. How much farther is Ian's mother's round-trip than his father's?

Ⓐ $6\frac{9}{10}$ miles

Ⓑ $16\frac{2}{5}$ miles

Ⓒ $7\frac{1}{10}$ miles

Ⓓ $17\frac{7}{10}$ miles

24. **Multi-Step** Mrs. Holbrook's delivery truck consumes 12 gallons of gasoline in three days. If $2\frac{4}{5}$ gallons of gas are consumed on the first day, and $3\frac{7}{10}$ gallons are consumed on the second day, how much is consumed on the third day?

Ⓐ $6\frac{1}{2}$ gallons

Ⓑ $9\frac{1}{5}$ gallons

Ⓒ $5\frac{1}{2}$ gallons

Ⓓ $8\frac{3}{10}$ gallons

Name _____

5.8 Use Properties of Addition

© Houghton Mifflin Harcourt Publishing Company

? Essential Question

How can properties help you add fractions with unequal denominators?

Connect You can use properties of addition to help you add fractions with unequal denominators.

Commutative Property: $\frac{1}{2} + \frac{3}{5} = \frac{3}{5} + \frac{1}{2}$

Associative Property: $\left(\frac{2}{9} + \frac{1}{8}\right) + \frac{3}{8} = \frac{2}{9} + \left(\frac{1}{8} + \frac{3}{8}\right)$

Remember

Parentheses ( ) tell which operation to do first.

Unlock the Problem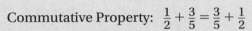

Jane and her family are driving to Big Lagoon State Park. On the first day, they travel $\frac{1}{3}$ of the total distance. On the second day, they travel $\frac{1}{3}$ of the total distance in the morning and then $\frac{1}{6}$ of the total distance in the afternoon. How much of the total distance has Jane's family driven by the end of the second day?

Use the Associative Property.

Day 1 + Day 2

$$\frac{1}{3} + \left(\frac{1}{3} + \frac{1}{6}\right) = \left(\boxed{} + \boxed{}\right) + \boxed{}$$

Write the number sentence to represent the problem. Use the Associative Property to group fractions with equal denominators together.

$$= \boxed{} + \boxed{}$$

Use mental math to add the fractions with equal denominators.

$$= \boxed{} + \boxed{}$$

Write equivalent fractions with equal denominators. Then add.

$$= \boxed{}$$

So, Jane's family has driven _____ of the total distance by the end of the second day.

Math Talk

Mathematical Processes

Explain Why grouping the fractions differently makes it easier to find the sum.

🔑 Example Add. $\left(2\frac{5}{8} + 1\frac{2}{3}\right) + 1\frac{1}{8}$

Use the Commutative Property and the Associative Property.

$$\left(2\frac{5}{8} + 1\frac{2}{3}\right) + 1\frac{1}{8} = \left(\boxed{} + \boxed{}\right) + \boxed{}$$

Use the Commutative Property to put fractions with equal denominators next to each other.

$$= \boxed{} + \left(\boxed{} + \boxed{}\right)$$

Use the Associative Property to group fractions with equal denominators together.

$$= \boxed{} + \boxed{}$$

Use mental math to add the fractions with equal denominators.

$$= \boxed{} + \boxed{}$$

Write equivalent fractions with equal denominators.
Then add.

$$= \boxed{} = \boxed{}$$

Rename and simplify.

Try This!

Subtraction is not commutative or associative. When you subtract, perform operations in parentheses first. Then subtract from left to right.

a. $\frac{7}{8} - \frac{1}{2} - \frac{1}{8} = $ _____ $- \frac{1}{8} = $ _____

b. $\left(\frac{7}{8} - \frac{1}{2}\right) - \frac{1}{8} = $ _____ $- \frac{1}{8} = $ _____

c. $\frac{7}{8} - \left(\frac{1}{2} - \frac{1}{8}\right) = \frac{7}{8} - $ _____ $= $ _____

Explain how you can use your answers to conclude that subtraction is not associative.

_____

_____

Share and Show

Use the properties and mental math to solve. Write your answer in simplest form.

1. $\left(2\frac{5}{8} + \frac{5}{6}\right) + 1\frac{1}{8}$

2. $\frac{5}{12} + \left(\frac{5}{12} + \frac{3}{4}\right)$

3. $\left(3\frac{1}{4} + 2\frac{5}{6}\right) + 1\frac{3}{4}$

Name _____

Problem Solving

Use the properties and mental math to solve. Write your answer in simplest form.

4. $\left(\frac{2}{7} + \frac{1}{3}\right) + \frac{2}{3}$

5. $\left(\frac{1}{5} + \frac{1}{2}\right) + \frac{2}{5}$

6. $\left(\frac{1}{6} + \frac{3}{7}\right) + \frac{2}{7}$

7. **Explain** why grouping the fractions differently makes it easier to find the sum.

_____

_____

Problem Solving Real World

Use the map to solve 8–9.

8. **H.O.T.** **Multi-Step** On one afternoon, Mario walks from his house to the library. That evening, Mario walks from the library to the mall, and then to Kyle's house. **Describe** how you can use the properties to find how far Mario walks.

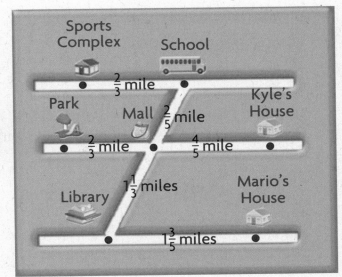

Sports Complex
School
$\frac{2}{3}$ mile
Park
Mall $\frac{2}{5}$ mile
Kyle's House
$\frac{2}{3}$ mile $\frac{4}{5}$ mile
$1\frac{1}{3}$ miles
Mario's House
Library
$1\frac{3}{5}$ miles

_____

_____

_____

_____

9. **H.O.T.** **Pose a Problem** Write and solve a new problem that uses the distances between four locations.

_____

_____

_____

Daily Assessment Task

Fill in the bubble completely to show your answer.

10. During a scavenger hunt, Ben's team completed four tasks in the following times: $2\frac{1}{3}$ hours, $1\frac{1}{2}$ hours, $1\frac{1}{3}$ hours, and $1\frac{1}{3}$ hours. How long did it take Ben's team to complete the scavenger hunt?

    Ⓐ $6\frac{1}{2}$ hours

    Ⓑ $5\frac{1}{2}$ hours

    Ⓒ 6 hours

    Ⓓ 5 hours

11. **Use Symbols** Elijah wants to add $\left(2\frac{3}{5} + 8\frac{1}{6}\right) + 5\frac{1}{5}$. He rewrites the problem as $\left(8\frac{1}{6} + 2\frac{3}{5}\right) + 5\frac{1}{5}$. Then he uses the Associative Property to rewrite the problem. Which shows his next step?

    Ⓐ $8\frac{1}{6} + \left(2\frac{3}{5} + 5\frac{1}{5}\right)$

    Ⓑ $\left(8\frac{1}{6}\right)\left(2\frac{3}{5} + 5\frac{1}{5}\right)$

    Ⓒ $\left(8\frac{1}{6} + 2\frac{3}{5} + 5\frac{1}{5}\right)$

    Ⓓ $\left(2\frac{3}{5} + 8\frac{1}{6}\right)\left(5\frac{1}{5}\right)$

12. **Multi-Step** Glen finds the sum of $\left(3\frac{3}{10} + 4\frac{1}{3}\right) + 2\frac{1}{10}$ and Ana finds the sum of $\left(4\frac{1}{3} + 3\frac{3}{10}\right) + 2\frac{1}{10}$. What is the total sum of their answers?

    Ⓐ $9\frac{11}{15}$ Ⓒ $18\frac{7}{15}$

    Ⓑ $9\frac{1}{15}$ Ⓓ $19\frac{7}{15}$

 TEXAS Test Prep

13. Use the properties and mental math to solve.

    $$\frac{11}{12} - \left(\frac{2}{3} - \frac{1}{12}\right)$$

    Ⓐ $\frac{7}{12}$

    Ⓑ $\frac{1}{3}$

    Ⓒ $\frac{1}{4}$

    Ⓓ $\frac{1}{6}$

Homework and Practice

Name _____

5.8 Use Properties of Addition

Use the properties and mental math to solve. Write your answer in simplest form.

1. $(\frac{3}{7} + \frac{2}{3}) + \frac{1}{3}$ _____

2. $\frac{4}{7} + (\frac{1}{6} + \frac{2}{7})$ _____

3. $(\frac{4}{5} + \frac{1}{2}) + \frac{2}{5}$ _____

4. $(3\frac{5}{8} + \frac{1}{6}) + 2\frac{1}{8}$ _____

5. $2\frac{1}{6} + (2\frac{1}{4} + 1\frac{1}{6})$ _____

6. $(\frac{1}{7} + \frac{1}{6}) + \frac{3}{7}$ _____

7. $(\frac{3}{4} + \frac{7}{12}) + \frac{5}{12}$ _____

8. $\frac{3}{5} + (2\frac{1}{5} + 1\frac{1}{4})$ _____

9. $(3\frac{1}{2} + 1\frac{3}{5}) + 1\frac{1}{2}$ _____

10. Write a word problem for the addends $\frac{7}{10}$, $\frac{1}{5}$, and $\frac{9}{10}$. Explain how you solved your problem.

_____

_____

_____

Problem Solving Real World

11. Last night, Hailey spent $\frac{4}{5}$ hour on math homework, $\frac{1}{2}$ hour on science homework, and $\frac{3}{5}$ hour on social studies homework. How long did Hailey spend on homework last night?

12. The rainfall totals at the airport for the last three months were $2\frac{1}{6}$ inches, $1\frac{2}{3}$ inches, and $1\frac{1}{6}$ inches. What was the total rainfall for the last three months?

_____   _____

Fill in the bubble completely to show your answer.

13. Shelly volunteered at the pet shelter $2\frac{1}{2}$ hours in June, $1\frac{2}{3}$ hours in July, and the same amount of hours in August as in June. How many hours did Shelly volunteer this summer?

   (A) $4\frac{1}{6}$ hours

   (B) 5 hours

   (C) $6\frac{2}{3}$ hours

   (D) $5\frac{2}{3}$ hours

14. Erica uses a recipe for cookies that calls for $2\frac{3}{4}$ cups of flour and $1\frac{1}{2}$ cups of sugar. Erica doubles the recipe and adds the flour and sugar to a mixing bowl. Which is the amount of dry ingredients in the bowl?

   (A) $5\frac{3}{4}$ cups

   (B) $8\frac{1}{2}$ cups

   (C) $4\frac{1}{4}$ cups

   (D) $9\frac{1}{2}$ cups

15. Stefan wants to add $(3\frac{5}{7} + 1\frac{1}{5}) + 2\frac{1}{7}$. He uses the Commutative Property to rewrite the problem. Which shows this step?

   (A) $(3\frac{5}{7} + 1\frac{1}{5} + 2\frac{1}{7})$

   (B) $3\frac{5}{7} + (1\frac{1}{5} + 2\frac{1}{7})$

   (C) $(1\frac{1}{5} + 3\frac{5}{7}) + 2\frac{1}{7}$

   (D) $(2\frac{1}{7} + 1\frac{1}{5}) + 3\frac{5}{7}$

16. Habib is making a frame for a rectangular picture that is $2\frac{1}{4}$ feet by $3\frac{3}{8}$ feet. How many feet of wood trim should Habib buy to make the frame?

   (A) $6\frac{3}{4}$ feet

   (B) $10\frac{1}{4}$ feet

   (C) $11\frac{1}{4}$ feet

   (D) $5\frac{5}{8}$ feet

17. **Multi-Step** Juliana used $10\frac{1}{2}$ yards of yarn to make three yarn dolls. She used $4\frac{1}{2}$ yards of yarn for the first doll and $2\frac{1}{5}$ yards for the second doll. How much yarn did Juliana use for the third doll?

   (A) $3\frac{4}{5}$ yards

   (B) $2\frac{4}{5}$ yards

   (C) $3\frac{1}{5}$ yards

   (D) $2\frac{1}{5}$ yards

18. **Multi-Step** Yuan finds the sum of $\frac{3}{10} + (\frac{1}{5} + \frac{1}{10})$. Then he adds $\frac{1}{15}$ to the sum. What is Yuan's final sum?

   (A) $\frac{3}{5}$

   (B) $\frac{1}{5}$

   (C) $\frac{1}{3}$

   (D) $\frac{2}{3}$

Name _____

 Module 5 Assessment

Vocabulary

Choose the best term from the box.

Vocabulary
common denominator
common multiple
equivalent fraction

1. A _____ is a common
   multiple of two or more denominators. (p. 213)

Concepts and Skills

Estimate the sum or difference. ⬤ TEKS 5.3.A

2. $\frac{8}{9} + \frac{4}{7}$

3. $3\frac{2}{5} - \frac{5}{8}$

4. $1\frac{5}{6} + 2\frac{2}{11}$

**Use the least common denominator to write an equivalent
fraction for each fraction.** ⬤ TEKS 5.3

5. $\frac{2}{5}, \frac{1}{10}$ least common
   denominator: _____

6. $\frac{5}{6}, \frac{3}{8}$ least common
   denominator: _____

7. $\frac{1}{3}, \frac{2}{7}$ least common
   denominator: _____

_____   _____   _____

**Use models or strategies to find the sum or difference. Write your answer
in simplest form.** ⬤ TEKS 5.3.H, 5.3.K

8. $\frac{11}{18} - \frac{1}{6}$

9. $\frac{2}{7} + \frac{2}{5}$

10. $\frac{3}{4} - \frac{3}{10}$

**Use the properties and mental math to solve. Write your answer in
simplest form.** ⬤ TEKS 5.3.H

11. $\left(\frac{3}{8} + \frac{2}{3}\right) + \frac{1}{3}$

12. $1\frac{4}{5} + \left(2\frac{3}{20} + \frac{3}{5}\right)$

13. $3\frac{5}{9} + \left(1\frac{7}{9} + 2\frac{5}{12}\right)$

14. Samuel walks in the Labor Day parade. He walks $3\frac{1}{4}$ miles along the parade route and $2\frac{5}{6}$ miles home. How many miles does Samuel walk? 👉 TEKS 5.3.K

  Ⓐ $\frac{5}{10}$ mile

  Ⓑ $6\frac{1}{12}$ miles

  Ⓒ $5\frac{1}{2}$ miles

  Ⓓ $5\frac{11}{12}$ miles

15. Mrs. Michaels bakes a pie for her book club meeting. The shaded part of the diagram shows the amount of pie left after the meeting. That evening, Mr. Michaels eats $\frac{1}{4}$ of the whole pie. Which fraction represents the amount of pie remaining? 👉 TEKS 5.3.H, 5.3.K

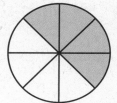

  Ⓐ $\frac{1}{4}$

  Ⓑ $\frac{3}{8}$

  Ⓒ $\frac{5}{8}$

  Ⓓ $\frac{3}{4}$

16. Aaron is practicing for a triathlon. On Sunday, he bikes $12\frac{5}{8}$ miles and swims $5\frac{2}{3}$ miles. On Monday, he runs $6\frac{3}{8}$ miles. How many total miles does Aaron cover on the two days? 👉 TEKS 5.3.K

  Ⓐ $23\frac{1}{6}$ miles

  Ⓑ $25\frac{7}{12}$ miles

  Ⓒ $24\frac{7}{12}$ miles

  Ⓓ $24\frac{2}{3}$ miles

17. Mario is painting his walls. He needs a total of $5\frac{2}{3}$ gallons of paint for the job. He has $3\frac{3}{4}$ gallons of paint. How much more paint does he need? 👉 TEKS 5.3.K

  Ⓐ $2\frac{5}{6}$ gallons

  Ⓑ $9\frac{1}{12}$ gallons

  Ⓒ $2\frac{1}{12}$ gallons

  Ⓓ $1\frac{11}{12}$ gallons

TEKS Number and Operations—5.3.I
MATHEMATICAL PROCESSES
5.1.E

6.1 Find Part of a Group

Essential Question How can you find a fractional part of a group?

Unlock the Problem (Real World)

Maya collects stamps. She has 20 stamps in her collection. Four-fifths of her stamps have been canceled. How many of the stamps in Maya's collection have been canceled?

Find $\frac{4}{5}$ of 20.

- Put 20 counters on your MathBoard.

  Since you want to find $\frac{4}{5}$ of the stamps, you should arrange the

  20 counters in _____ equal groups.

- Draw the counters in equal groups below. How many counters are in

  each group? _____

- Each group represents _____ of the stamps. Circle $\frac{4}{5}$ of the counters.

  How many groups did you circle? _____

  How many counters did you circle? _____

  $\frac{4}{5}$ of 20 = _____, or $\frac{4}{5} \times 20 =$ _____

So, _____ of the stamps have been canceled.

Math Talk
Mathematical Processes

How many groups would you circle if $\frac{3}{5}$ of the stamps were canceled? **Explain.**

🔑 Example

Max's stamp collection has stamps from different countries. He has 12 stamps from Canada. Of those twelve, $\frac{2}{3}$ of them have pictures of Queen Elizabeth II. How many stamps have the queen on them?

- Draw an array to represent the 12 stamps by drawing an ✗ for each stamp. Since you want to find $\frac{2}{3}$ of the stamps, your array should

  show _____ rows of equal size.

- Circle _____ of the 3 rows to show $\frac{2}{3}$ of 12. Then count the number of ✗s in the circle.

  There are _____ ✗s circled.

- Complete the number sentences.

  $\frac{2}{3}$ of 12 = _____, or $\frac{2}{3} \times 12$ = _____

So, there are _____ stamps with a picture of Queen Elizabeth II.

Share and Show

1. Complete the model to solve.

$\frac{7}{8}$ of 16, or $\frac{7}{8} \times 16$

a. How many rows of counters are there? _____

b. How many counters are in each row? _____

c. Circle _____ rows to solve the problem.

d. How many counters are circled? _____

$\frac{7}{8}$ of 16 = _____, or $\frac{7}{8} \times 16$ = _____

Use a model to solve.

2. $\frac{2}{3} \times 18$ = _____

3. $\frac{2}{5} \times 15$ = _____

4. $\frac{2}{3} \times 6$ = _____

Name _____

Problem Solving

Use a model to solve.

5. $\frac{5}{8} \times 24 =$ _____

6. $\frac{3}{4} \times 24 =$ _____

7. $\frac{4}{7} \times 21 =$ _____

8. On your MathBoard, use counters to find $\frac{4}{6}$ of 12. **Explain** why the answer is the same as when you found $\frac{2}{3}$ of 12.

_____

_____

Problem Solving (Real World)

Use the table for 9–10.

9. **Representations** Four-fifths of Zack's stamps have pictures of animals. How many stamps with pictures of animals does Zack have? Use a model to solve.

_____

Stamps Collected	
Name	**Number of Stamps**
Zack	30
Teri	18
Paco	24

10. **H.O.T.** **Write Math** ▶ Zack, Teri, and Paco combined the foreign stamps from their collections for a stamp show. Out of their collections, $\frac{3}{10}$ of Zack's stamps, $\frac{5}{6}$ of Teri's stamps, and $\frac{3}{8}$ of Paco's stamps were from foreign countries. How many stamps were in their display? **Explain** how you solved the problem.

_____

_____

_____

11. **H.O.T.** **Multi-Step** Paula has 24 stamps in her collection. Among her stamps, $\frac{1}{3}$ have pictures of animals. Out of her stamps with pictures of animals, $\frac{3}{4}$ of those stamps have pictures of birds. How many stamps have pictures of birds on them?

_____

Mathematical Processes
Model • Reason • Communicate

Fill in the bubble completely to show your answer.

12. **Apply** Eduardo has 30 pairs of socks in a drawer. Of those, 6 pairs are matched and the rest are mismatched. He is packing $\frac{1}{2}$ of his mismatched pairs in his suitcase for a trip. How many pairs is Eduardo packing for his trip?

(A) 6

(C) 12

(B) 4

(D) 18

13. **Use Diagrams** Which problem does the model represent?

(A) $\frac{2}{3} \times 15$

(C) $\frac{3}{4} \times 15$

(B) $\frac{1}{2} \times 15$

(D) $\frac{1}{3} \times 15$

14. **Multi-Step** Amy has 25 different hair ribbons. She bought 4 of them in a store, but she made the rest herself. Of the hair ribbons she made, $\frac{1}{3}$ have sparkles on them. How many hair ribbons with sparkles did Amy make?

(A) 9

(C) 3

(B) 7

(D) 14

⭐ TEXAS Test Prep

15. Barry bought 21 stamps from a hobby shop. He gave $\frac{3}{7}$ of them to his sister. How many stamps did he have left?

(A) 9 stamps

(B) 6 stamps

(C) 3 stamps

(D) 12 stamps

6.1 Find Part of a Group

Use a model to solve.

1. $\frac{3}{5} \times 10 =$ _____

2. $\frac{2}{3} \times 15 =$ _____

3. $\frac{3}{8} \times 16 =$ _____

4. $\frac{5}{6} \times 30 =$ _____

5. $\frac{5}{7} \times 14 =$ _____

6. $\frac{3}{5} \times 25 =$ _____

7. $\frac{3}{4} \times 16 =$ _____

8. $\frac{2}{5} \times 20 =$ _____

9. $\frac{4}{7} \times 35 =$ _____

10. $\frac{2}{3} \times 21 =$ _____

11. $\frac{3}{4} \times 28 =$ _____

12. $\frac{8}{9} \times 27 =$ _____

13. Will the product of a fraction less than one and a whole number be less than or greater than the whole number? **Explain.**

_____

_____

_____

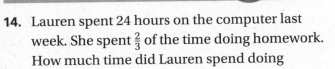

Problem Solving Real World

14. Lauren spent 24 hours on the computer last week. She spent $\frac{2}{3}$ of the time doing homework. How much time did Lauren spend doing homework?

_____

15. A display at the natural science museum contains 21 plant and animal fossils. $\frac{4}{7}$ of the fossils in the display are animal fossils. How many fossils in the display are animal fossils?

_____

Fill in the bubble completely to show your answer.

16. Today, the fifth-grade class will explore all 36 fossil displays at the museum. They explore $\frac{4}{9}$ of the displays in the morning. How many displays are left for the class to explore in the afternoon?

- Ⓐ 20
- Ⓑ 16
- Ⓒ 18
- Ⓓ 32

17. There are 32 students in Mr. Samuelson's class. $\frac{5}{8}$ of the students are boys. How many of the students in the class are girls?

- Ⓐ 27
- Ⓑ 3
- Ⓒ 20
- Ⓓ 12

18. Miguel uses counters to solve $\frac{5}{8} \times 16$.

How many counters will Miguel circle for the product?

- Ⓐ 10
- Ⓑ 6
- Ⓒ 5
- Ⓓ 12

19. Which problem does the model represent?

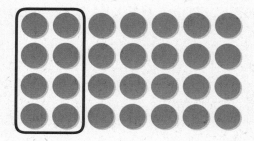

- Ⓐ $\frac{5}{7} \times 28$
- Ⓑ $\frac{2}{5} \times 28$
- Ⓒ $\frac{4}{7} \times 28$
- Ⓓ $\frac{2}{7} \times 28$

20. Multi-Step The members of the parents' association are making 6 batches of brownies and 12 batches of fruit bars for the bake sale. They need $\frac{1}{2}$ cup of sugar for each batch. How much sugar do they need?

- Ⓐ 9 cups
- Ⓑ 36 cups
- Ⓒ 3 cups
- Ⓓ 6 cups

21. Multi-Step Natalie had 64 beads. She used 24 beads to make a bracelet. She used $\frac{7}{8}$ of the remaining beads to make a necklace. How many beads does Natalie have left?

- Ⓐ 40
- Ⓑ 21
- Ⓒ 5
- Ⓓ 35

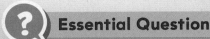

6.2 Multiply Fractions and Whole Numbers

TEKS Number and Operations—5.3.I

MATHEMATICAL PROCESSES

5.1.D, 5.1.E

? Essential Question

How can you use a model to show the product of a fraction and a whole number?

Investigate

Martin is planting a vegetable garden. Each row is two meters long. He wants to plant carrots along $\frac{3}{4}$ of each row. How many meters of each row will he plant with carrots?

Multiply. $\frac{3}{4} \times 2$

Materials ■ fraction strips ■ MathBoard

A. Place two 1-whole fraction strips side-by-side to represent the length of the garden.

B. Find 4 fraction strips all with the same denominator that fit exactly under the two wholes.

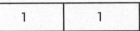

| 1 | 1 |

C. Draw a picture of your model.

D. Circle $\frac{3}{4}$ of 2 on the model you drew.

E. Complete the number sentence. $\frac{3}{4} \times 2 =$ _____

So, Martin will plant carrots along _____ meters of each row.

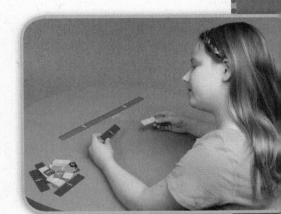

Draw Conclusions

1. **Explain** why you placed four fraction strips with the same denominator under the two 1-whole strips.

_____

_____

2. **Explain** how you would model $\frac{3}{10}$ of 2?

_____

_____

Make Connections

You can also use a model to multiply a fraction by a whole number.

Margo was helping clean up after a class party. There were 3 boxes remaining with pizza in them. Each box had $\frac{3}{8}$ of a pizza left. How much pizza was left in all?

Materials ■ fraction circles

STEP 1 Find $3 \times \frac{3}{8}$. Model three 1-whole fraction circles to represent the number of boxes containing pizza.

STEP 2 Place $\frac{1}{8}$ fraction circle pieces on each circle to represent the amount of pizza that was left in each box. Shade the fraction circles below to show your model.

Each circle shows _____ eighths of a whole.

The 3 circles show _____ eighths of a whole.

STEP 3 Complete the number sentences.

$$\frac{3}{8} + \frac{3}{8} + \frac{3}{8} = \underline{\hspace{2cm}}$$

$$3 \times \frac{3}{8} = \underline{\hspace{2cm}}$$

So, Margo had _____ boxes of pizza left.

Math Talk

Mathematical Processes

Explain how you would know there is more than one pizza left.

Share and Show

MATH BOARD

Use the model to find the product.

✓ 1. $\frac{5}{6} \times 3 =$ _____

	1		1		1
$\frac{1}{2}$	$\frac{1}{2}$	$\frac{1}{2}$	$\frac{1}{2}$	$\frac{1}{2}$	$\frac{1}{2}$

✓ 2. $2 \times \frac{5}{6} =$ _____

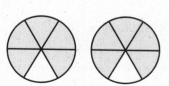

Name _____

H.O.T. Pose a Problem

3. Tarique drew the model below for a problem. Write 2 problems that can be solved using this model. One of your problems should involve multiplying a whole number by a fraction and the other problem should involve multiplying a fraction by a whole number.

Pose problems.

Solve your problems.

4. **H.O.T.** **Multi-Step** How could you change the model to give you an answer of $4\frac{4}{5}$? **Explain** and write a new equation.

_____

_____

_____

_____

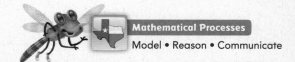

Daily Assessment Task

Fill in the bubble completely to show your answer.

5. Carly mixes vinegar and baking soda for a science project. She has a spoon that measures $\frac{1}{4}$ teaspoon. If she fills the spoon 6 times, how much baking soda will she have?

   Ⓐ $\frac{1}{10}$ teaspoon

   Ⓑ $\frac{2}{3}$ teaspoon

   Ⓒ $1\frac{1}{2}$ teaspoons

   Ⓓ $1\frac{3}{4}$ teaspoons

6. **Use Tools** Which multiplication problem does the model represent?

1		1		1		1	
$\frac{1}{2}$	$\frac{1}{2}$	$\frac{1}{2}$	$\frac{1}{2}$	$\frac{1}{2}$	$\frac{1}{2}$	$\frac{1}{2}$	$\frac{1}{2}$

   Ⓐ $\frac{1}{2} \times 8$　　　　Ⓒ $\frac{2}{3} \times 3$

   Ⓑ $\frac{3}{8} \times 4$　　　　Ⓓ $\frac{1}{4} \times 4$

7. **Multi-Step** Josh brought 4 small spinach pies to his baseball team party. At the end of the party, $\frac{3}{5}$ of each pie was left. If Josh gave 2 whole pies away, what part of a pie did he have left to take home?

   Ⓐ $\frac{2}{5}$　　　　　　Ⓒ $\frac{5}{6}$

   Ⓑ $\frac{1}{3}$　　　　　　Ⓓ $\frac{1}{2}$

⭐ TEXAS Test Prep

8. Katana has a shelf that is 5 feet long. She wants to paint a design along $\frac{7}{10}$ of the shelf. How many feet of the shelf will Katana paint a design?

   Ⓐ $1\frac{2}{5}$ feet

   Ⓑ $1\frac{1}{5}$ feet

   Ⓒ $3\frac{1}{2}$ feet

   Ⓓ $4\frac{3}{10}$ feet

Homework and Practice

Name _____

6.2 Multiply Fractions and Whole Numbers

Use the model to find the product.

1. $\frac{9}{10} \times 2 =$ _____

1	1

| $\frac{1}{5}$ | $\frac{1}{5}$ | $\frac{1}{5}$ | $\frac{1}{5}$ | $\frac{1}{5}$ | $\frac{1}{5}$ | $\frac{1}{5}$ | $\frac{1}{5}$ | $\frac{1}{5}$ | $\frac{1}{5}$ |

2. $\frac{3}{4} \times 3 =$ _____

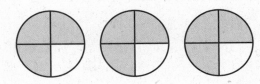

3. $\frac{5}{8} \times 3 =$ _____

1	1	1

| $\frac{1}{8}$ | $\frac{1}{8}$ | $\frac{1}{8}$ | $\frac{1}{8}$ | $\frac{1}{8}$ | $\frac{1}{8}$ | $\frac{1}{8}$ | $\frac{1}{8}$ | $\frac{1}{8}$ | $\frac{1}{8}$ | $\frac{1}{8}$ | $\frac{1}{8}$ | $\frac{1}{8}$ | $\frac{1}{8}$ | $\frac{1}{8}$ | $\frac{1}{8}$ | $\frac{1}{8}$ | $\frac{1}{8}$ | $\frac{1}{8}$ | $\frac{1}{8}$ | $\frac{1}{8}$ | $\frac{1}{8}$ | $\frac{1}{8}$ | $\frac{1}{8}$ |

4. $\frac{5}{6} \times 4 =$ _____

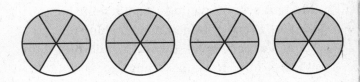

5. $\frac{7}{12} \times 2 =$ _____

1	1

| $\frac{1}{6}$ | $\frac{1}{6}$ | $\frac{1}{6}$ | $\frac{1}{6}$ | $\frac{1}{6}$ | $\frac{1}{6}$ | $\frac{1}{6}$ | $\frac{1}{6}$ | $\frac{1}{6}$ | $\frac{1}{6}$ | $\frac{1}{6}$ | $\frac{1}{6}$ |

6. $\frac{7}{10} \times 2 =$ _____

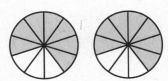

Problem Solving

7. Chef Talbot is baking 6 blueberry pies. If he uses $\frac{3}{4}$ pint of blueberries in each pie, how many pints of blueberries will he need?

_____

8. Mr. McGregor pours $\frac{3}{8}$ pound of dirt in each of his 4 flower pots. How much dirt does Mr. McGregor use to fill the 4 pots?

_____

Fill in the bubble completely to show your answer.

9. Which multiplication problem does the model represent?

1				1			
$\frac{1}{4}$	$\frac{1}{4}$	$\frac{1}{4}$	$\frac{1}{4}$	$\frac{1}{4}$	$\frac{1}{4}$	$\frac{1}{4}$	$\frac{1}{4}$

Ⓐ $\frac{1}{8} \times 2$

Ⓑ $\frac{7}{8} \times 2$

Ⓒ $\frac{1}{2} \times 4$

Ⓓ $\frac{1}{4} \times 8$

10. Which multiplication problem does the model represent?

Ⓐ $\frac{5}{12} \times 3$

Ⓑ $\frac{7}{12} \times 3$

Ⓒ $\frac{3}{12} \times 5$

Ⓓ $\frac{1}{2} \times 3$

11. Marianne is completing a 4-mile route for charity. Every $\frac{1}{10}$ mile is marked along the route. For each mile, she runs $\frac{7}{10}$ mile and walks $\frac{3}{10}$ mile. How many miles does Marianne run?

Ⓐ $1\frac{1}{10}$ miles

Ⓑ $2\frac{4}{5}$ miles

Ⓒ $1\frac{1}{5}$ miles

Ⓓ $2\frac{2}{5}$ miles

12. Terrance runs 5 miles each week. His brother runs $\frac{5}{6}$ the distance Terrance runs in one week. How far does Terrance's brother run in one week?

Ⓐ $3\frac{1}{3}$ miles

Ⓑ $4\frac{1}{6}$ miles

Ⓒ $5\frac{1}{6}$ miles

Ⓓ 4 miles

13. Multi-Step Colton's recipe makes 2 dozen brownies. His recipe calls for $\frac{7}{8}$ cup of vegetable oil. How much oil will Colton need to make 6 dozen brownies?

Ⓐ $2\frac{5}{8}$ cups

Ⓑ $1\frac{3}{4}$ cups

Ⓒ $5\frac{1}{4}$ cups

Ⓓ $3\frac{1}{2}$ cups

14. Multi-Step Kiesha brought 3 loaves of cornbread to a football party. $\frac{5}{12}$ of each loaf was eaten. If Kiesha gave 1 whole loaf of the leftover bread to the party hosts, what part of a loaf did she have left to take home?

Ⓐ $\frac{3}{4}$

Ⓑ $\frac{1}{4}$

Ⓒ $\frac{1}{2}$

Ⓓ $\frac{7}{12}$

Name _____

6.3 Fraction and Whole-Number Multiplication

? Essential Question

How can you find the product of a fraction and a whole number without using a model?

❓ Unlock the Problem Real World

Charlene has five 1-pound bags of different color sands. For an art project, she will use $\frac{3}{8}$ pound of each bag of sand to create a colorful sand-art jar. How much sand will be in Charlene's sand-art jar?

- How much sand is in each bag?

  _____

- Will Charlene use all of the sand in each bag? Explain.

  _____

🔑 **Multiply a fraction by a whole number.**

MODEL

- Shade the model to show 5 groups of $\frac{3}{8}$.

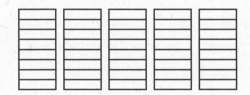

- Rearrange the shaded pieces to fill as many wholes as possible.

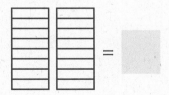

RECORD

- Write an expression to represent the problem.

  $5 \times \dfrac{3}{8}$ **Think:** I need to find 5 groups of 3 eighth-size pieces.

- Multiply the number of eighth-size pieces in each whole by 5. Then write the answer as the total number of eighth-size pieces.

  $\dfrac{\boxed{} \times \boxed{}}{8} = \dfrac{\boxed{}}{\boxed{}}$

- Write the answer as a mixed number in simplest form.

  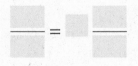

So, there are _____ pounds of sand in Charlene's sand-art jar.

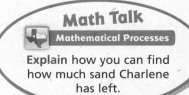

Math Talk
Mathematical Processes

Explain how you can find how much sand Charlene has left.

Example Multiply a whole number by a fraction.

Kirsten brought in 4 loaves of bread to make sandwiches for the class picnic. Her classmates used $\frac{2}{3}$ of the bread. How many loaves of bread were used?

MODEL

- Shade the model to show $\frac{2}{3}$ of 4.

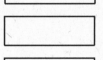

Think: I can cut the loaves into thirds and show $\frac{2}{3}$ of them being used.

- Rearrange the shaded pieces to fill as many wholes as possible.

So, _____ loaves of bread were used.

RECORD

- Write an expression to represent the problem.

$$\frac{2}{3} \times 4$$

Think: I need to find $\frac{2}{3}$ of 4 wholes.

- Multiply 4 by the number of third-size pieces in each whole. Then write the answer as the total number of third-size pieces.

- Write the answer as a mixed number.

Share and Show

Find the product. Write the product in simplest form.

1. $3 \times \frac{2}{5} =$ _____

- Multiply the numerator by the whole number. Write the product over the denominator.

- Write the answer as a mixed number in simplest form.

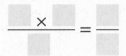

2. $\frac{2}{3} \times 5 =$ _____   3. $6 \times \frac{2}{3} =$ _____   4. $\frac{5}{7} \times 4 =$ _____

258

Name _____

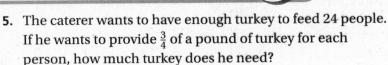
5. The caterer wants to have enough turkey to feed 24 people. If he wants to provide $\frac{3}{4}$ of a pound of turkey for each person, how much turkey does he need?

(A) 72 pounds   (C) 18 pounds

(B) 24 pounds   (D) 6 pounds

a. What do you need to find? _____

_____

b. What operation will you use? _____

c. What information are you given? _____

_____

d. Solve the problem.

e. Complete the sentences.

The caterer wants to serve 24 people

_____ of a pound of turkey each.

He will need _____ × _____, or

_____ pounds of turkey.

f. Fill in the bubble for the correct answer choice.

 Algebra Find the unknown digit.

6. $\dfrac{\blacksquare}{2} \times 8 = 4$

$\blacksquare =$ _____

7. $\blacksquare \times \dfrac{5}{6} = \dfrac{20}{6}$, or $3\frac{1}{3}$

$\blacksquare =$ _____

8. $\dfrac{1}{\blacksquare} \times 18 = 3$

$\blacksquare =$ _____

9. **H.O.T.** **Multi-Step** Patty wants to run $\frac{5}{6}$ of a mile every day for 5 days. Keisha wants to run $\frac{3}{4}$ of a mile every day for 6 days. Who will run the greater distance?

_____

Math on the Spot

Daily Assessment Task

Fill in the bubble completely to show your answer.

10. A heavy-duty snowmaking machine makes $\frac{3}{4}$ inch of snow each minute. How many inches of snow can the machine make in 8 minutes?

    (A) 8 inches

    (B) 6 inches

    (C) $7\frac{1}{4}$ inches

    (D) $4\frac{1}{2}$ inches

11. **Connect** Which has the same product as $\frac{2}{3} \times 8$?

    (A) $\frac{5}{6} \times 7$

    (B) $\frac{1}{4} \times 13$

    (C) $\frac{3}{8} \times 2$

    (D) $\frac{1}{3} \times 16$

12. **Multi-Step** A baker made 5 pounds of icing. He used $\frac{4}{9}$ of the icing to decorate cakes. How much of the icing is left over?

    (A) 1 pound

    (B) $1\frac{5}{9}$ pounds

    (C) $1\frac{2}{3}$ pounds

    (D) $2\frac{7}{9}$ pounds

⭐ TEXAS Test Prep

13. Doug has 33 feet of rope. He wants to use $\frac{2}{3}$ of it for his canoe. How many feet of rope will he use for his canoe?

    (A) 66 feet

    (B) 22 feet

    (C) 33 feet

    (D) 11 feet

Name _____

6.3 Fraction and Whole-Number Multiplication

Find the product. Write the product in simplest form.

1. $\frac{3}{7} \times 4 =$ _____

2. $\frac{3}{5} \times 5 =$ _____

3. $\frac{2}{3} \times 8 =$ _____

4. $16 \times \frac{3}{4} =$ _____

5. $9 \times \frac{5}{6} =$ _____

6. $6 \times \frac{3}{8} =$ _____

7. $\frac{2}{9} \times 5 =$ _____

8. $\frac{4}{7} \times 3 =$ _____

9. $\frac{3}{10} \times 7 =$ _____

Find the unknown digit.

10. $\frac{\blacksquare}{4} \times 8 = 2$

$\blacksquare =$ _____

11. $\blacksquare \times \frac{5}{7} = \frac{30}{7}$, or $4\frac{2}{7}$

$\blacksquare =$ _____

12. $\frac{1}{\blacksquare} \times 24 = 4$

$\blacksquare =$ _____

13. $\frac{1}{\blacksquare} \times 9 = 3$

$\blacksquare =$ _____

14. $\blacksquare \times \frac{4}{9} = \frac{20}{9}$, or $2\frac{2}{9}$

$\blacksquare =$ _____

15. $\frac{\blacksquare}{4} \times 4 = 3$

$\blacksquare =$ _____

Problem Solving

16. Sandra exercised $\frac{2}{3}$ hour every day for two weeks while she was on vacation. How many hours did Sandra exercise during her vacation?

_____

17. Mike bought 15 baseball cards. Rookie players are featured on $\frac{3}{5}$ of the cards. How many cards feature rookie players?

_____

Fill in the bubble completely to show your answer.

18. The florist arranges a bouquet with 12 flowers. He decides that $\frac{3}{4}$ of the flowers in the bouquet will be carnations. How many carnations will the florist need to complete the bouquet?

   (A) 10

   (B) 9

   (C) 6

   (D) 3

19. The average rainfall for each week for the last 4 weeks was $\frac{7}{12}$ inch. How much rain fell during the last 4 weeks?

   (A) $2\frac{1}{3}$ inches

   (B) $4\frac{1}{12}$ inches

   (C) 2 inches

   (D) $\frac{11}{12}$ inch

20. Eric practiced for his piano recital $\frac{3}{4}$ hour every day last week. How many hours did Eric practice last week?

   (A) $3\frac{3}{4}$ hours

   (B) 7 hours

   (C) $5\frac{1}{4}$ hours

   (D) $2\frac{1}{2}$ hours

21. Which does not have the same product as $4 \times \frac{5}{9}$?

   (A) $4 \times \frac{9}{5}$

   (B) $5 \times \frac{4}{9}$

   (C) $2 \times \frac{10}{9}$

   (D) $10 \times \frac{2}{9}$

22. **Multi-Step** Rose bought a dozen eggs. She used $\frac{2}{3}$ of the eggs to make custard and $\frac{1}{4}$ of the eggs to make an omelet. How many eggs does Rose have left?

   (A) 9

   (B) 4

   (C) 3

   (D) 1

23. **Multi-Step** Meredith's class has 21 students. Meredith rides the bus home with $\frac{2}{3}$ of the students in her class. How many students in Meredith's class do not ride the bus home with her?

   (A) 14

   (B) 16

   (C) 7

   (D) 6

6.4 Divide Fractions and Whole Numbers

TEKS Number and Operations—5.3.J, 5.3.L
MATHEMATICAL PROCESSES
5.1.C, 5.1.F

? Essential Question

How do you divide a whole number by a fraction and divide a fraction by a whole number?

Investigate

Materials ■ fraction strips

A. Mia walks a 2-mile fitness trail. She stops to exercise every $\frac{1}{5}$ mile. How many times does Mia stop to exercise?

- Draw a number line from 0 to 2. Divide the number line into fifths. Label each fifth on your number line.

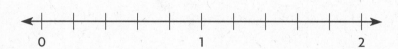

- Skip count by fifths from 0 to 2 to find $2 \div \frac{1}{5}$.

  There are _____ one-fifths in 2 wholes.

You can use the relationship between multiplication and division to explain and check your solution.

- Record and check the quotient.

  $2 \div \frac{1}{5} =$ _____ because _____ $\times \frac{1}{5} = 2$.

So, Mia stops to exercise _____ times.

B. Roger has 2 yards of string. He cuts the string into pieces that are $\frac{1}{3}$ yard long. How many pieces of string does Roger have?

- Model 2 using 2 whole fraction strips.

- Then place enough $\frac{1}{3}$ strips to fit exactly under the

  2 wholes. There are _____ one-third-size pieces in 2 wholes.

- Record and check the quotient.

  $2 \div \frac{1}{3} =$ _____ because _____ $\times \frac{1}{3} = 2$.

So, Roger has _____ pieces of string.

Make Connections

You can use fraction strips to divide a fraction by a whole number.

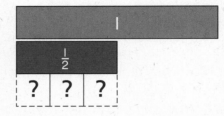

Calia shares half of a package of clay equally among herself and each of 2 friends. What fraction of the whole package of clay will each friend get?

STEP 1 Place a $\frac{1}{2}$ strip under a 1-whole strip to show the $\frac{1}{2}$ package of clay.

STEP 2 Find 3 fraction strips, all with the same denominator, that fit exactly under the $\frac{1}{2}$ strip.

Each piece is _____ of the whole.

Think: How much of the whole is each piece when $\frac{1}{2}$ is divided into 3 equal pieces?

STEP 3 Record and check the quotient.

$\frac{1}{2} \div 3 =$ _____ because _____ $\times 3 = \frac{1}{2}$.

So, each friend will get _____ of the whole package of clay.

Math Talk
Mathematical Processes

When you divide a fraction by a whole number, how does the quotient compare to the dividend? **Explain.**

Share and Show

Divide and check the quotient.

1.

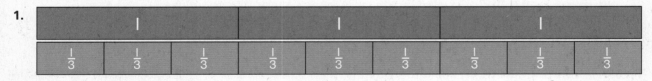

$3 \div \frac{1}{3} =$ _____ because _____ $\times \frac{1}{3} = 3$.

2.

Think: What label should I write for each tick mark?

$3 \div \frac{1}{6} =$ _____ because

_____ $\times \frac{1}{6} = 3$.

3.

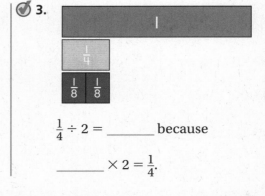

$\frac{1}{4} \div 2 =$ _____ because

_____ $\times 2 = \frac{1}{4}$.

Name _____

H.O.T. **Sense or Nonsense?**

4. Emilio and Julia used different ways to find $\frac{1}{2} \div 4$. Emilio used a model to find the quotient. Julia used a related multiplication equation to find the quotient. Whose answer makes sense? Whose answer is nonsense? **Explain** your reasoning.

Emilio's Work

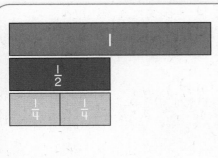

$\frac{1}{2} \div 4 = \frac{1}{4}$

_____

_____

_____

_____

Julia's Work

If $\frac{1}{2} \div 4 =$ ■, then ■ $\times 4 = \frac{1}{2}$.

I know that $\frac{1}{8} \times 4 = \frac{1}{2}$.

So, $\frac{1}{2} \div 4 = \frac{1}{8}$ because $\frac{1}{8} \times 4 = \frac{1}{2}$.

_____

_____

_____

_____

_____

5. For the answer that is nonsense, describe how to find the correct answer.

_____

_____

6. **H.O.T.** **Multi-Step** If you were going to find $\frac{1}{2} \div 5$, **explain** how you would find the quotient using fraction strips. Write an equation to show the quotient.

_____

_____

_____

Daily Assessment Task

Fill in the bubble completely to show your answer.

7. Ants are lined up along the edges of your sandwich at a picnic. If the sandwich is 9 inches around and each ant is $\frac{1}{6}$ of an inch, how many ants are lined up around the sandwich?

    (A) 15 ants

    (B) 16 ants

    (C) 27 ants

    (D) 54 ants

8. **Use Tools** Which is the division problem modeled by the picture?

$\frac{1}{3}$	$\frac{1}{3}$	$\frac{1}{3}$	$\frac{1}{3}$	$\frac{1}{3}$	$\frac{1}{3}$	$\frac{1}{3}$	$\frac{1}{3}$	$\frac{1}{3}$

    (A) $4 \div \frac{1}{12}$

    (B) $3 \div \frac{1}{4}$

    (C) $3 \div \frac{1}{3}$

    (D) $12 \div \frac{1}{3}$

9. **Multi-Step** Maddie divided 6 by $\frac{1}{2}$, and then divided that answer by $\frac{1}{3}$. What was her final answer?

    (A) 9   (C) 12

    (B) 1   (D) 36

TEXAS Test Prep

10. Reid has 4 bags of soil. He uses $\frac{1}{3}$ of a bag to fill each planter. How many planters can Reid fill with the bags of soil?

    (A) $1\frac{1}{3}$

    (B) 12

    (C) $3\frac{2}{3}$

    (D) $4\frac{1}{3}$

Name _Eduardo   Carjul_

6.4 Divide Fractions and Whole Numbers

Divide and check the quotient.

1.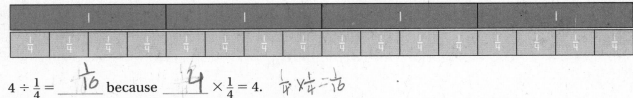

$4 \div \frac{1}{4} =$ _$\frac{1}{16}$_ because _4_ $\times \frac{1}{4} = 4$. $\frac{1}{4} \times \frac{1}{4} = \frac{1}{16}$

2.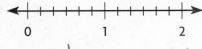

$2 \div \frac{1}{6} =$ _$\frac{1}{12}$_ because _2_ $\times \frac{1}{6} = 2$.

$\frac{1}{6} \times \frac{1}{2} = \frac{1}{12}$

3.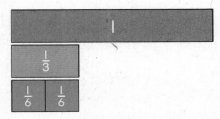

$\frac{1}{3} \div 2 =$ _$\frac{1}{6}$_ because _$\frac{1}{6}$_ $\times 2 = \frac{1}{3}$.

$\frac{1}{6} \times \frac{1}{2} = \frac{1}{6}$

4.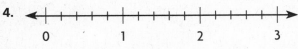

$3 \div \frac{1}{5} =$ _$\frac{1}{15}$_ because _3_ $\times \frac{1}{5} = 3$.

$\frac{1}{5} \times \frac{1}{3} = \frac{1}{15}$

5.

$\frac{1}{5} \div 2 =$ _$\frac{1}{10}$_ because _$\frac{1}{10}$_ $\times 2 = \frac{1}{5}$.

Problem Solving Real World

6. Julie buys a board that is 6 feet long. She wants to cut it into pieces that are $\frac{1}{2}$ foot each. How many pieces will Julie have after she cuts the board?

$\frac{1}{2} \times \frac{1}{6} = \frac{1}{12}$

7. Mr. Morales makes four batches of cookies for family math night. He divides half of a pound of butter equally into 4 mixing bowls. How much butter is in each bowl?

Fill in the bubble completely to show your answer.

8. Which is the division problem modeled by the picture?

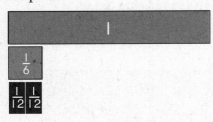

(A) $\frac{1}{2} \div 6$

(B) $\frac{1}{6} \div 12$

(C) $\frac{1}{6} \div 2$

(D) $\frac{1}{12} \div 2$

9. Which is the division problem modeled by the picture?

(A) $3 \div \frac{1}{8}$

(B) $24 \div \frac{1}{4}$

(C) $3 \div \frac{1}{24}$

(D) $8 \div \frac{1}{3}$

10. Evan brings 8 liters of juice to be served at family math night. He pours $\frac{1}{5}$ liter into each glass. How many glasses of juice can be served?

(A) 8

(B) 40

(C) 13

(D) 10

11. Marissa is painting one of her bedroom walls. She marks off $\frac{1}{4}$ of the wall. Then she divides the marked section into 3 equal parts and paints one part blue. What fraction of the whole wall is blue?

(A) $\frac{1}{3}$

(B) $\frac{1}{4}$

(C) $\frac{1}{7}$

(D) $\frac{1}{12}$

12. **Multi-Step** Rex combines $\frac{1}{4}$ cup sugar and $\frac{1}{4}$ cup flour into a small bowl. Then he divides the amount in the small bowl into 4 empty mixing bowls. What amount of dry ingredients is in each mixing bowl?

(A) $\frac{1}{16}$ cup

(B) $\frac{1}{2}$ cup

(C) $\frac{1}{8}$ cup

(D) 2 cups

13. **Multi-Step** Jamie divided 8 by $\frac{1}{2}$, and then multiplied that answer by $\frac{1}{4}$. What was her final answer?

(A) 4

(B) 1

(C) 64

(D) 32

Name _____

6.5 PROBLEM SOLVING • Use Multiplication

 Essential Question

How can the strategy *draw a diagram* help you solve fraction division problems by writing a multiplication sentence?

Unlock the Problem

Erica makes 6 submarine sandwiches and cuts each sandwich into thirds. How many $\frac{1}{3}$-size sandwich pieces does she have?

Read

What do I need to find?

I need to find _____

_____

_____.

What information am I given?

I need to use the size of each _____ of

sandwich and the number of _____ she cuts.

Plan

What is my plan or strategy?

I can _____ to
organize the information from the problem.
Then I can use the organized information to find

_____

_____.

Solve

Since Erica cuts 6 submarine sandwiches, my diagram needs to show 6 rectangles to represent the sandwiches. I can divide each of the 6 rectangles into thirds.

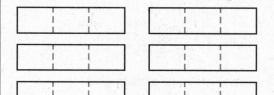

To find the total number of thirds in the 6 rectangles, I can multiply the number of thirds in each rectangle by the number of rectangles.

$$6 \div \frac{1}{3} = 6 \times \underline{} = \underline{}$$

Math Talk

Mathematical Processes

Explain how you can use multiplication to check your answer.

So, Erica has _____ one-third-size sandwich pieces.

Roberto is cutting 3 blueberry pies into halves to give to his neighbors. How many neighbors will get a $\frac{1}{2}$-size pie piece?

Read	Solve
What do I need to find?	
What information am I given?	
Plan	
What is my plan or strategy?	

So, _____ neighbors will get a $\frac{1}{2}$-size pie piece.

- **Explain** how the diagram you drew for the division problem helps you write a multiplication sentence.

_____

_____

Name _____

1. A chef has 5 blocks of butter. Each block weighs 1 pound. She cuts each block into fourths. How many $\frac{1}{4}$-pound pieces of butter does the chef have?

   First, draw rectangles to represent the blocks of butter.

   Then, divide each rectangle into fourths.

   Finally, multiply the number of fourths in each block by the number of blocks.

   So, the chef has _____ one-fourth-pound pieces of butter.

Write Math ▶

Show Your Work

2. **What if** the chef had 3 blocks of butter and cut the blocks into thirds? How many $\frac{1}{3}$-pound pieces of butter would the chef have?

   _____

Problem Solving

3. **H.O.T.** **Multi-Step** Julie makes a drawing that is $\frac{1}{4}$ the size of the original drawing. Sahil makes a drawing that is $\frac{1}{3}$ the size of the original. A tree in the original drawing is 12 inches tall. What will be the difference between the height of the tree in Julie and Sahil's drawings?

4. **H.O.T.** **Use Tools** Brianna has a sheet of paper that is 6 feet long. She cuts the length of paper into sixths and then cuts the length of each of these $\frac{1}{6}$-pieces into thirds. How many pieces does she have? How many inches long is each piece?

   _____

Daily Assessment Task

Fill in the bubble completely to show your answer.

5. A structure is made out of foam cubes that are each $\frac{1}{4}$ foot tall. The height of the structure is 8 feet. How many cubes were used to build the structure?

   (A) 2 cubes

   (B) 16 cubes

   (C) 8 cubes

   (D) 32 cubes

6. **Use Diagrams** Terrance needs to divide 9 by $\frac{1}{2}$. How can he find the quotient?

   (A) Draw 9 rectangles and divide each in halves. Count the halves.

   (B) Draw 9 rectangles and shade $\frac{1}{2}$ of each. Count the shaded parts.

   (C) Shade a rectangle to show $\frac{1}{2}$, and then divide the shaded part into 9 parts. Find the amount shaded.

   (D) Draw a rectangle with a length of 9 and a width of $\frac{1}{2}$. Find the area.

7. **Multi-Step** Dorothy has a ribbon that is 3 feet long, and a ribbon that is 8 feet long. She needs to cut the ribbon into pieces that are $\frac{1}{4}$ foot long. How many pieces will she have in all?

   (A) 12 pieces

   (B) 32 pieces

   (C) 11 pieces

   (D) 44 pieces

 TEXAS Test Prep

8. Adrian made 3 carrot cakes. He cut each cake into fourths. How many $\frac{1}{4}$-size cake pieces does he have?

   (A) 16   (C) 1

   (B) 12   (D) $1\frac{1}{3}$

6.6 Fraction and Whole-Number Division

TEKS Number and Operations—5.3.J, 5.3.L
MATHEMATICAL PROCESSES
5.1.E, 5.1.F

 Essential Question

How can you divide unit fractions by whole numbers and whole numbers by unit fractions?

Unlock the Problem

Three friends share a $\frac{1}{4}$-pound block of fudge equally. What fraction of a pound of fudge does each friend get?

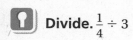 **Divide.** $\frac{1}{4} \div 3$

- Let the rectangle represent a 1-pound block of fudge. Divide the rectangle into fourths and then divide each fourth into three equal parts.

  The rectangle is now divided into _____ equal parts.

- When you divide one fourth into 3 equal parts, you are finding one of three equal parts or $\frac{1}{3}$ of $\frac{1}{4}$. Shade $\frac{1}{3}$ of $\frac{1}{4}$.

  The shaded part is _____ of the whole rectangle.

So, each friend gets _____ of a pound of fudge.

$\frac{1}{4}$

$\frac{1}{4} \div 3 = $ _____

Example

Brad has 9 pounds of ground turkey to make turkey burgers for a picnic. How many $\frac{1}{3}$-pound turkey burgers can he make?

Math Talk
Mathematical Processes

Will the number of turkey burgers be less than or greater than 9? Explain.

Divide. $9 \div \frac{1}{3}$

- Draw 9 rectangles to represent each pound of ground turkey. Divide each rectangle into thirds.

  When you divide the _____ rectangles into thirds, you are finding the number of thirds in 9 rectangles or

  finding 9 groups of _____ . There are _____ thirds.

  _omplete the number sentence.

  _rad can make _____ one-third-pound turkey burgers.

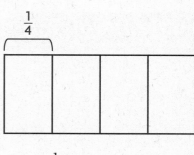

$9 \div \frac{1}{3} = $ _____ $\times$ _____ $=$ _____

1. Use the model to complete the number sentence.

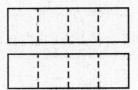

$$2 \div \frac{1}{4} = 2 \times \underline{\hspace{1cm}} = \underline{\hspace{1cm}}$$

2. Use the model to divide.

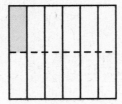

$$\frac{1}{6} \div 2 = \underline{\hspace{1cm}}$$

Problem Solving

Divide.

3. $5 \div \frac{1}{3}$

4. $8 \div \frac{1}{2}$

5. $\frac{1}{7} \div 4$

6. $\frac{1}{3} \div 4$

7. $\frac{1}{4} \div 12$

8. $6 \div \frac{1}{5}$

9. **Write Math** ▶ **Communicate** Describe how the model shows that dividing by $\frac{1}{2}$ is the same as multiplying by 2.

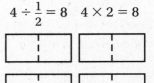

$$4 \div \frac{1}{2} = 8 \quad 4 \times 2 = 8$$

_____

_____

10. **H.O.T.** **Describe** how the model shows that dividing by 2 is the same as finding $\frac{1}{2}$ of $\frac{1}{4}$.

$$\frac{1}{4} \div 2 = \frac{1}{8}$$

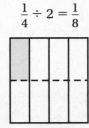

_____

_____

Name _____

11. **H.O.T.** **Multi-Step** The slowest mammal is the three-toed sloth. The top speed of a three-toed sloth on the ground is about $\frac{1}{4}$ foot per second. The top speed of a giant tortoise on the ground is about $\frac{1}{3}$ foot per second. How much longer would it take a three-toed sloth than a giant tortoise to travel 10 feet on the ground?

Ⓐ 10 seconds Ⓒ 40 seconds

Ⓑ 30 seconds Ⓓ 70 seconds

a. What do you need to find? _____

_____

b. What operations will you use to solve the problem? _____

_____

c. Show the steps you used to solve the problem.

d. Complete the sentences.

A three-toed sloth would travel 10 feet in

_____ seconds.

A giant tortoise would travel 10 feet in

_____ seconds.

Since _____ − _____ = _____,
it would take a three-toed sloth

_____ seconds longer to travel 10 feet.

e. Fill in the bubble for the correct answer choice.

12. Robert divides 8 cups of almonds into $\frac{1}{8}$-cup servings. How many servings does he have?

_____

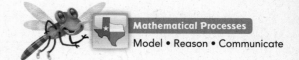
Daily Assessment Task

Fill in the bubble completely to show your answer.

13. Your friend asks you to watch his iguana. He gives you $\frac{1}{3}$ pound of food for 4 days. He tells you if you feed the iguana the same amount each day, you will have no food left over. How much food should you feed the iguana each day?

Ⓐ $\frac{1}{7}$ pound

Ⓑ 7 pounds

Ⓒ 12 pounds

Ⓓ $\frac{1}{12}$ pound

14. **Representations** Jake modeled a division problem. Which problem does his model represent?

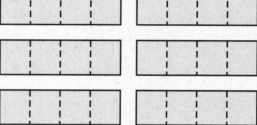

Ⓐ $6 \div \frac{1}{4} = 24$

Ⓑ $6 \times \frac{1}{4} = 1\frac{1}{2}$

Ⓒ $\frac{1}{4} \div 6 = \frac{1}{24}$

Ⓓ $6 \div 4 = 1\frac{1}{2}$

15. **Multi-Step** Five people are going to share $\frac{1}{4}$ gallon of juice. After the juice is poured equally, Sheila gives her glass to Maria. How much juice does Maria have?

Ⓐ $\frac{1}{40}$ gal

Ⓑ $\frac{4}{16}$ gal

Ⓒ $\frac{1}{10}$ gal

Ⓓ $\frac{1}{20}$ gal

⭐ TEXAS Test Prep

16. Tina cuts $\frac{1}{3}$ yard of fabric into 4 equal parts. What is the length of each part?

Ⓐ 12 yards

Ⓒ $3\frac{2}{3}$ yards

Ⓑ $1\frac{1}{3}$ yards

Ⓓ $\frac{1}{12}$ yard

6.6 Fraction and Whole-Number Division

Divide.

1. $6 \div \dfrac{1}{3}$

_____

2. $4 \div \dfrac{1}{8}$

_____

3. $\dfrac{1}{3} \div 9$

_____

4. $7 \div \dfrac{1}{2}$

_____

5. $8 \div \dfrac{1}{3}$

_____

6. $\dfrac{1}{4} \div 4$

_____

7. $9 \div \dfrac{1}{4}$

_____

8. $\dfrac{1}{7} \div 2$

_____

9. $10 \div \dfrac{1}{5}$

_____

10. $5 \div \dfrac{1}{5}$

_____

11. $\dfrac{1}{5} \div 12$

_____

12. $\dfrac{1}{9} \div 5$

_____

Problem Solving

13. Cooks at a food booth at the state fair made an extra-large 8-foot long burrito. If they cut the burrito into $\frac{1}{4}$-foot servings, how many people will the extra-large burrito serve?

_____

14. A serving of the burrito contains $\frac{1}{4}$ pound of meat. Franklin and two friends share his serving equally. How much meat does each friend get?

_____

Fill in the bubble completely to show your answer.

15. Toby used the model below to help him divide.

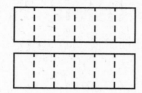

Which problem was he trying to solve?

Ⓐ $\frac{1}{6} \div 2$

Ⓑ $2 \div 6$

Ⓒ $2 \div \frac{1}{6}$

Ⓓ $2 \times \frac{1}{6}$

16. Which model shows the solution for $\frac{1}{2} \div 3$?

Ⓐ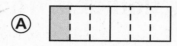

Ⓑ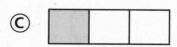

Ⓒ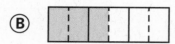

Ⓓ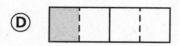

17. Analise cuts $\frac{1}{2}$ yard of rope into 8 equal parts. What is the length of each part?

Ⓐ $\frac{1}{16}$ yard

Ⓑ $\frac{1}{10}$ yard

Ⓒ $\frac{1}{4}$ yard

Ⓓ $\frac{1}{6}$ yard

18. The dragon costume for the new year celebration is 9 yards long. If Brittany sews a button on each $\frac{1}{6}$-yard section, how many buttons will she sew?

Ⓐ 63

Ⓑ 56

Ⓒ 15

Ⓓ 54

19. Multi-Step Ruby has a collection of 16 stuffed animals. She gives $\frac{1}{4}$ of her collection to her younger brother. Then she gives half of the remaining animals to her baby sister. How many animals does Ruby give her sister?

Ⓐ 4

Ⓑ 2

Ⓒ 6

Ⓓ 8

20. Multi-Step Ahmad and Kiera are mixing paints for the students in their art class. They mix 2 pints of blue paint, 2 pints of white paint, and 1 pint of green paint. How many $\frac{1}{3}$-pint containers can they fill with the mixed paint?

Ⓐ 15

Ⓑ 12

Ⓒ 6

Ⓓ $1\frac{2}{3}$

Module 6 Assessment

Concepts and Skills

1. Explain how you would model $5 \times \frac{2}{3}$. ◆ TEKS 5.3.I

_____

_____

Divide. Use a model. ◆ TEKS 5.3.J, 5.3.L

2. $3 \div \frac{1}{2} =$ _____

3. $1 \div \frac{1}{4} =$ _____

4. $\frac{1}{2} \div 2 =$ _____

5. $\frac{1}{3} \div 4 =$ _____

6. $2 \div \frac{1}{6} =$ _____

7. $\frac{1}{4} \div 3 =$ _____

Find the product. Write the product in simplest form. Use a model. ◆ TEKS 5.3.I

8. $\frac{2}{3} \times 6$

9. $\frac{4}{5} \times 7$

10. $8 \times \frac{5}{7}$

11. $2 \times \frac{3}{11}$

12. $5 \times \frac{2}{3}$

13. $\frac{7}{12} \times 8$

Fill in the bubble completely to show your answer.

14. Michelle cuts $\frac{1}{4}$ yard of ribbon into 4 equal pieces. What is the length of each piece? ⬇ TEKS 5.3.J, 5.3.L

   Ⓐ $\frac{1}{16}$ yard

   Ⓑ 16 yards

   Ⓒ 1 yard

   Ⓓ $\frac{1}{8}$ yard

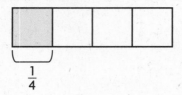

15. Holly had 30 pencils. She gave 6 pencils to her friends. Three-eighths of her remaining pencils need to be sharpened. How many of Holly's pencils need to be sharpened? ⬇ TEKS 5.3.I

   Ⓐ 24

   Ⓑ 9

   Ⓒ 3

   Ⓓ 16

16. Caleb and 2 friends are sharing $\frac{1}{2}$ quart of milk equally. What fraction of a quart of milk does each person get? ⬇ TEKS 5.3.L

   Ⓐ $\frac{2}{3}$ quart

   Ⓑ $\frac{3}{2}$ quarts

   Ⓒ $\frac{1}{4}$ quart

   Ⓓ $\frac{1}{6}$ quart

17. Thomas makes 5 sandwiches that he cuts into thirds. How many $\frac{1}{3}$-size sandwich pieces does he have? ⬇ TEKS 5.3.L

   Ⓐ 8

   Ⓑ $\frac{4}{3}$

   Ⓒ 2

   Ⓓ 15

Name _____

Vocabulary

Vocabulary

common denominator

common multiple

Choose the best term from the box.

1. A _____ is a number that is a
   multiple of two or more numbers. (p. 213)

Concepts and Skills

**Use a common denominator to write an equivalent
fraction for each fraction.** ⬇ TEKS 5.3

2. $\frac{2}{5}, \frac{1}{8}$ common
   denominator: _____

   _____

3. $\frac{3}{4}, \frac{1}{2}$ common
   denominator: _____

   _____

4. $\frac{2}{3}, \frac{1}{6}$ common
   denominator: _____

   _____

Find the sum or difference. Write your answer in simplest form. ⬇ TEKS 5.3.K

5. $\frac{5}{6} + \frac{5}{8}$

6. $3\frac{2}{3} - 1\frac{2}{5}$

7. $7\frac{3}{5} + 3\frac{9}{20}$

Find the product. Write the product in simplest form. Use a model. ⬇ TEKS 5.3.I

8. $\frac{3}{5} \times 8 =$ _____

9. $\frac{1}{4} \times 10 =$ _____

10. $\frac{5}{7} \times 15 =$ _____

11. $\frac{5}{6} \times 2 =$ _____

12. $\frac{1}{5} \times 10 =$ _____

13. $7 \times \frac{1}{6} =$ _____

Divide. Use a model or strategy. ⬇ TEKS 5.3.J, 5.3.L

14. $2 \div \frac{1}{3} =$ _____

15. $1 \div \frac{1}{5} =$ _____

16. $\frac{1}{4} \div 3 =$ _____

Fill in the bubble completely to show your answer.

17. Natasha bought $\frac{1}{4}$ pound of green grapes and $\frac{2}{3}$ pound of red grapes. She ate $\frac{1}{2}$ pound of the grapes. What is the total amount of grapes Natasha has left? 🔻 TEKS 5.3.K

Ⓐ 1 pound

Ⓑ $\frac{5}{12}$ pound

Ⓒ $\frac{3}{7}$ pound

Ⓓ $\frac{6}{12}$ pound

18. Ashton picked 6 pounds of pecans. He used $\frac{1}{3}$ of the pecans in a soup recipe. Ashton puts the pecans that are left in $\frac{1}{4}$-pound bags. How many bags of pecans does he have? 🔻 TEKS 5.3.I, 5.3.L

Ⓐ 16

Ⓑ 2

Ⓒ 8

Ⓓ 1

19. Isabella has $2\frac{1}{4}$ cups of granola and adds $1\frac{1}{2}$ cups of raisins. She then adds $1\frac{1}{4}$ cups of almonds to the mix. She divides the mix into $\frac{1}{4}$-cup servings. How many $\frac{1}{4}$-cup servings does she have? 🔻 TEKS 5.3.K, 5.3.L

Ⓐ $1\frac{1}{4}$

Ⓑ 16

Ⓒ 5

Ⓓ 20

20. Melvin walked $\frac{5}{8}$ mile to the library. He then walked $\frac{3}{10}$ mile from the library to the store. About how far did Melvin walk? 🔻 TEKS 5.3.A

Ⓐ about $1\frac{1}{2}$ miles

Ⓑ about 1 mile

Ⓒ about $\frac{1}{2}$ mile

Ⓓ about 2 miles

Fill in the bubble completely to show your answer.

21. Mrs. Friedmon baked a walnut cake for her class. The models below show how much cake she brought to school and how much she had left at the end of the day.

Before School   After School

Which fraction represents the difference between the amounts of cake Mrs. Friedmon had before school and after school? TEKS 5.3.H, 5.3.K

(A) $\frac{5}{8}$

(B) $1\frac{1}{2}$

(C) $1\frac{5}{8}$

(D) $2\frac{1}{2}$

22. Julie spends $\frac{3}{4}$ hour studying on Monday and $\frac{1}{6}$ hour studying on Tuesday. How many hours does Julie study on those two days?
TEKS 5.3.H, 5.3.K

(A) $\frac{1}{3}$ hour

(B) $\frac{2}{5}$ hour

(C) $\frac{5}{6}$ hour

(D) $\frac{11}{12}$ hour

1

| $\frac{1}{4}$ | $\frac{1}{4}$ | $\frac{1}{4}$ | $\frac{1}{6}$ |

| $\frac{1}{12}$ | $\frac{1}{12}$ | $\frac{1}{12}$ | $\frac{1}{12}$ | $\frac{1}{12}$ | $\frac{1}{12}$ | $\frac{1}{12}$ | $\frac{1}{12}$ | $\frac{1}{12}$ | $\frac{1}{12}$ |

23. A chef makes 4 different quiches as the special of the day. At the end of day, each dish had $\frac{3}{8}$ of the quiche left. How much quiche was bought in all? TEKS 5.3.I

(A) $\frac{3}{2}$

(B) $\frac{3}{32}$

(C) $\frac{5}{2}$

(D) $\frac{5}{8}$

24. Paulo had $2\frac{1}{4}$ feet of red twine. He had $1\frac{5}{12}$ feet of blue twine. He used some twine to make a craft. He has $1\frac{11}{12}$ feet of twine left. How much twine did Paulo use for his craft? TEKS 5.3.K

Ⓐ $2\frac{3}{12}$ feet

Ⓑ $1\frac{3}{4}$ feet

Ⓒ $5\frac{7}{12}$ feet

Ⓓ $2\frac{9}{12}$ feet

25. Which property or properties does the problem below use? TEKS 5.3.H

$$\left(\frac{2}{3} + \frac{3}{5}\right) + \frac{1}{3} = \frac{3}{5} + \left(\frac{2}{3} + \frac{1}{3}\right)$$

Ⓐ Commutative Property and Identity Property

Ⓑ Associative Property and Distributive Property

Ⓒ Commutative Property and Associative Property

Ⓓ Distributive Property

26. Li cuts $\frac{1}{4}$ foot of ribbon into 3 equal parts. What is the length of each part? TEKS 5.3.J, 5.3.L

Ⓐ $2\frac{1}{4}$ feet

Ⓑ $\frac{3}{12}$ foot

Ⓒ $\frac{4}{9}$ foot

Ⓓ Not Here

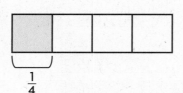

27. Draw a diagram and write a story problem to represent $6 \div \frac{1}{5}$.
TEKS 5.3.J

_____

_____

_____

Algebraic Reasoning

Show What You Know ✓

Check your understanding of important skills.

Name _____

▶ **Relate Multiplication and Division**

1. Since 3 × _____ = 12,

   then 12 ÷ 3 = _____ .

2. Since 48 ÷ 6 = _____ ,

   then _____ × 6 = 48.

3. Since 7 × _____ = 70,

   then 70 ÷ 7 = _____ .

4. Since 54 ÷ 9 = _____ ,

   then _____ × 9 = 54.

▶ **Missing Factors** Find the missing factor.

5. 4 × _____ = 24

6. 6 × _____ = 36

7. _____ × 9 = 63

8. _____ × 5 = 40

9. _____ × 8 = 16

10. 11 × _____ = 88

▶ **Area** Write the area of each figure.

11.

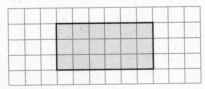

_____ square units

12.

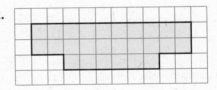

_____ square units

13.

_____ square units

14.

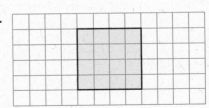

_____ square units

GO DIGITAL **Assessment Options:** Soar to Success Math

Vocabulary Builder

▶ **Visualize It** ••••••••••••••••••••••••••••••

Match the ✓ words with their examples.

What is it?		What are some examples?

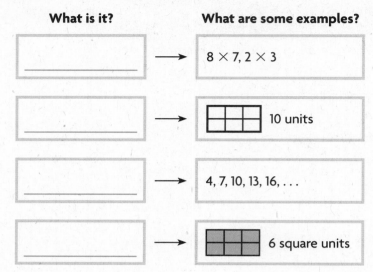

_____ → 8 × 7, 2 × 3

_____ → [grid] 10 units

_____ → 4, 7, 10, 13, 16, . . .

_____ → [shaded grid] 6 square units

Review Words

✓ area
✓ factor
  parentheses
✓ pattern
✓ perimeter

Preview Words

equation
numerical expression
volume

▶ **Understand Vocabulary** •••••••••••••••••••••

Complete the sentences with the words.

1. A _____ is an ordered set of numbers or objects.

2. _____ is the distance around a closed plane figure.

3. A _____ is a mathematical phrase that has numbers and operation signs but does not have an equal sign.

4. _____ is the measure of the number of unit squares.

5. An _____ is an algebraic or numerical sentence that shows that two quantities are equal.

6. _____ are the symbols used to show which operation or operations in an expression should be done first.

7. _____ is the measure of the space a solid figure occupies.

8. A _____ is a number multiplied by another number to find a product.

GO DIGITAL • Interactive Student Edition
  • Multimedia eGlossary

Name _____

Reading When you read a story, you interpret the words, sentences, and paragraphs. When you read math, you have to go beyond words. Often you must analyze graphs and tables to get the information you need.

Read the problem. Study the input/output table.

Vann works part-time for the Transit Authority. He earns $12 an hour. The input column of the input/output table shows the number of hours, *x*, that he works. The output column shows how much he earns, *y*. What is the rule for the table?

The rule shows how the input, *x*, is related to the output, *y*.

number of hours

amount earned

Rule: ?	
Input (*x*)	Output (*y*)
1	$12	1 × $12
2	$24	2 × $12
3	$36	3 × $12
4	$48	4 × $12

Think

The rule for this table is multiply by $12. $y = x \cdot \$12$

Writing Keith drives a limo to the airport. He can take 4 passengers at a time. Write a problem that can be answered by using this information and an input/output table. Ask a classmate to solve the problem.

_____

_____

_____

_____

Make It Even

Object of the Game Make an expression equal to an even number.

Materials

- Number/Symbol Cards: 3 sets labeled 0–9, 2 sets labeled +, −

Number of Players 2

Set Up

Give each player a set of symbol cards. Shuffle the number cards and place them face down in a stack.

How to Play

1 Each player draws 3 number cards from the stack. Players use the number cards and one or two of his or her symbol cards to make an expression.

2 A player's score is the value of the expression. If the value is an even number, the score is doubled.

3 Return all the cards to the deck and shuffle. Repeat steps 1–2.

4 The player with the highest score after 4 rounds wins.

7.1 Factors and Divisibility

TEKS Algebraic Reasoning—5.4.A
MATHEMATICAL PROCESSES
5.1.C, 5.1.D, 5.1.F

? Essential Question

How can you tell whether one number is a factor of another number?

🔑 Unlock the Problem (Real World)

Students in Carlo's art class painted 32 square tiles for a mosaic. They will arrange the tiles to make a rectangle. Can the rectangle have 32 tiles arranged into 3 equal rows, without gaps or overlaps?

A **composite number** is a whole number greater than 1 that has more than two factors. You can use models and division to find factors of composite numbers.

🔑 One Way Draw a model.

Think: Try to arrange the tiles into 3 equal rows to make a rectangle.

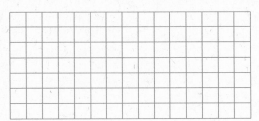

A rectangle _____ have 32 tiles arranged into 3 equal rows.

▲ Mosaics are decorative patterns made with pieces of glass or other materials.

🔑 Another Way Use division.

If 3 is a factor of 32, then the unknown factor in $3 \times \blacksquare = 32$ is a whole number.

3)3 2

Think: Divide to see whether the unknown factor is a whole number.

> **Math Idea**
>
> A factor of a number divides the number evenly. This means the quotient is a whole number and the remainder is 0.

The unknown factor in $3 \times \blacksquare = 32$ _____ a whole number.

So, a rectangle _____ have 32 tiles arranged in 3 rows.

> **Math Talk**
> Mathematical Processes
>
> **Explain** how the model relates to the quotient and remainder for $32 \div 3$.

Divisibility Rules A number is **divisible** by another number if the quotient is a counting number and the remainder is 0.

Some numbers have a divisibility rule. You can use a divisibility rule to tell whether one number is a factor of another.

 Is 6 a factor of 72?

Think: If 72 is divisible by 6, then 6 is a factor of 72.

Test for divisibility by 6:

Is 72 even? _____

What is the sum of the digits of 72?

_____ + _____ = _____

Is the sum of the digits divisible by 3?

_____

72 is divisible by _____.

So, 6 is a factor of 72.

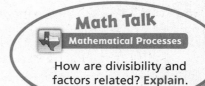

Divisibility Rules	
Number	**Divisibility Rule**
2	The number is even.
3	The sum of the digits is divisible by 3.
5	The last digit is 0 or 5.
6	The number is even and divisible by 3.
9	The sum of the digits is divisible by 9.

Math Talk
Mathematical Processes

How are divisibility and factors related? **Explain.**

Share and Show

1. Is 4 a factor of 28? Draw a model to help.

Think: Can you make a rectangle with 28 squares in 4 equal rows?

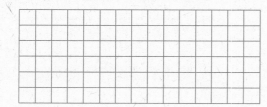

4 _____ a factor of 28.

Is 5 a factor of the number? Write *yes* or *no*.

2. 27

✓ **3.** 30

4. 36

✓ **5.** 53

_____   _____   _____   _____

Name _____

List all the factor pairs in the table. Use a model or paper and pencil to help.

6.

Factors of 24	
_____ × _____ = _____	_____ , _____
_____ × _____ = _____	_____ , _____
_____ × _____ = _____	_____ , _____
_____ × _____ = _____	_____ , _____

7.

Factors of 39	
_____ × _____ = _____	_____ , _____
_____ × _____ = _____	_____ , _____

List all the factor pairs for the number. Make a table to help.

8. 56

_____

_____

9. 64

_____

_____

10. **H.O.T.** **What's the Error?** George said if 2 and 4 are factors of a number, then 8 is a factor of the number. Is he correct? **Explain.**

_____

Problem Solving (Real World)

Use the table to solve 11–12.

11. **Multi-Step** Dirk bought a set of stamps. The number of stamps in the set he bought is divisible by 2, 3, 5, 6, and 9. Which set is it?

_____

12. **H.O.T.** **Multi-Step** Geri wants to put 6 stamps on some pages in her stamp book and 9 stamps on other pages. **Explain** how she could do this with the stamp set for Sweden.

Stamps Sets	
Country	**Number of stamps**
Germany	90
Sweden	78
Japan	63
Canada	25

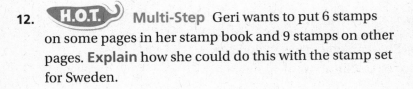

_____

_____

_____

Daily Assessment Task

Fill in the bubble completely to show your answer.

13. There are 54 people attending a party. Carla is arranging chairs and tables. How should she arrange the chairs so that there will be an equal number of people seated at each table?

Ⓐ 12 chairs at each table

Ⓑ 8 chairs at each table

Ⓒ 9 chairs at each table

Ⓓ 10 chairs at each table

14. **Analyze** Jake organizes 48 marbles into packs. He places the same number of marbles into each pack. How could he arrange the marbles?

Ⓐ 8 or 10 in each pack

Ⓑ 9 or 12 in each pack

Ⓒ 10 or 12 in each pack

Ⓓ 8 or 12 in each pack

15. **Multi-Step** Megan has 34 rocks in her rock collection. She wants to put 5 rocks in some cases and 7 rocks in other cases. How could she arrange the rocks?

Ⓐ Have 6 cases of 5 rocks, and 1 case of 7 rocks.

Ⓑ Have 4 cases of 5 rocks, and 2 cases of 7 rocks.

Ⓒ Have 2 cases of 5 rocks, and 4 cases of 7 rocks.

Ⓓ Have 5 cases of 5 rocks, and 2 cases of 7 rocks.

 TEXAS Test Prep

16. Mrs. Mastrioni bought a set of 80 stamps. She wanted to give all the stamps to her students as a reward. She could give equal numbers of stamps to

Ⓐ 2 or 3 students.

Ⓑ 2 or 6 students.

Ⓒ 2, 4, 5, or 8 students.

Ⓓ 2, 4, 8, or 9 students.

Name _____

7.1 Factors and Divisibility

List all the factor pairs in the table.

1.

Factors of 30	
_____ × _____ = _____	_____ , _____
_____ × _____ = _____	_____ , _____
_____ × _____ = _____	_____ , _____
_____ × _____ = _____	_____ , _____

2.

Factors of 15	
_____ × _____ = _____	_____ , _____
_____ × _____ = _____	_____ , _____

List all the factor pairs for the number. Make a table to help.

3. 18

_____

_____

4. 45

_____

_____

5. 36

_____

_____

6. 63

_____

_____

Problem Solving Real World

7. Planners for the city's botanical garden are planting a rose garden. They want to plant 56 rose bushes. Can they arrange the rose bushes into 4 equal rows? **Explain.**

_____

_____

_____

_____

8. A marching band with 75 members makes two rectangular marching formations. One rectangle has 6 rows and the other rectangle has 9 rows. **Explain** how the members can form the two rectangles.

_____

_____

_____

_____

Lesson Check

⭐ **TEXAS** Test Prep

Fill in the bubble completely to show your answer.

9. Which number is divisible by 2, 3, and 6?

Ⓐ 60

Ⓑ 33

Ⓒ 46

Ⓓ 21

10. Jo Beth organizes 63 party favors into gift bags. She places the same number of favors in each bag. How could she arrange the favors?

Ⓐ 3 or 6 in each bag

Ⓑ 6 or 9 in each bag

Ⓒ 7 or 8 in each bag

Ⓓ 7 or 9 in each bag

11. A package of marbles contains 20 blue marbles, 38 red marbles, 48 green marbles, and 16 yellow marbles. Which color of marbles can be divided evenly between 6 people?

Ⓐ blue

Ⓑ red

Ⓒ green

Ⓓ yellow

12. The fifth-grade students participating in the math competition will be evenly divided into teams of 3 students each. How many students could be participating?

Ⓐ 25

Ⓑ 21

Ⓒ 23

Ⓓ 26

13. **Multi-Step** The librarian has 94 books to organize. He wants to put 5 books on some shelves and 6 books on other shelves. How could he arrange the books?

Ⓐ Have 8 shelves of 5 books, and 9 shelves of 6 books.

Ⓑ Have 9 shelves of 5 books, and 8 shelves of 6 books.

Ⓒ Have 5 shelves of 6 books, and 6 shelves of 5 books.

Ⓓ Have 7 shelves of 5 books, and 6 shelves of 6 books.

14. **Multi-Step** A group of 72 students went on a field trip. The students traveled in vans, with an equal number of girls and boys in each van. If 42 boys went on the trip, how many vans were there?

Ⓐ 9

Ⓑ 8

Ⓒ 7

Ⓓ 6

Name _____

7.2 Prime and Composite Numbers

 Essential Question

How can you tell whether a number is prime or composite?

🔑 Unlock the Problem Real World

Students are arranging square tables to make one larger, rectangular table at a fundraiser for an animal shelter. If the students want to choose from the greatest number of ways to arrange the tables, should they use 12 or 13 square tables?

🔲 **Use a grid to show all the possible arrangements of 12 and 13 tables.**

Label each drawing with the factors modeled.

● What are the factors of 12?
_____

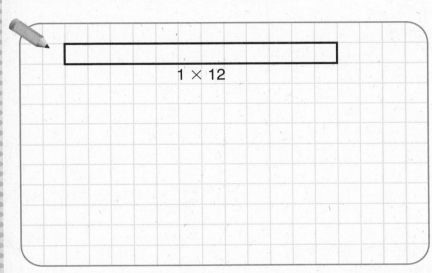

1×12

> **⚠ ERROR Alert**
>
> The same factors in a different order should be counted only once. For example, 3×4 and 4×3 are the same factor pair.

So, there are more ways to arrange _____ tables.

Math Talk
Mathematical Processes

Explain how knowing whether 12 and 13 are prime or composite could have helped you solve the problem above.

- A **prime number** is a whole number greater than 1 that has exactly two factors, 1 and itself.

- A composite number is a whole number greater than 1 that has more than two factors.

Factors of 12: _____ , _____ , _____ , _____ , _____ , _____

Factors of 13: _____ , _____

12 is a _____ number, and 13 is a _____ number.

Divisibility You can use divisibility rules to help tell whether a number is prime or composite. If a number is divisible by any number other than 1 and itself, then the number is composite.

> **Math Idea**
> The number 1 is neither prime nor composite, since it has only one factor: 1.

🔑 Tell whether 51 is *prime* or *composite*.

Is 51 divisible by 2? _____

Is 51 divisible by 3? _____

Think: 51 is divisible by a number other than 1 and 51.
51 has more than two factors.

So, 51 is _____.

Share and Show MATH BOARD

Tell whether the number is *prime* or *composite*.

1. 11
   Think: Does 11 have other factors besides 1 and itself?

   _____

2. 73

   _____

✓ 3. 69

   _____

✓ 4. 42

   _____

Problem Solving

> **Math Talk**
> **Mathematical Processes**
> Is the product of two prime numbers prime or composite? Explain.

H.O.T. **Analyze** Write *true* or *false* for each statement. Explain or give an example to support your answer.

5. The number 1 is not prime.

   _____
   _____

6. A composite number cannot have three factors.

   _____
   _____

7. Only odd numbers are prime numbers.

   _____
   _____

8. Every multiple of 7 is a composite number.

   _____
   _____

9. **H.O.T.** Name a 2-digit odd number that is prime. Name a 2-digit odd number that is composite.

   _____

Problem Solving (Real World)

Eratosthenes was a Greek mathematician who lived more than 2,200 years ago. He invented a method of finding prime numbers, which is now called the Sieve of Eratosthenes.

10. Multi-Step Follow the steps below to circle all prime numbers less than 100. Then list the prime numbers.

STEP 1

Cross out 1, since 1 is not prime.

STEP 2

Circle 2, since it is prime. Cross out all other multiples of 2.

STEP 3

Circle the next number that is not crossed out. This number is prime. Cross out all the multiples of this number.

STEP 4

Repeat Step 3 until every number is either circled or crossed out.

1	2	3	4	5	6	7	8	9	10
11	12	13	14	15	16	17	18	19	20
21	22	23	24	25	26	27	28	29	30
31	32	33	34	35	36	37	38	39	40
41	42	43	44	45	46	47	48	49	50
51	52	53	54	55	56	57	58	59	60
61	62	63	64	65	66	67	68	69	70
71	72	73	74	75	76	77	78	79	80
81	82	83	84	85	86	87	88	89	90
91	92	93	94	95	96	97	98	99	100

So, the prime numbers less than 100 are

_____

_____

_____

_____

_____

_____

_____

11. **H.O.T.** **Explain** why the multiples of any number other than 1 are not prime numbers.

_____

_____

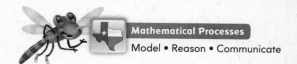
Daily Assessment Task

Fill in the bubble completely to show your answer.

12. **Reasoning** Talia's locker combination consists of three prime numbers. The sum of these numbers is also a prime number. Which of these might be her combination?

   (A) 3 - - 8 - - 17

   (B) 2 - - 3 - - 19

   (C) 7 - - 13 - - 3

   (D) 11 - - 2 - - 5

13. A certain number is a whole number. If the number is also composite, what *must* be true about the number?

   (A) It is odd.

   (B) It has more than two factors.

   (C) It has exactly two factors.

   (D) It has two or more digits.

14. **Multi-Step** The sum of three prime numbers is 12. What could the numbers be?

   (A) 3, 7, 2

   (B) 6, 6, 0

   (C) 3, 5, 7

   (D) 3, 4, 5

TEXAS Test Prep

15. The number 2 is

   (A) prime.

   (B) composite.

   (C) neither prime nor composite.

   (D) both prime and composite.

7.2 Prime and Composite Numbers

Tell whether the number is *prime* or *composite*.

1. 19 _____

2. 81 _____

3. 52 _____

4. 23 _____

5. 33 _____

6. 60 _____

7. 31 _____

8. 25 _____

Write *true* or *false* for each statement. Explain or give an example to support your answer.

9. A prime number is always greater than 1.

_____

_____

10. The number 17 is a prime number.

_____

_____

11. Every multiple of 5 is a composite number.

_____

_____

_____

12. A number can be both prime and composite.

_____

_____

_____

Problem Solving Real World

13. The students in math class use square tiles to make arrays. Celia says they can make more arrays with 8 tiles than with 9 tiles because 8 has more factors. Is Celia correct? **Explain**.

_____

_____

_____

Fill in the bubble completely to show your answer.

14. Four boys compare the numbers on their football jerseys. Parker has the number 55. Nick has 47. Marshall has 16, and Leon has 9. Whose jersey has a prime number?

   Ⓐ Parker

   Ⓑ Nick

   Ⓒ Marshall

   Ⓓ Leon

15. Harlan played her favorite game app three times this morning. In each game, the number of points she scored was a prime number. When she adds the points for the three games together, the sum is also a prime number. Which of these might be her scores?

   Ⓐ 17, 19, 20

   Ⓑ 11, 17, 21

   Ⓒ 21, 23, 13

   Ⓓ 29, 19, 23

16. Esteban made a list of prime numbers less than 40. He listed the numbers in order from least to greatest. Which number did Esteban put on his list after 29?

   Ⓐ 41

   Ⓑ 23

   Ⓒ 33

   Ⓓ 31

17. Carolyn found that the difference between two prime numbers is a composite number. Which could be the prime numbers?

   Ⓐ 2, 5

   Ⓑ 13, 2

   Ⓒ 23, 19

   Ⓓ 13, 11

18. **Multi-Step** Trisha spins a spinner. The pointer lands on three prime numbers. She says the sum is less than 12. Which could be the numbers?

   Ⓐ 2, 3, 5

   Ⓑ 2, 4, 5

   Ⓒ 2, 7, 3

   Ⓓ 0, 9, 1

19. **Multi-Step** Felix found the sum of two prime numbers and one composite number to be 45. The difference between the greatest and least number is 4. Which could be the three numbers?

   Ⓐ 13, 17, 15

   Ⓑ 18, 14, 13

   Ⓒ 15, 14, 16

   Ⓓ 11, 19, 12

TEKS Algebraic
Reasoning—5.4.E
MATHEMATICAL PROCESSES
5.1.D, 5.1.E

7.3 Numerical Expressions

 Essential Question

How can you use a numerical expression to describe a situation?

Unlock the Problem

A **numerical expression** is a mathematical phrase that has numbers and operation signs but does not have an equal sign. Some numerical expressions have parentheses.

Doug went fishing for 3 days. Each day he put $15 in his pocket. At the end of each day, he had $5 left. How much money did Doug spend by the end of the trip?

- Underline the events for each day.
- Circle the number of days these events happened.

Which expression matches the meaning of the words?

Think: Each day he took $15 and had $5 left. He did this for 3 days.

($15 − $5) ← **Think:** What expression can you write to show how much money Doug spends in one day?

_____

3 × ($15 − $5) ← **Think:** What expression can you write to show how much money Doug spends in three days?

Math Talk
Mathematical Processes

Explain how the expression of what Doug spent in three days compares to the expression of what he spent in one day.

Example

Which problem matches the expression $20 − ($12 + $3)?

Kim has $20 to spend for her fishing trip. She spends $12 on a fishing pole. Then she finds $3. How much money does Kim have now?

List the events in order.

First: Kim has $20.

Next: _____ .

Then: _____ .

Do these words
match the expression? _____

Kim has $20 to spend for her fishing trip. She spends $12 on a fishing pole and $3 on bait. How much money does Kim have now?

List the events in order.

First: Kim has $20.

Next: _____ .

Then: _____ .

Do these words
match the expression? _____

Circle the expression that matches the words.

1. Teri had 18 worms. She gave 4 worms to Susie and 3 worms to Jamie.

   $(18 - 4) + 3$ $18 - (4 + 3)$

2. Rick had $8. He then worked 4 hours for $5 each hour.

   $\$8 + (4 \times \$5)$ $(\$8 + 4) \times \$5$

Write an expression to match the words.

3. Greg walks dogs for 5 days. He walks 4 dogs each morning and 3 dogs each afternoon.

   _____

4. Lynda has 27 fewer fish than Jack. Jack has 80 fish.

   _____

Write words to match the expression.

5. $34 - 17$

   _____

   _____

6. $6 \times (12 - 4)$

   _____

   _____

Problem Solving

Write an expression to match the words.

7. José has 9 pens. He buys 3 more. He shares all the pens equally among 6 friends.

   _____

8. Monique had $20. She spent $5 on lunch and $10 at the bookstore.

   _____

 Write words to match the expression.

9. $(\$8 + \$14) - (4 \times \$5)$

   _____

   _____

10. $(12 \times 6) - (3 \times 2)$

   _____

   _____

   _____

Connect **Draw a line to match the expression with the words.**

11. Fred catches 25 fish. Then he releases 10 fish and catches 8 more.

   Nick has 25 pens. He gives 10 pens to one friend and 8 pens to another friend.

   Jan catches 25 fish and lets 10 fish go.

   • $25 - 10$

   • $25 - (10 + 8)$

   • $(25 - 10) + 8$

Name _____

Use the rule and the table for 12–13.

Aquarium Fish

Type of Fish	Length (in inches)
Lemon Tetra	2
Strawberry Tetra	3
Giant Danio	5
Tiger Barb	3
Swordtail	5

12. **Represent** Write a numerical expression to represent the total number of lemon tetras that could be in a 20-gallon aquarium.

_____

13. **H.O.T.** There are tiger barbs in a 15-gallon aquarium and giant danios in a 30-gallon aquarium. Write a numerical expression to represent the total number of fish that could be in both aquariums.

_____

▲ The rule for the number of fish in an aquarium is to allow 1 gallon of water for each inch of length.

Write Math ▶ Show Your Work

14. **H.O.T.** Write a word problem for an expression that is three times as great as $(15 + 7)$. Then write the expression.

_____

_____

_____

_____

15. **What's the Question?** Lu has 3 swordtails in her aquarium. She buys 2 more swordtails.

_____

_____

16. **Multi-Step** Tammy has 26 stamps. She buys 19 more stamps. She shares all the stamps equally among 9 friends. Write an expression to match the words. How many stamps does each friend get?

_____

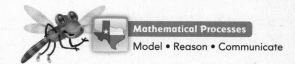
Daily Assessment Task

Fill in the bubble completely to show your answer.

17. Daniel started a video game with 30 tokens. He earned 8 more tokens for jumping on a star, but lost 6 tokens for falling into a hole. When he passed a checkpoint, his number of tokens doubled! Then he spent 20 tokens to buy a flashlight. Which expression shows how many tokens he has left?

    (A) $2 \times (30 + 8 - 6 - 20)$

    (B) $2 \times (30 + 8) - (20 + 6)$

    (C) $2 \times 30 + 8 - 6 - 20$

    (D) $2 \times (30 + 8 - 6) - 20$

18. Enrique brought $30 to the mall and spent $14 on a soccer ball and $6 on lunch. Which expression represents the situation?

    (A) $30 \div (14 - 6)$

    (B) $30 - (14 + 6)$

    (C) $30 \div (14 - 6)$

    (D) $30 - 14 + 30 - 6$

19. **Multi-Step** Terrel has 8 nickels. Heather has twice as many nickels as Terrel. Heather spends 4 nickels to buy a pencil. Each nickel is worth 5 cents. Which expression shows how many cents Heather has left?

    (A) $5 + 2 + 8 - 4$ (C) $5 \times (2 \times 8 - 4)$

    (B) $5 \times (2 \times 8) - 4$ (D) $5 \times 2 + 8 - 4$

⭐ TEXAS Test Prep

20. Josh has 3 fish in each of 5 buckets. Then he releases 4 fish. Which expression matches the words?

    (A) $(3 \times 4) - 5$

    (B) $(5 \times 4) - 3$

    (C) $(5 \times 3) - 4$

    (D) $(5 - 3) \times 4$

306

Name _____

7.3 Numerical Expressions

Write an expression to match the words.

1. Frank had $25 in his checking account. He withdrew $15 cash and $9 to pay a bill.

_____

2. Patricia charges $12 to rake the yard. She charges $5 per hour to bag the piles of leaves for 2 hours.

_____

Write words to match the expressions.

3. $(5 \times 2) \times (3 \times 15)$

_____

_____

4. $36 + (2 \times 3)$

_____

_____

_____

5. $(5 + 10) \div 5$

_____

_____

_____

6. $(12 \times 2) + (4 \times 3)$

_____

_____

_____

Problem Solving

7. Dominick makes a design with 5 rows of 6 tiles. He frames the same design in 7 different frames to sell at the craft fair. Write an expression to match the words. How many tiles does Dominick use?

_____

8. Tim buys three 6-packs of apple juice boxes and five 4-packs of cranberry juice boxes for his party. Write an expression to match the words. How many boxes of juice does Tim buy?

_____

Fill in the bubble completely to show your answer.

Use the price list for 9–11.

Ultimate Amusement Park	
Ticket	Price
Child admission	$12
Adult admission	$15
Funland ride	$2 each
Thrill ride	$3 each

9. Which expression shows the cost of one adult admission ticket and 9 thrill ride tickets?

(A) $15 + (9 × $3)

(B) $12 + (9 × $3)

(C) $15 + (9 + $3)

(D) ($15 × 9) + $3

10. Bandar and Courtney each paid $12 for admission. They bought 14 thrill ride tickets. Which expression shows their cost?

(A) $12 + (14 × $3)

(B) (2 × $12) + (14 × $3)

(C) (2 × $12) + 14

(D) $12 + (14 + $3)

11. Riley bought a child admission ticket and 6 funland ride tickets. He used a coupon for a $5 discount. Which expression shows Riley's total cost?

(A) $12 + (6 × $2)

(B) $12 + ($6 + $2) − $5

(C) $12 + (6 × $2) − $5

(D) $12 + (6 × $2) + $5

12. **Multi-Step** The classroom has 12 chairs on the right side of the room, 15 chairs on the left, and 9 chairs stacked in the back. Mrs. Kim wants to divide the chairs evenly into 3 groups. Which expression represents the situation?

(A) 12 + 15 + 9 × 3

(B) 12 + 15 + (9 ÷ 3)

(C) 12 + 15 + 9 + 3

(D) (12 + 15 + 9) ÷ 3

13. **Multi-Step** Mr. Richardson is driving to a town 85 miles away. He drives 35 miles per hour for 2 hours before stopping for lunch. He drives 6 more miles and stops for gas. Which expression shows how many miles Mr. Richardson has left to drive?

(A) 85 − (35 × 2) − 6

(B) 85 − 35 − 2 − 6

(C) (85 − 35) × 2 − 6

(D) 85 − 35 + 2 − 6

TEKS Algebraic
Reasoning—5.4.F
MATHEMATICAL PROCESSES
5.1.B, 5.1.F, 5.1.G

7.4 Simplify Numerical Expressions

Essential Question

In what order must operations be simplified to find the solution to a problem?

Connect Remember that a numerical expression is a mathematical phrase that uses only numbers and operation symbols.

$(5 - 2) \times 7$ $72 \div 9 + 16$ $(24 - 15) + 32$

To **simplify**, or find the value of, a numerical expression with more than one operation, you must follow rules called the **order of operations**. The order of operations tells you in what order you should simplify an expression.

Order of Operations

1. Perform operations in parentheses.
2. Multiply and divide from left to right.
3. Add and subtract from left to right.

Unlock the Problem

A cake recipe calls for 4 cups of flour and 2 cups of sugar. To triple the recipe, how many cups of flour and sugar are needed in all?

Simplify 3 × 4 + 3 × 2 to find the total number of cups.

A Heather did not follow the order of operations correctly.

Heather
$3 \times 4 + 3 \times 2$ First, I added.
$3 \times 7 \times 2$ Then, I multiplied.
42

B Follow the order of operations by multiplying first and then adding.

Name_____
$3 \times 4 + 3 \times 2$

Explain why Heather's answer is not correct.

_____

So, _____ cups of flour and sugar are needed.

Simplify Expressions with Parentheses To simplify an expression with parentheses, follow the order of operations. Perform the operations in parentheses first. Multiply from left to right. Then add and subtract from left to right.

 **Example**

Each batch of cupcakes Lena makes uses 3 cups of flour, 1 cup of milk, and 2 cups of sugar. Lena wants to make 5 batches of cupcakes. How many cups of flour, milk, and sugar will she need in all?

Write the expression. $5 \times (3 + 1 + 2)$

First, perform the operations in parentheses. $5 \times ($ _____ $)$

Then multiply.   _____

So, Lena will use _____ cups of flour, milk, and sugar in all.

Share and Show

Simplify the numerical expression.

1. $10 + 36 \div 9$

   Think: I need to divide first.

   _____

2. $10 + (25 - 10) \div 5$

   _____

3. $9 - (3 \times 2) + 8$

   _____

Problem Solving

Math Talk
Mathematical Processes

Raina simplified the expression $5 \times 2 + 2$ by adding first and then multiplying. Will her answer be correct? **Explain.**

4. **H.O.T.** **Use Symbols** Write $12 + 17 - 3 \times 2$ with parentheses so it has a value of 23.

_____

5. **H.O.T.** **Multi-Step** The value of $100 - 30 \div 5$ with parentheses can have a value of 14 or 94. **Explain.**

_____

_____

Name _____

6. **Multi-Step** A movie theater has 4 groups of seats. The largest group of seats, in the middle, has 20 rows, with 20 seats in each row. There are 2 smaller groups of seats on the sides, each with 20 rows and 6 seats in each row. A group of seats in the back has 5 rows, with 30 seats in each row. How many seats are in the movie theater?

back

side	middle	side

a. What do you need to know?

_____

_____

b. What operation can you use to find the number of seats in the back group of seats? Write the expression.

_____

c. What operation can you use to find the number of seats in both groups of side seats? Write the expression.

_____

d. What operation can you use to find the number of seats in the middle group? Write the expression.

_____

e. Write an expression to represent the total number of seats in the theater.

_____

_____

f. How many seats are in the theater? Show the steps you use to solve the problem.

_____

_____

7. **Multi-Step** In the wild, an adult giant panda eats about 30 pounds of food each day. Write and simplify a numerical expression that shows how many pounds of food 6 pandas eat in 3 days.

_____

8. **H.O.T.** **Connect** Write and simplify two equivalent numerical expressions that show the Distributive Property of Multiplication.

_____

_____

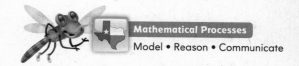

Daily Assessment Task

Fill in the bubble completely to show your answer.

9. The books in an unusual library are labeled with numerical expressions. Katrina needs to find the book with a numerical expression that has a value of 12. Which one should she choose?

   Ⓐ $(6 + 26) - (4 \times 5)$

   Ⓑ $2 \times (15 - 7)$

   Ⓒ $10 + 8 - 36 \div 9$

   Ⓓ $(25 - 4) \div 7$

10. Franco needs to simplify $3 \times (8 - 4) + 7$. What should be his first step?

    Ⓐ Add 7 to 4.

    Ⓑ Subtract 4 from 8.

    Ⓒ Multiply 3 by 7.

    Ⓓ Add 3 to 7.

11. **Multi-Step** Sarah simplified each of the expressions shown. What is the difference between the values of the two expressions?

    $$3 \times 12 - 9 + 10 \qquad 3 \times (12 - 9) + 10$$

    Ⓐ 9

    Ⓒ 12

    Ⓑ 18

    Ⓓ 22

 TEXAS Test Prep

12. Which expression has a value of 6?

    Ⓐ $(6 \div 3) \times 4 + 8$

    Ⓑ $27 - 9 \div 3 \times (4 + 1)$

    Ⓒ $(18 + 12) \times 6 - 4$

    Ⓓ $71 - 5 \times (9 + 4)$

7.4 Simplify Numerical Expressions

Simplify the numerical expression.

1. $10 - (2 \times 4) + 12$

2. $14 + 35 \div 7$

3. $11 + (31 - 4) \div 9$

4. $25 - 4 \times 5$

5. $3 \times (6 + 3) - 15$

6. $30 - 14 \div 2$

Rewrite the expression with parentheses to equal the given value.

7. $12 + 6 \div 2 + 4$; value: 13

8. $42 - 24 \div 6$; value: 3

9. $9 + 16 - 2 \times 4$; value: 17

10. $60 - 3 + 2 \times 5$; value: 35

11. $18 + 9 \div 3$; value: 21

12. $5 \times 2 + 4 + 3$; value: 45

Problem Solving

13. Julian paid his library fines. He paid $2 each for 4 overdue books and $16 for a lost book. Write and simplify a numerical expression that shows how much Julian paid in library fines.

14. For 5 days in a row last week, Addison read 9 pages of a poetry book and 16 pages of her favorite novel. Write and simplify a numerical expression that shows how many pages Addison read last week.

Fill in the bubble completely to show your answer.

15. Mrs. Harrison writes a numerical expression on the board that has a value of 16. Which expression does Mrs. Harrison write?

Ⓐ $(15 + 3) - 14 \div 2$

Ⓑ $20 - 4 \div 2$

Ⓒ $3 \times (5 + 1)$

Ⓓ $18 + 13 - (5 \times 3)$

16. Omar wants to simplify the expression below. What should be his first step?

$$6 \times (3 + 9) - 5$$

Ⓐ Multiply 6 by 3.

Ⓑ Subtract 5 from 9.

Ⓒ Add 9 to 3.

Ⓓ Subtract 5 from 6.

17. Which is the value of the numerical expression below?

$$30 \div (3 + 2) \times 8$$

Ⓐ 96

Ⓑ 48

Ⓒ 26

Ⓓ 40

18. Becka says that when she simplifies the expression below, the value is 6 less than her age. What is Becka's age?

$$(7 + 11) - 8 \div 2$$

Ⓐ 20

Ⓑ 14

Ⓒ 26

Ⓓ 11

19. Multi-Step Kalani and Porter each simplified one of the expressions below. If they add their results together, what will be their sum?

Kalani: $4 \times 11 - 5 + 12$

Porter: $4 \times 11 - (5 + 12)$

Ⓐ 78

Ⓑ 44

Ⓒ 102

Ⓓ 54

20. Multi-Step Nicole simplified the expression below. Then she multiplied the value of the expression by 5. What is Nicole's product?

$$36 + 6 \div 3 + 2$$

Ⓐ 16

Ⓑ 80

Ⓒ 40

Ⓓ 200

7.5 **Grouping Symbols**

TEKS Algebraic
Reasoning—5.4.E, 5.4.F
MATHEMATICAL PROCESSES
5.1.A, 5.1.G

Essential Question

 In what order must operations be simplified to find a solution when there are parentheses within brackets?

Unlock the Problem

Mary's weekly allowance is $8 and David's weekly allowance is $5. Every week they each spend $2 on lunch. Write a numerical expression to show how many weeks it will take them together to save enough money to buy a video game for $45.

- Underline Mary's weekly allowance and how much she spends.
- Circle David's weekly allowance and how much he spends.

 Use parentheses and brackets to write an expression.

You can use parentheses and brackets to group operations that go together. Operations in parentheses and brackets are performed first.

STEP 1 Write an expression to represent how much Mary and David save each week.

- How much money does Mary save each week?

   Think: Each week Mary gets $8 and spends $2.

   (_____)

- How much money does David save each week?

   Think: Each week David gets $5 and spends $2.

   (_____)

- How much money do Mary and David save together each week? _____

STEP 2 Write an expression to represent how many weeks it will take Mary and David to save enough money for the video game.

- How many weeks will it take Mary and David to save enough for a video game?

   Think: I can use brackets to group operations a second time. $45 is divided by the total amount of money saved each week.

   _____ ÷ [_____]

Math Talk
Mathematical Processes

Explain why brackets are placed around the part of the expression that represents the amount of money Mary and David save each week.

Simplify Expressions with Grouping Symbols When simplifying an expression with different grouping symbols (parentheses and brackets), perform the operation in the innermost set of grouping symbols first, simplifying the expression from the inside out.

🔑 Example

John gets $6 for his weekly allowance and spends $4 of it. His sister Tina gets $7 for her weekly allowance and spends $3 of it. Their mother's birthday is in 4 weeks. If they save the same amount each week, how much money can they save together in that time to buy her a present?

- Write the expression using parentheses and brackets.
$4 \times [(\$6 - \$4) + (\$7 - \$3)]$

- Perform the operations in the parentheses first.
$4 \times [\underline{\hspace{1cm}} + \underline{\hspace{1cm}}]$

- Next perform the operations in the brackets.
$4 \times \underline{\hspace{1cm}}$

- Then multiply.
$\underline{\hspace{1cm}}$

So, John and Tina will be able to save _____ for their mother's birthday present.

- **H.O.T.** **What if** only Tina saves money? Will this change the numerical expression? **Explain.**

_____

Share and Show

Simplify the numerical expression.

1. $12 + [(15 - 5) + (9 - 3)]$

$12 + [10 + \underline{\hspace{1cm}}]$

$12 + \underline{\hspace{1cm}}$

_____

✅ **2.** $5 \times [(26 - 4) - (4 + 6)]$

_____

✅ **3.** $36 \div [(18 - 10) - (8 - 6)]$

_____

Problem Solving

4. **H.O.T.** **Use Symbols** Write the expression $2 \times 8 + 20 - 12 \div 6$ with parentheses and brackets two different ways so its value is less than 10 and greater than 50.

_____

316

Name _____

5. **Reasoning** Dan has a flower shop. Each day he displays 24 roses. He gives away 10 and sells the rest. Each day he displays 36 carnations. He gives away 12 and sells the rest. What expression can you use to find out how many roses and carnations Dan sells in a week?

a. What information are you given?

_____

_____

b. What are you being asked to do?

_____

_____

c. What expression shows how many roses Dan sells in one day?

_____

d. What expression shows how many carnations Dan sells in one day?

_____

e. Write an expression to represent the total number of roses and carnations Dan sells in one day.

_____

f. Write the expression that shows how many roses and carnations Dan sells in a week.

_____

6. **Multi-Step** Simplify the expression to find out how many roses and carnations Dan sells in a week.

_____

7. **H.O.T.** How could you change the story in Problem 5 so there is only one expression inside parentheses?

_____

_____

Math on the Spot

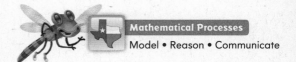

Daily Assessment Task

Fill in the bubble completely to show your answer.

8. A gift shop had 500 colored pencils. The shop sold 3 sets of 20 colored pencils, 6 sets of 12 colored pencils, and 10 sets of 18 colored pencils. Which expression shows how many colored pencils are left?

   (A) $3 \times 20 + 6 \times 12 + 10 \times 18 - 500$

   (B) $500 - [3 \times (20 + 6) \times (12 + 10) \times 18)]$

   (C) $500 + [(3 \times 20) + (6 \times 12) + (10 \times 18)]$

   (D) $500 - [(3 \times 20) + (6 \times 12) + (10 \times 18)]$

9. Anya buys 8 oranges every Monday morning at the farmer's market. She gives 6 away and eats the rest. Every Friday she buys 6 oranges, gives 5 away, and eats the rest. Simplify the expression $52 \times [(8 - 6) + (6 - 5)]$ to find the number of oranges Anya eats in a year.

   (A) 104   (C) 156

   (B) 208   (D) 260

10. **Multi-Step** A company can produce 300 ballpoint pens or 550 gel pens each hour. Each weekday, the company produces ballpoint pens for 5 hours and gel pens for 8 hours. How many pens does the company produce in 5 weekdays?

    (A) 7,500   (C) 29,500

    (B) 24,500   (D) 5,900

⭐ TEXAS Test Prep

11. Which expression has a value of 4?

    (A) $[(4 \times 5) + (9 + 7)] + 9$

    (B) $[(4 \times 5) + (9 + 7)] \div 9$

    (C) $[(4 \times 5) - (9 + 7)] \times 9$

    (D) $[(4 + 5) + (9 + 7)] - 9$

Name _____

 # Module 7 Assessment

Vocabulary

Vocabulary

Choose the best term from the box.

Vocabulary
composite number
numerical expression
prime number

1. A _____ is a whole number greater than 1 that has exactly two factors, 1 and itself. (p. 297)

2. A _____ is a mathematical phrase that has numbers and operation signs but does not have an equal sign. (p. 303)

Concepts and Skills

Decide if the number is prime or composite. If it is composite, list the factor pairs. TEKS 5.4.A

3. 54

4. 28

_____

_____

_____

_____

Tell whether the number is prime or composite. TEKS 5.4.A

5. 33

6. 47

7. 91

8. 81

_____

_____

_____

_____

Simplify the numerical expression. TEKS 5.4.F

9. $18 - (8 \times 3) \div 4$

10. $35 - [(4 \times 5) + (2 \times 5)]$

_____

_____

TEXAS Test Prep

11. Students in a math contest are asked to simplify a numerical expression. The correct answer is 34. Which could be the expression? ⚑ TEKS 5.4.F

   Ⓐ $6 + 3 \times 4 - 2$

   Ⓑ $6 + 3 \times (4 - 2)$

   Ⓒ $(6 + 3) \times 4 - 2$

   Ⓓ $6 + (3 \times 4) - 2$

12. Ana writes the expression $(8 \times 4) + (6 \times 3)$ to represent the number of cards in her sports card collection. Which could be Ana's sports card collection? ⚑ TEKS 5.4.E

   Ⓐ 8 soccer cards and 4 baseball cards in one box, 6 soccer cards and 3 baseball cards in another box

   Ⓑ 8 soccer cards separated into 4 boxes, 6 baseball cards separated into 3 boxes

   Ⓒ 8 boxes with 4 soccer cards in each box, 6 boxes with 3 baseball cards in each box

   Ⓓ 12 soccer cards, 9 baseball cards

13. A florist has 9 daffodils and twice as many tulips. He donates the flowers equally to 3 parks. Which expression represents the number of flowers each park receives? ⚑ TEKS 5.4.E

   Ⓐ $(9 \times 2) \div 3$

   Ⓑ $[9 + (2 \times 9)] \div 3$

   Ⓒ $[9 \times (2 \times 9)] \div 3$

   Ⓓ $[9 \times (2 \times 9)] \div 3$

14. David washes 10 cars and waxes 4 cars every Saturday. He earns $5 for each car he washes and $12 for each car he waxes. How much money does he earn on 3 Saturdays in dollars? Simplify the expression $3 \times [(10 \times 5) + (4 \times 12)]$ to find the answer. ⚑ TEKS 5.4.F

Record your answer and fill in the bubbles on the grid. Be sure to use the correct place value.

⓪	⓪	⓪		⓪	⓪
①	①	①		①	①
②	②	②		②	②
③	③	③		③	③
④	④	④		④	④
⑤	⑤	⑤		⑤	⑤
⑥	⑥	⑥		⑥	⑥
⑦	⑦	⑦		⑦	⑦
⑧	⑧	⑧		⑧	⑧
⑨	⑨	⑨		⑨	⑨

TEKS Algebraic
Reasoning—5.4.B
MATHEMATICAL PROCESSES
5.1.C, 5.1.D

8.1 Equations

? Essential Question

How can you use a pan balance to model and solve an equation with an unknown quantity?

Investigate

Hands On

Materials ■ pan balance, connecting cubes

A *pan balance* weighs objects whose weights are unknown by balancing them with objects whose weights are known. When the two pans are balanced, the objects have the same weight.

You can use a pan balance to model and solve an equation. An equation is a mathematical sentence that shows that two amounts are equal.

A. Use a pan balance to model and solve the equation $11 = 8 + x$. Place 11 connecting cubes in the left pan of a pan balance. Place 8 connecting cubes in the right pan. Are the pans balanced? **Explain.**

_____

_____

_____

B. Use your pan balance to find the value of x in the equation. Add cubes to the right pan, one at a time, until the pans are balanced. What is the value of x?

_____

Complete the picture of the pan balance below by drawing blocks to show how you balanced the equation.

Make Connections

You can use what you have learned about the order of operations to simplify both sides of an equation before you model and solve the equation.

Example Use the pan balance to solve $4 + 2 \times 3 = 7 + y$.

STEP 1 Use the order of operations to simplify the equation.

$4 + 2 \times 3 = 7 + y$ Multiply first.

$4 + 6 = 7 + y$ Then add.

STEP 2 Model the equation.

$10 = 7 + y$

STEP 3 Solve the equation. Complete the pan balance picture by drawing squares to balance the equation.

$10 = 7 +$ _____ $y =$ _____

Share and Show

Use the pan balance to model and solve the equation.

1. $1 + b = 3 + 8$

$b =$ _____

2. $7 + 6 = 8 + k$

_____ $= k$

Math Talk
Mathematical Processes

How can you tell that your solution to an equation is correct?

Which value of *m*, 4, 8, or 10, makes the equation true?

3. $5 + 4 + 4 = 9 + m$

_____ $= m$

4. $3 + m + 2 = 7 + 4 + 2$

$m =$ _____

5. **H.O.T.** **Explain** why there is only one solution to the equation $8 = w + 5$.

_____

_____

Name _____

Problem Solving Real World

When two pans are balanced, the objects on the pans have the same weight. Use the pan balances to solve 6–8.

6.  **Multi-Step** Zane found the weight of 6 blocks on the first pan balance. He wants to find the weight of the green cylinder on the second pan balance. How can Zane find the weight of the green cylinder? What is the weight of the green cylinder? **Explain.**

   _____

   _____

   _____

   _____

   _____

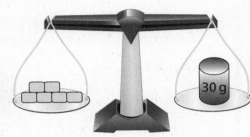

1 block = _____ grams

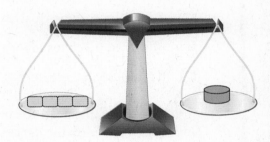

1 green cylinder = _____ grams

7. **Write Math** ▶ **What if** a pyramid and a block together have the same weight as 2 cylinders? How could Zane use the information from Problem 6 to find the weight of 1 pyramid? **Explain.**

   _____

   _____

   _____

Write Math ▶ **Show Your Work** · · · · · · · · ·

8. **What if** the weight on the right side of the first balance weighed the same as 3 blocks? What is the weight of one block? Of one green cylinder?

   _____

9.  **Multi-Step** Lucia placed 12 spheres on one side of a pan balance and 10 triangular prisms on the other side. Each side weighs 60 grams. What is the weight of one sphere? One triangular prism?

   _____

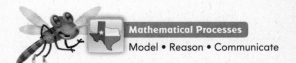
Daily Assessment Task

Fill in the bubble completely to show your answer.

10. **Reasoning** On the right side of a balance, there are two birds that each weigh 12 ounces. On the left side, there is a bird that weighs 14 ounces, and a bird with an unknown weight. If both sides of the balance have the same weight, how much does the unknown bird weigh?

Ⓐ 5 oz   Ⓒ 10 oz

Ⓑ 48 oz   Ⓓ 12 oz

11. **Use Tools** How would you balance the pan balance?

Ⓐ Take away 8 cubes from the left side of the balance.

Ⓑ Add 11 more cubes to the right side of the balance.

Ⓒ Add 27 more cubes to the right side of the balance.

Ⓓ It is already balanced.

12. **Multi-Step** Kevin placed 10 cubes on the right side of a pan balance. He placed 4 cubes on the left side. Then he doubled the number of cubes on the right side. Find the number of cubes that he must add to the left side to balance the pans.

Ⓐ 14   Ⓒ 16

Ⓑ 6   Ⓓ 24

 **TEXAS Test Prep**

13. What is the weight of 1 cube?

Ⓐ 28 ounces   Ⓒ 14 ounces

Ⓑ 10 ounces   Ⓓ 7 ounces

326

8.1 Equations

Use the pan balance to model and solve the equation.

1. $8 + 7 = 5 + x$

_____ $= x$

2. $2 + z = 4 + 10$

$z =$ _____

Which value of p, 4, 6, or 8, makes the equation true?

3. $6 + 4 + 3 = 7 + p$

_____ $= p$

4. $5 + p + 7 = 5 + 6 + 5$

$p =$ _____

Which value of g, 8, 9, or 10, makes the equation true?

5. $3 \times 2 + 4 = 2 + g$

_____ $= g$

6. $3 + 2 \times 6 = g + 5$

$g =$ _____

Problem Solving

7. Carlo places 8 apple slices on one side of a pan balance and 12 orange slices on the other side. Each side weighs 48 grams. What is the weight of one apple slice? One orange slice?

_____

8. On another pan balance, Carlo places 3 of the apple slices and 4 of the orange slices on the left side. He places 1 apple slice on the right side. How many orange slices will Carlo need to place on the right side so that pans are balanced?

_____

Fill in the bubble completely to show your answer.

9. How would you balance the pan balance?

   Ⓐ   Add 4 cubes to the left side of the balance.

   Ⓑ   Take away 4 cubes from the right side of the balance.

   Ⓒ   Move 4 cubes from the right side of the balance to the left side of the balance.

   Ⓓ   Move 8 cubes from the right side of the balance to the left side of the balance.

10. Brandy places weights measuring 1 gram, 5 grams, and 10 grams on the right side of a pan balance. She has a box of 2-gram weights and a box of 4-gram weights. Which combination of weights cannot be placed on the left side if Brandy wants the pans to balance?

   Ⓐ   four 4-gram weights

   Ⓑ   eight 2-gram weights

   Ⓒ   two 4-gram weights and four 2-gram weights

   Ⓓ   three 4-gram weights and one 2-gram weight

11. On the left side of a pan balance, there are two model cars that each weigh 8 ounces. On the right side, there is a model truck that weighs 12 ounces and a model car with an unknown weight. If both sides of the balance have the same weight, how much does the unknown model car weigh?

   Ⓐ 28 oz   Ⓒ 20 oz

   Ⓑ 4 oz   Ⓓ 8 oz

12. **Multi-Step** Casey placed 14 cubes on the right side of a pan balance. She placed 5 cubes on the left side. Then she removed half the cubes on the right side. Find the number of cubes that Casey must add to the left side to balance the pans.

   Ⓐ 9   Ⓒ 5

   Ⓑ 7   Ⓓ 2

13. **Multi-Step** The total weight of the shape blocks on both sides of Michael's pan balance equals 30 grams. Circles weigh 5 grams, squares weigh 10 grams, and triangles weigh 3 grams. The right side has a circle and a square. How many triangles are on the left side?

   Ⓐ 5   Ⓒ 6

   Ⓑ 4   Ⓓ 10

14. **Multi-Step** Will placed 12 cubes on the right side of a pan balance. He placed 3 cubes on the left side. Then he added 14 cubes on the left side. Find the number of cubes he must add to the right side to balance the pans.

   Ⓐ 5   Ⓒ 23

   Ⓑ 9   Ⓓ 3

Name _____

TEKS Algebraic Reasoning—5.4
MATHEMATICAL PROCESSES
5.1.A, 5.1.B, 5.1.E

Essential Question

How can you solve addition and subtraction equations?

Unlock the Problem

Yara is going camping in the Everglades National Park. Her backpack with camping gear weighs 17 pounds. When she adds her camera gear, the total weight of her backpack is 25 pounds. How much does Yara's camera gear weigh?

- What does the backpack weigh without the camera gear?

_____

- What do you need to find?

_____

🔑 **Write a related equation.**

The problem describes a part-part-whole relationship. A strip diagram can help you understand this relationship and write an equation. Let *c* represent the weight (in pounds) of the camera gear.

17	c

25

STEP 1

Use the strip diagram to write an equation.

Weight of   Total
the two parts   weight

$$17 + c = 25$$

STEP 2

Write a subtraction equation that is related to the addition equation.

Equation: _____

Subtract: $c =$ _____

So, Yara's camera gear weighs _____ pounds.

- **What if** Yara's backpack with camping gear weighs 15 pounds and the camera gear weighs 6 pounds? How much does her backpack with camping gear and camera gear weigh? How would the strip diagram above change?

_____

_____

Math Talk
Mathematical Processes

Explain how you can tell that your solution to an equation is true.

🔑 Example Use a related equation.

Kent has a collection of CDs. He gives 5 CDs to his brother. He then has 8 CDs left in his collection. How many CDs did Kent have before he gave some to his brother?

STEP 1 Draw a strip diagram.

- Write the missing labels in the strip diagram, where c is the number of CDs in Kent's collection before he gave some away.

- Use the model to write the equation.

Total number of CDs	Number given away	Number of CDs left

$$c \quad - \quad \rule{2cm}{0.4pt} \quad = \quad \rule{1.5cm}{0.4pt}.$$

- How many CDs did Kent give away?

  _____

- What operation will you use to show the CDs that Kent gave away?

  _____

_____
c

STEP 2 Use the strip diagram to write a related addition equation. Then add to solve.

Equation: _____

Add: $c =$ _____

So, Kent had _____ CDs before he gave some away.

Share and Show

MATH BOARD

Use the strip diagram to write an equation. Then solve.

✓ 1. Janine went to the beach 22 times during July and August. Six of those times were in August. How many times did she go in July?

6	d

22

Equation: _____ _____ $= d$

✓ 2. Ariana has some crayons and her friend has 7 fewer crayons. If her friend has 15 crayons, how many crayons, c, does Ariana have?

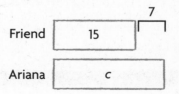

Friend | 15 | 7

Ariana | c

Equation: _____ $c =$ _____

3. **Explain** how a strip diagram helps you understand the problem and write an equation.

_____

_____

_____

Name _____

 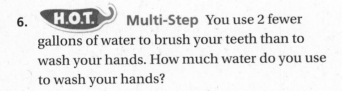
Use the bar graph to solve 4–6. Draw a strip diagram to write each equation. Then solve.

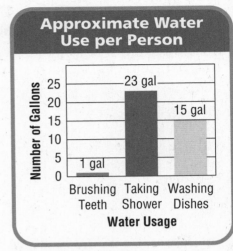

Approximate Water Use per Person

4. **H.O.T.** **Multi-Step** Taking a shower uses about 13 fewer gallons of water than taking a bath. About how many gallons of water are used for taking a bath?

   In your equation, let b represent the number of gallons of water needed for a bath.

   _____

5. **H.O.T.** **Multi-Step** Stephan did some chores before heading to practice. He washed the dishes and washed a load of laundry. He used about 44 gallons of water in all. How many gallons of water did he use to wash a load of laundry?

   In your equation, let w represent the number of gallons of water needed for a load of laundry.

   _____

Write Math ▶ **Show Your Work**

6. **H.O.T.** **Multi-Step** You use 2 fewer gallons of water to brush your teeth than to wash your hands. How much water do you use to wash your hands?

   In your equation, let h represent the number of gallons of water used to wash your hands.

   _____

7. **Apply** Wes had some money in his wallet and $39 in his pocket. He had $76 in all. He could represent his money by using the equation $39 + m = 76$. How much did Wes have in his wallet?

   _____

Daily Assessment Task

Fill in the bubble completely to show your answer.

8. Stan spent $18 on giant carrots at the Giant Vegetable Store. He also bought a bag of giant peas, but the bag had no price tag. Stan was charged a total of $23. Which equation can help you find the cost of the peas?

Ⓐ $18 + 23 = p$

Ⓑ $18 - 23 = p$

Ⓒ $18 + p = 23$

Ⓓ $23 + p = 18$

9. **Representations** Morgan has 28 pieces of jewelry, 10 of which are necklaces. The rest of the jewelry pieces are bracelets. Which equation can you use to find the number of bracelets, b, she has?

Ⓐ $b = 10 - 28$

Ⓑ $b = 28 - 10$

Ⓒ $28 = b - 10$

Ⓓ $10 = b + 28$

10. **Multi-Step** Joseph bought 5 folders for school that cost $3 each. He also bought a new backpack. If the total cost was $35, how much did the backpack cost?

Ⓐ $5

Ⓑ $15

Ⓒ $20

Ⓓ $50

⭐TEXAS Test Prep

11. A football team scored 16 points, which was 12 fewer points than their opponents scored. How many points, y, did their opponents score?

Ⓐ $y = 24$ Ⓒ $y = 4$

Ⓑ $y = 28$ Ⓓ $y = 18$

8.2 Addition and Subtraction Equations

Use the strip diagram to write an equation. Then solve.

1. Kiki had 17 mystery books. She got some more mystery books as a gift. Now she has a total of 21 mystery books. How many books did Kiki receive as a gift?

17	p

21

Equation: _____ _____ $= p$

2. Joe scored 45 points. He scored 12 fewer points than Randy. How points did Randy score?

Joe | 45 | 12 |

Randy | s |

Equation: _____ $s =$ _____

3. The pet store had some goldfish. Eight goldfish were sold. There are 28 goldfish left. How many goldfish did the pet store have before some were sold?

8	28

f

Equation: _____ $f =$ _____

4. Joaquin and Erik worked together on a project. Erik worked 13 hours. Together, they worked 22 hours. How many hours did Joaquin work?

13	h

22

Equation: _____ _____ $= h$

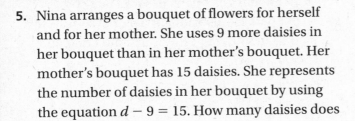

Problem Solving Real World

5. Nina arranges a bouquet of flowers for herself and for her mother. She uses 9 more daisies in her bouquet than in her mother's bouquet. Her mother's bouquet has 15 daisies. She represents the number of daisies in her bouquet by using the equation $d - 9 = 15$. How many daisies does Nina's bouquet have?

_____

6. Kierra has 49 pennies in a drawer and some pennies in a jar. She has 81 pennies in all. She represents the number of pennies by using the equation $49 + j = 81$. How many pennies does Kierra have in the jar?

_____

Lesson Check

Fill in the bubble completely to show your answer.

7. Last weekend, Ryan earned $27 babysitting. He earned $19 on Friday and the rest of the money on Saturday. Which equation can you use to find the amount, m, Ryan earned on Saturday?

Ⓐ $m = \$27 + \$19$

Ⓑ $\$19 = m + \$27$

Ⓒ $\$27 = m - \$19$

Ⓓ $m = \$27 - \$19$

8. Fatima used a coupon to pay for a pair of jeans. The original price of the jeans was $25. The coupon reduced the price to $16. Which equation can you use to help you find the value of the coupon?

Ⓐ $\$16 + c = \$25$

Ⓑ $\$25 + \$16 = c$

Ⓒ $\$25 + c = \$16$

Ⓓ $\$16 - c = \$25$

9. Hailey received 33 text messages on Saturday, which were 18 fewer messages than she received on Sunday. How many text messages, t, did Hailey receive on Sunday?

Ⓐ $t = 15$

Ⓑ $t = 25$

Ⓒ $t = 51$

Ⓓ $t = 41$

10. At the second bus stop, 26 people got off the bus, which were 9 more than the number of people that got off at the first bus stop. How many people, p, got off the bus at the first stop?

Ⓐ $p = 17$

Ⓑ $p = 35$

Ⓒ $p = 23$

Ⓓ $p = 15$

11. **Multi-Step** There were 14 dogs adopted from the animal shelter last week. This week, 8 dogs were adopted. There are 5 dogs left. How many dogs, d, did the shelter have for adoption?

Ⓐ $d = 27$

Ⓑ $d = 22$

Ⓒ $d = 13$

Ⓓ $d = 17$

12. **Multi-Step** Lorenzo spent $47 at the shoe store. He bought 3 pairs of socks that cost $6 per pair. He also bought a pair of shoes. He paid $4 in sales tax. How much did Lorenzo's shoes, s, cost?

Ⓐ $s = \$25$

Ⓑ $s = \$22$

Ⓒ $s = \$34$

Ⓓ $s = \$29$

8.3 Multiplication and Division Equations

TEKS Algebraic Reasoning—5.4.B

MATHEMATICAL PROCESSES
5.1.F, 5.1.G

? Essential Question

How can you model and solve multiplication and division equations?

Unlock the Problem

Jake is buying a movie ticket and a box of popcorn for $12. The ticket costs 2 times as much as the popcorn. How much does the popcorn cost? How much does the ticket cost?

The cost of the ticket is $2 \times p$, where p is the price of the popcorn.

● How does knowing that a ticket costs 2 times as much as the popcorn help you choose an operation to write an expression?

_____

_____

🔑 Use a related equation.

STEP 1

Complete the strip diagram to represent the popcorn and ticket cost.

The popcorn costs p. Label the strip for the popcorn. It represents 1 unit.

The cost of the ticket is _____ times as much. Label the strips for the ticket.

What is the total cost? _____

How many units are shown in the model? _____

Popcorn [_____]

Ticket [_____ | _____]

Popcorn and ticket [_____]

Popcorn: 1 unit = _____

Popcorn + ticket: 3 units = _____

STEP 2

Use the strip diagram to write a multiplication equation.

$$\underset{\text{Cost of popcorn and ticket}}{3 \times p} = \underset{\text{Total cost}}{\rule{2cm}{0.4pt}}$$

To find a missing factor, write a division equation that is related to the multiplication equation. Then divide.

$$\rule{2cm}{0.4pt} \div 3 = p \qquad \rule{2cm}{0.4pt} = p$$

So, 1 bag of popcorn costs _____.

The cost of 1 ticket is 2 times the cost of 1 bag of popcorn.

So, 1 ticket costs _____.

Math Idea

You can write $3 \times p$ as $3 \times p$, $3p$, $3(p)$, or $3 \cdot p$.

Example Use a related equation.

Katrina buys a package of trading cards. She divides the cards
into 4 equal piles. Each pile contains 12 cards. The equation
that describes the number of cards in the package is $c \div 4 = 12$.
How many cards were in the package when Katrina bought it?

  Write a related equation.

MODEL

- Use a strip diagram to represent the
  problem.

  c

  | 12 | 12 | 12 | 12 |

So, the package Katrina bought had _____ trading cards in it.

SOLVE

- Write a related multiplication equation.

  Multiplication equation: _____

  $c = $ _____

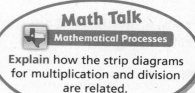
Math Talk
Mathematical Processes

Explain how the strip diagrams
for multiplication and division
are related.

Share and Show

MATH BOARD

Use the strip diagrams to write an equation. Then solve.

1. The cost of 3 pencils is 96 cents. Each pencil
costs the same. What is the cost of 1 pencil, p?

| p | p | p |

96

Equation: _____ = 96 $p =$ _____

One pencil costs _____ cents.

2. A gardener is planting 6 rows of spring bulbs.
Each row has 15 bulbs. How many bulbs is he
planting? Let b equal the total number of bulbs.

| 15 | 15 | 15 | 15 | 15 | 15 |

b

Equation: _____ $b =$ _____

He is planting _____ bulbs.

Problem Solving

Practice: Copy and Solve Use a strip diagram or a related equation
to solve. Check your solution.

3. $128 = 8 \times d$ **4.** $r \div 9 = 17$ **5.** $6m = 78$ **6.** $7 = b \div 17$

7. Write Math ▶ How can you justify that $j = 348$ is the solution
to $j \div 12 = 29$? **Explain.**

Name _____

Use the table to complete 8–9. Use a strip diagram to write each equation. Then solve.

Snack Bar Menu	
Large Popcorn	$8
Medium Drink	$5
Fruit Snack	$4
Yogurt Bars	$3
Family Combo	$18

8. **Multi-Step** On Friday, the snack bar made $992 selling large buckets of popcorn. How many large buckets of popcorn did the snack bar sell on Friday?

   In your equation, let p represent the number of large buckets of popcorn sold.

   _____

9. **H.O.T. Multi-Step** On Thursday, the snack bar made total of $340 in medium drink sales and a total of $216 in yogurt bar sales. Which item did the snack bar sell more of on Thursday? **Explain** how you found your answer.

   _____

   _____

   _____

   _____

Write Math ▶ Show Your Work

10. **H.O.T. Multi-Step** Asher wants to buy a video game console. In order to save the money needed to buy it in 5 months, he divides the cost by 5. He finds he needs to save $37 a month. What is the total cost, c, of the game console?

   _____

   _____

11. **Representations** Mariah bought a bag of buttons. She divides the buttons equally among 15 containers. Each container has 10 buttons. How many buttons does Mariah have?

   In your equation, let b represent the number of buttons Mariah has.

   _____

Daily Assessment Task

Fill in the bubble completely to show your answer.

12. Mr. Tune took a vacation to Neptune. His vacation lasted for 144 hours. A day on Neptune lasts for 16 hours. Which equation and solution shows how many days Mr. Tune's vacation lasted?

(A) $16d = 144$; $d = 9$

(B) $d = 16 \times 144$; $d = 2{,}304$

(C) $16 + d = 144$; $d = 128$

(D) $d = 16 + 144$; $d = 160$

13. Which equation does the strip diagram represent?

12	12	12	12	12	12

a

(A) $6a = 12$ (C) $12a = 6$

(B) $a \div 6 = 12$ (D) $a + 6 = 12$

14. **Multi-Step** Noah bought 5 CDs and a DVD for a total of $57. The DVD cost $12. The CDs were each the same price. How much did Noah pay for each CD?

(A) $12   (C) $11

(B) $15   (D) $9

⭐ TEXAS Test Prep

15. Rick earned $133 for 7 hours of work. How much does Rick earn per hour? The equation $7p = 133$ can be used to find p, the amount Rick earns per hour.

(A) $19

(B) $6

(C) $931

(D) $69

8.3 Multiplication and Division Equations

Use a strip diagram or a related equation to solve.

Check your solution.

1. $c \div 5 = 13$

2. $112 = 7 \times b$

3. $4p = 68$

4. $9 = d \div 21$

5. $105 = 3 \times a$

6. $9g = 99$

7. $m \div 10 = 16$

8. $22 = n \div 7$

9. $92 = f \times 4$

10. $h \div 9 = 14$

11. $13 = j \div 8$

12. $165 = 11r$

Problem Solving

13. Sierra arranges fabric squares to sew together to make a blanket for her baby sister. She divides the fabric squares equally among 12 rows. Each row has 8 squares. How many fabric squares does Sierra have?

In your equation, let f represent the number of fabric squares Sierra has.

_____

14. A school district purchased 90 new computers. The computers were divided equally among 6 classrooms. How many new computers are in each classroom?

In your equation, let c represent the number of computers in each classroom.

_____

15. Write a real-world problem for the equation $4 \times y = 60$. Then solve.

_____

_____

_____

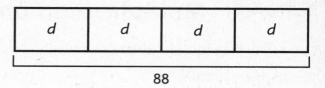
Fill in the bubble completely to show your answer.

16. Which equation does the strip diagram represent?

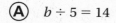

| 14 | 14 | 14 | 14 | 14 |

b

(A) $b \div 5 = 14$

(B) $14b = 5$

(C) $14 \div 5 = b$

(D) $5b = 14$

17. Which equation does the strip diagram represent?

| d | d | d | d |

88

(A) $d + 4 = 88$

(B) $d \div 4 = 88$

(C) $4d = 88$

(D) $d = 4 \times 88$

18. Dori earned 95 points on her science test. She received 5 points for each question she answered correctly. How many questions did Dori answer correctly? The equation $5q = 95$ can be used to find q, the number of questions answered correctly.

(A) 100

(B) 90

(C) 19

(D) 11

19. The Adams family drove 270 miles to reach their vacation destination. If they drove 45 miles each hour, how many hours did they drive? Which equation can you use to represent the problem?

(A) $h = 270 \times 45$

(B) $270 = 45h$

(C) $45 \div h = 270$

(D) $h + 45 = 270$

20. Multi-Step The movie theater has 176 seats. There are 9 rows of 18 seats plus an additional section of handicapped accessible seats. Write and solve an equation to find the number of handicapped accessible seats in the theater.

(A) 9

(B) 14

(C) 4

(D) 12

21. Multi-Step Sergei had $75 when he arrived at the mall. He spent $9 at the food court. Then he bought 3 posters that each cost the same amount. Sergei has $27 left. Write and solve an equation to find the cost of one poster.

(A) $9

(B) $3

(C) $13

(D) $7

8.4 Represent and Solve Multi-Step Problems

TEKS Algebraic Reasoning—5.4.B
MATHEMATICAL PROCESSES
5.1.B, 5.1.D

? Essential Question

How can you represent and solve multi-step problems using equations?

Unlock the Problem Real World

Shaniqua buys 140 small beads and 30 large beads to make bracelets. She makes 5 bracelets. She uses 13 beads on each bracelet. How many beads does Shaniqua have left?

• Underline the important information.

Example 1 Use multiple single-step equations.

STEP 1 Find the total number of beads Shaniqua buys.

total number of small beads   total number of large beads

$a \longleftarrow$ total number of beads Shaniqua buys

$140 + 30 = a$

_____ $= a$

STEP 2 Find the total number of beads Shaniqua uses to make 5 bracelets.

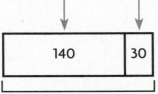 $\longleftarrow$ 5 bracelets with 13 beads

$d \longleftarrow$ total number of beads Shaniqua uses

$5 \times 13 = d$

_____ $= d$

STEP 3 Find the total number of beads Shaniqua has left.

beads left   beads used

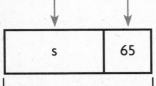

170 $\longleftarrow$ total number of beads Shaniqua buys

$170 - 65 = s$

_____ $= s$

So, Shaniqua has _____ beads left.

Try This! Sometimes you can use one multi-step equation to solve a problem.

Miguel sorts his seashell collection into boxes. He has 3 boxes with 15 periwinkle shells in each box. He has 2 boxes with 7 clamshells in each box. He gives his little brother 10 shells. How many shells does he have now?

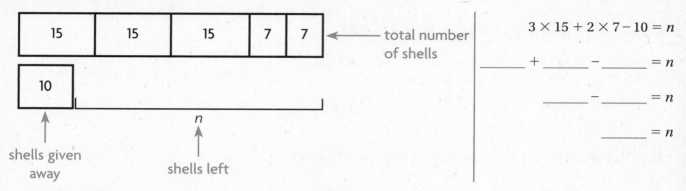

$3 \times 15 + 2 \times 7 - 10 = n$

_____ + _____ − _____ = n

_____ − _____ = n

_____ = n

← total number of shells

shells given away

shells left

🔑 Example 2

Meagan has two card-collection books. The first book has 8 cards on each of 14 pages. The second book has 6 cards on each of 15 pages. Which of the two books has more cards?

STEP 1 Solve the equation $b \div 8 = 14$ to find the number of cards in the first book.

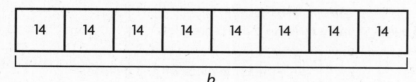

Write a related multiplication equation.

$14 \times$ _____ $= b$ $b =$ _____

STEP 2 Solve the equation $p \div 6 = 15$ to find the number of cards in the second book.

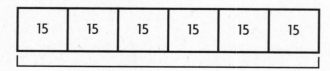

Write a related multiplication equation.

$15 \times$ _____ $= p$ $p =$ _____

STEP 3 Compare the number of cards in each book.

The first book has _____ cards.

The second book has _____ cards.

Since _____ > _____, the _____ book has more cards.

Math Talk

Mathematical Processes

Explain why you can use a related multiplication to solve a division problem.

Name _____

Use equations to solve each multi-step problem.

1. A caterer is making 3 trays of 24 sandwiches and 2 trays of 30 sandwiches. She receives an order for 35 sandwiches. How many sandwiches, s, does the caterer have left?

2. A baseball league has a total of 156 players. The players are divided into 12 equal teams. Each team has 3 coaches. All players and coaches receive 2 jerseys. How many jerseys, j, will each team receive?

Problem Solving
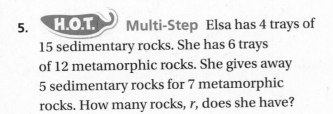

Write Math ▶ **Show Your Work** · · · · · · · ·

Use equations to solve.

3. **Multi-Step** A florist makes 4 floral arrangements that are exactly the same. He uses 4 bunches of 8 tulips and 2 bunches of 10 daisies. How many flowers, f, are in each arrangement?

4. **H.O.T.** **Multi-Step** Francois is rolling coins. He has 3 rolls of 40 quarters. He has 8 rolls of 50 dimes. He exchanges 2 rolls of dimes for 1 roll of quarters. How many coins, c, does Francois have?

5. **H.O.T.** **Multi-Step** Elsa has 4 trays of 15 sedimentary rocks. She has 6 trays of 12 metamorphic rocks. She gives away 5 sedimentary rocks for 7 metamorphic rocks. How many rocks, r, does she have?

6. **Analyze** Murial alternates her exercise. She runs 5 miles each day for 3 days and walks 4 miles each day for 2 days in one week. She rides her bike 8 miles each day for 4 days the next week. How many more miles, m, does Murial travel during the second week than the first week?

Daily Assessment Task

Fill in the bubble completely to show your answer.

7. **Apply** A volunteer took 3 cups and 7 quarts of a large bowl of soup home from a cooking class.. How much soup did this volunteer take? (Hint: There are 4 cups in a quart.)

   (A) 31 cups

   (B) 37 cups

   (C) 31 quarts

   (D) 42 quarts

8. What is the first step in solving the equation $4 + 10 \times 3 - 2 = n$?

   (A) Find $4 + 10$.

   (B) Find $3 - 2$.

   (C) Find 10×3.

   (D) Subtract n.

9. **Multi-Step** Evelyn has 4 boxes with 8 pieces of sidewalk chalk in each box. She has 3 boxes with 9 stickers in each box. She gets 5 more pieces of sidewalk chalk from her brother. If she places everything into a bin, how many items does she place in the bin?

   (A) 24

   (B) 55

   (C) 64

   (D) 72

⭐ TEXAS Test Prep

10. The cost of 3 pizzas is shared equally by 6 people. Each pizza costs $9. Each person contributes $5. Which equation could be used to find, m, the amount of money left?

   (A) $3 \times 9 - 6 \times 5 = m$

   (C) $6 \times 5 - 3 \times 9 = m$

   (B) $9 \div 3 - 6 \times 5 = m$

   (D) $3 \times 9 + 5 \times 6 = m$

344

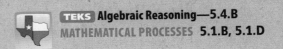
8.4 Represent and Solve Multi-Step Problems

Use equations to solve.

1. Last week, Mary picked 4 baskets of 8 tomatoes from her garden. This week, she picked 3 baskets of 13 tomatoes. How many more tomatoes, t, does Mary pick this week than last week?

2. A costume designer sews 4 rows of 16 beads on a princess costume, 5 rows of 15 beads on a butterfly costume, and 3 rows of 17 beads on a ballerina costume. How many more beads, b, are sewn on the costume with the most beads than are sewn on the costume with the least number of beads?

3. Venancio needs to paint 8 game boards for the carnival. Each game board is divided into 12 parts. He paints 5 parts of 8 game boards yellow, 3 parts of 6 game boards red, 2 parts of 7 game boards green, and 15 parts purple. How many more parts, p, does Venancio have left to paint?

4. Mr. Gates buys frozen yogurt bars for the grade 5 picnic. He buys 3 packages of 12 strawberry yogurt bars and 6 packages of 8 banana yogurt bars. He gives an equal number of frozen yogurt bars to each of 3 classes. How many frozen yogurt bars, y, does each class get?

Problem Solving

5. Rusty has a cap collection. He has 2 shelves with 9 football team caps on each shelf. He has 3 shelves with 11 baseball caps on each shelf. He gives his best friend 2 football caps and 3 baseball caps. How many caps, c, does Rusty have now?

6. Erin pays $3 for each of 4 headbands and $2 for each of 5 barrettes. How much more money, m, does Erin pay for all the headbands than for all the barrettes?

Fill in the bubble completely to show your answer.

7. Marty is using balloons to decorate for a party. She has 3 groups of 5 pink balloons and 4 groups of 3 yellow balloons. She also has 6 white balloons. Which equation could be used to find, b, the total number of balloons?

   (A) $3 \times 5 + 4 \times 3 = b$

   (B) $3 + 5 + 4 + 3 + 6 = b$

   (C) $3 \times 5 + 4 \times 3 + 6 = b$

   (D) $3 \times 5 \times 4 \times 3 = b$

8. For the bake sale, 6 people each bake two dozen oatmeal cookies. Each person eats 2 cookies and then delivers the remaining cookies to the bake sale. Which equation could be used to find, c, the number of oatmeal cookies at the bake sale?

   (A) $6 \times 2 \times 12 - 6 \times 2 = c$

   (B) $6 \times 12 - 6 \times 2 = c$

   (C) $2 \times 12 - 6 \times 2 = c$

   (D) $6 \times 2 - 6 \times 2 = c$

9. Jasper used 15 inches of blue ribbon, 14 inches of yellow ribbon, and 3 feet of red ribbon to decorate his box of cookies. How many inches of ribbon did Jasper use?

   (A) 65 inches

   (B) 32 inches

   (C) 93 inches

   (D) 29 inches

10. William used 10 ounces of plain milk and 4 pints of chocolate milk when making the restaurant milkshake recipe. How many ounces of milk did William use? (Hint: there are 16 ounces in a pint.)

    (A) 64 ounces

    (B) 40 ounces

    (C) 26 ounces

    (D) 74 ounces

11. **Multi-Step** Rona has 4 packs of 12 glitter pens. She has 7 packs of 8 scented pens. She gives her friend a pack of glitter pens in exchange for a new pack of scented pens. How many pens does Rona have now?

    (A) 92

    (B) 104

    (C) 100

    (D) 112

12. **Multi-Step** Bella has potted plants on her patio. She has 4 pots with 3 begonia plants in each pot. She has 3 pots with 8 petunias in each pot. She plants 7 more zinnia plants in another pot. How many plants does Bella have on her patio?

    (A) 25

    (B) 43

    (C) 36

    (D) 57

Module 8 Assessment

Concepts and Skills

1. Which value of n makes the equation, $n + 5 = 4 + 4$, true? ⬆TEKS 5.4.B

_____

Use the strip diagram to write an equation. Then solve. ⬆TEKS 5.4

2. Eric jogged 15 laps around a track. Margo jogged 5 laps. How many more laps did Eric jog than Margo?

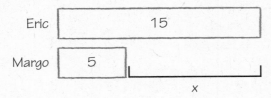

| Eric | 15 |
| Margo | 5 |

Equation: _____ $x =$ _____

3. Sadie hit 17 golf balls from her bucket. Then there were 33 golf balls left in the bucket. How many golf balls did Sadie have in her bucket before she hit any golf balls?

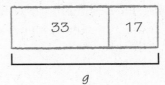

| 33 | 17 |

g

Equation: _____ $g =$ _____

Write an equation. Then solve. ⬆TEKS 5.4.B

4. A store sells 8 small, 18 medium, and 20 large sweatshirts. Each sweatshirt costs $16. How much money, m, is the store paid for all the sweatshirts they sell?

_____

5. A caterer makes sandwiches from 8 loaves of bread. Each loaf makes 10 sandwiches. The caterer puts 3 ounces of turkey on each sandwich. How many ounces, z, of turkey does the caterer use?

_____

6. A train has 34 passengers in each of 3 cars and 28 passengers in each of 4 cars. How many passengers, p, are on the train?

_____

7. There are 252 students at a school party. They are seated in groups of 9. Each group gets 3 bags of popcorn. How many bags of popcorn, p, are used for the party?

_____

8. Ryan has 5 boxes with 8 markers in each box. He has 7 boxes with 10 markers in each box. He gives his friend one box of 8 markers and one box of 10 markers. Which equation can be used to find the total number of markers, m, that Ryan has left? ⬇ TEKS 5.4.B

Ⓐ $7 \times 10 - 5 \times 8 - 8 - 10 = m$

Ⓑ $8 - 5 \times 8 + 10 - 7 \times 10 = m$

Ⓒ $5 \times 8 \div 7 \times 10 - 8 - 10 = m$

Ⓓ $5 \times 8 + 7 \times 10 - 8 - 10 = m$

9. Thora had $5 left in her pocket after spending $12 on snacks and souvenirs on a class trip. How much money did Thora take on the class trip? The equation $t - 12 = 5$ can be used to find t, the amount of money Thora took on the class trip. ⬇ TEKS 5.4

Ⓐ $17   Ⓒ $7

Ⓑ $14   Ⓓ $16

10. Students earned $368 selling c, calendars. They earned $456 selling m, mugs. The price of each mug and each calendar is $8. The equation $c = 368 \div 8$ represents the number of calendars they sold. The equation $m = 456 \div 8$ represents the number of mugs they sold. How many more mugs than calendars did students sell? ⬇ TEKS 5.4.B

Ⓐ 57

Ⓑ 103

Ⓒ 11

Ⓓ 46

11. There are 180 students at summer camp. Each cabin houses 12 students. There are 2 counselors for each cabin. Solve the equation $c = (180 \div 12) \times 2$ to find the number of c, counselors. ⬇ TEKS 5.4.B

Record your answer and fill in the bubbles on the grid. Be sure to use the correct place value.

⓪	⓪	⓪	.	⓪	⓪
①	①	①		①	①
②	②	②		②	②
③	③	③		③	③
④	④	④		④	④
⑤	⑤	⑤		⑤	⑤
⑥	⑥	⑥		⑥	⑥
⑦	⑦	⑦		⑦	⑦
⑧	⑧	⑧		⑧	⑧
⑨	⑨	⑨		⑨	⑨

Name _____

9.1 Formulas for Area and Perimeter

? **Essential Question** How can you use formulas to find the area and perimeter of shapes?

🔑 Unlock the Problem (Real World)

A **formula** is an equation that expresses a mathematical rule. You can use formulas to find the perimeter and area of rectangles.

Lloyd is planting a rectangular garden that measures 40 feet by 24 feet. He wants to put a fence around it to protect his vegetables from rabbits. How many feet of fencing does he need?

 Use a formula to find the perimeter.

$P = l + w + l + w$ ____ P = perimeter; l = length; w = width

$P = 40 +$ _____ $+$ _____ $+$ _____ ____ Replace the unknowns with the lengths and the widths.

$P =$ _____ ____ Add.

The perimeter is _____ feet. So, Lloyd needs _____ feet of fencing.

Lloyd needs to find how large his garden is so he can order enough mulch for the garden. What is the area of Lloyd's garden?

> **Remember**
> Area is measured in square units, such as square feet or sq ft.

 Use a formula to find the area.

$A = l \times w$ ____ A = area; l = length; w = width

$A =$ _____ $\times$ _____ ____ Replace the unknowns with the length and the width.

$A =$ _____ ____ Multiply.

So, the area of Lloyd's garden is _____ square feet.

Try This!

You can also use the formula $P = 2l + 2w$ to find the perimeter. What is the perimeter of a rectangle that is 12 feet long and 16 feet wide?

$P = 2 \times$ _____ $+ 2 \times$ _____ ____ Replace the unknowns with the length and the width.

$P =$ _____

The perimeter is _____ feet.

> **Math Talk**
> **Mathematical Processes**
> Explain how you can use the properties of operations to rewrite $P = l + w + l + w$ as $P = 2l + 2w$.

You can find the area of complex figures by separating them into two or more simpler shapes.

Example Find the area.

STEP 1 Separate the figure into a rectangle and a square.

STEP 2 Find the area of the rectangle.

$A = l \times w$

$A =$ _____

$A =$ _____

The area of the rectangle is _____ square meters.

STEP 3 Find the area of the square.

$A =$ _____

$A =$ _____

$A =$ _____

The area of the square is _____ square meters.

STEP 4 Find the area of the complex figure by adding the areas.

$A =$ _____ + _____

$A =$ _____

So, the area of the complex figure is _____ square meters.

Share and Show

MATH BOARD

✓ **1.** Find the perimeter of the square.

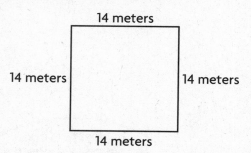

14 meters
14 meters   14 meters
14 meters

$P =$ _____ + _____ + _____ + _____

$P =$ _____

The perimeter is _____ meters.

✓ **2.** Find the area of the rectangle.

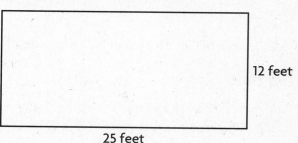

12 feet

25 feet

$A =$ _____ × _____

$A =$ _____

The area is _____ square feet.

Problem Solving

3. **H.O.T.** **Explain** how you can use *s* to write the formula for the perimeter of a square with side length *s*.

_____

_____

4. **H.O.T.** A rectangle has an area of 96 square feet. If the length of the rectangle is 12 feet, what is the width of the rectangle?

_____

_____

_____

Problem Solving Real World

5. Brent plans to stain a deck that is 14 feet by 8 feet. If one can of stain covers an area of 100 square feet, how many cans of stain will he need? **Explain**.

_____

_____

6. **H.O.T.** **Multi-Step** Latoya uses 50 feet of wood to make a rectangular garden bed. If the length of the garden bed is 10 feet, what is the width?

_____

_____

_____

7. **H.O.T.** **What's the Error?** Maggie wants to fence off two side-by-side sections of her garden. Each section is 14 feet long and 6 feet wide. She says she needs 80 feet of fencing. **Explain** what is wrong with her thinking. How much fencing does she really need?

_____

_____

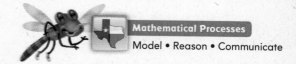

Daily Assessment Task

Fill in the bubble for the correct answer choice.

8. **Apply** Tina is fixing a rectangular sign. She plans to place metal trim around the sign edges. The rectangle measures 32 inches by 9 inches. How much trim will Tina need?

Ⓐ 36 inches

Ⓑ 41 inches

Ⓒ 72 inches

Ⓓ 82 inches

9. A rectangle has a length of 5 meters and a width of 4 meters. Which equation can you use to find the perimeter?

Ⓐ $P = 4 \times 5$

Ⓑ $P = 4 \times 4$

Ⓒ $P = 4 + 4 + 5 + 5$

Ⓓ $P = 4 + 5$

10. **Multi-Step** Lana had an "L" shaped piece of felt. Her mom cut it into two rectangles. One rectangle measured 4 inches by 9 inches, and the other measured 4 inches by 3 inches. What is the total area of the two rectangles?

Ⓐ 40 square inches

Ⓑ 48 square inches

Ⓒ 72 square inches

Ⓓ 24 square inches

⭐ TEXAS Test Prep

11. Mai wants to tile the floor of her kitchen. Each tile has an area of 1 square foot. The floor of her kitchen is 11 feet by 16 feet. How many tiles does she need?

Ⓐ 150

Ⓑ 54

Ⓒ 176

Ⓓ 352

Name _____

9.2 Formulas for Volume

TEKS Algebraic
Reasoning—5.4.G
Also 5.6.A, 5.6.B
MATHEMATICAL PROCESSES
5.1.B, 5.1.D, 5.1.E

? Essential Question

How can you use formulas to find the volume of rectangular prisms?

Connect The base of a rectangular prism is a rectangle. You know that area is measured in square units, and that the area of a rectangle can be found by multiplying the length and the width.

Volume is the measure of the amount of space a solid figure occupies. Volume is measured in **cubic units**, such as cubic feet or cu ft. When you build a prism and add each layer of cubes, you are adding a third dimension, height.

The area of the base

is _____ sq units.

🔑 🔒 Unlock the Problem (Real World)

Margo is modeling a building using 1-centimeter cubes. The model has a rectangular base and a height of the 5 cubes. What is the volume of the rectangular prism that Margo built?

Use centimeter cubes to show Margo's model. Count the total number of cubes after each layer. Use the information to complete the table.

Height (in layers)	1	2	3	4	5
Volume (in cubic centimeters)	8	16			

+8
+8
+8
+8
8

- What multiplication pattern do the numbers in the table show?

_____

- Why do we multiply by 8?

_____

You can find the volume of a prism in cubic units by multiplying the number of square units in the base shape by the number of layers, or its height.

- Write a formula for finding the volume of a rectangular prism. Use *B* for the area of the base and *h* for the height.

_____

So, the volume of Margo's rectangular prism is _____ cubic centimeters.

Relate Height to Volume

You can use the formula for the area of a rectangle to rewrite the formula for the volume of a rectangular prism.

- What are the dimensions of the base of the box?

_____

- What operation can you use to find the area of the base shape?

_____

Toni stacks cube-shaped beads that measure 1 centimeter on each edge in a storage box. The box can hold 6 layers of 24 cubes with no gaps or overlaps. What is the volume of Toni's storage box?

 One Way Use $V = Bh$.

The volume of each bead is _____ cubic cm.

The storage box has a base with an area of _____ square cm.

The height of the storage box is _____ centimeters.

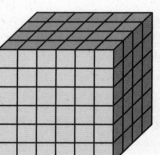

The volume of the storage box is

(_____ × _____), or _____ cubic cm.
   Base area

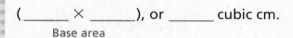 Another Way Use length, width, and height.

The base is a rectangle. Replace B with an expression for the area of the base shape.

$V = B \times h$ B = base area; l = length; w = width

$V = ($_____ × _____$) \times h$
    Base area

The base has a length of _____ centimeters

and a width of _____ centimeters. The height

is _____ centimeters. The volume of the storage box is

(_____ × _____) × _____ , or _____ × _____ , or _____ cubic cm.
  Base area

So, the volume of Toni's storage box is _____ cubic cm.

> **Math Talk**
> **Mathematical Processes**
>
> **Describe** one way you can check if the volume you calculated using the formulas is correct.

Name _____

Find the volume.

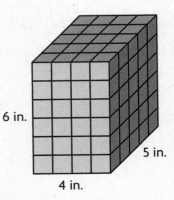

1. The length of the rectangular prism is _____.

   The width is _____. So, the area of the base is _____.

   The height is _____. So, the volume of the prism is _____.

6 in.

5 in.

4 in.

2.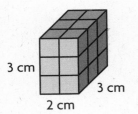

3 cm

3 cm

2 cm

Volume: _____

3.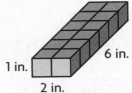

1 in.

6 in.

2 in.

Volume: _____

Problem Solving

4. **H.O.T.** **Connect** What happens to the volume of a rectangular prism if you double the height? Give an example.

_____

5. **H.O.T.** **Write Math** ▶ **Explain** how the two formulas for the volume of a rectangular prism $V = Bh$ and $V = l \times w \times h$ are related. Use a model with centimeter cubes to justify your reasoning.

_____

_____

Problem Solving Real World

6. **H.O.T.** **Multi-Step** Rich is building a travel crate for his dog, Thomas, a beagle-mix who is about 30 inches long, 12 inches wide, and 24 inches tall. For Thomas to travel safely, his crate needs to be a rectangular prism that is about 12 inches greater than his length and width, and 6 inches greater than his height. What is the volume of the travel crate that Rich should build?

_____

_____

Daily Assessment Task

Fill in the bubble completely to show your answer.

7. Sandra orders a box of cube-shaped beads. The beads are neatly stacked in layers, with the same number of beads in each layer. Each layer is 12 beads across and 7 beads wide. There are 4 layers. How many beads does she receive?

Ⓐ 23 beads Ⓒ 76 beads

Ⓑ 336 beads Ⓓ 88 beads

8. Which equation can you use to find the number of cubes in the rectangular prism?

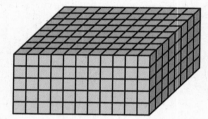

Ⓐ $V = 11 \times 8 \times 5$ Ⓒ $V = 11 \times 8 + 5$

Ⓑ $V = 11 + 8 + 5$ Ⓓ $V = 2(11 \times 8 \times 5)$

9. **Multi-Step** How many cubic units of material were used to make the two rectangular prisms?

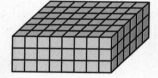 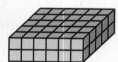

Ⓐ 144 cubic units Ⓒ 8,640 cubic units

Ⓑ 60 cubic units Ⓓ 204 cubic units

 TEXAS Test Prep

10. What is the volume of the rectangular prism at the right?

Ⓐ 125 cu in. Ⓒ 155 cu in.

Ⓑ 35 cu in. Ⓓ 175 cu in.

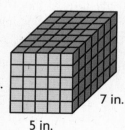

5 in.

7 in.

5 in.

TEKS Algebraic Reasoning—5.4.G
Also 5.6.A, 5.6.B
MATHEMATICAL PROCESSES 5.1.B, 5.1.D, 5.1.E

Name _____

9.2 Formulas for Volume

Find the volume.

1.

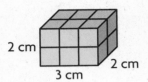

2 cm 2 cm 3 cm

Volume: _____

2.

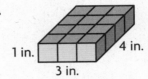

1 in. 4 in. 3 in.

Volume: _____

3.

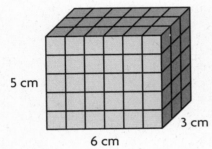

5 cm 3 cm 6 cm

Volume: _____

4.

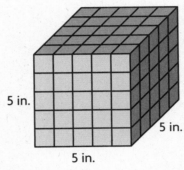

5 in. 5 in. 5 in.

Volume: _____

5.

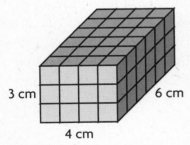

3 cm 6 cm 4 cm

Volume: _____

6.

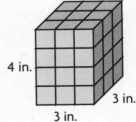

4 in. 3 in. 3 in.

Volume: _____

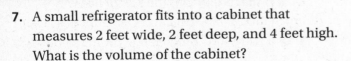
Problem Solving **Real World**

7. A small refrigerator fits into a cabinet that measures 2 feet wide, 2 feet deep, and 4 feet high. What is the volume of the cabinet?

_____

_____

8. Mr. Otis built a storage shed. The shed has a length of 5 meters, a width of 3 meters, and a height of 4 meters. His goal was for the shed to have a volume greater than 50 cubic meters. Did Mr. Otis meet his goal? **Explain**.

_____

_____

Fill in the bubble completely to show your answer.

9. What is the volume of the rectangular prism shown below?

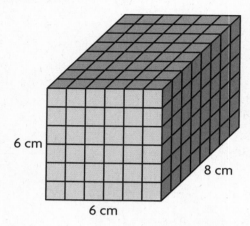

6 cm
8 cm
6 cm

Ⓐ 48 cu cm

Ⓑ 84 cu cm

Ⓒ 288 cu cm

Ⓓ 384 cu cm

10. Hannah used centimeter cubes to build the model shown below.

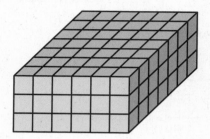

Which equation can you use to find the volume of Hannah's model?

Ⓐ $V = 6 + 7 + 3$

Ⓑ $V = (6 \times 7) + 3$

Ⓒ $V = (6 + 7) \times 3$

Ⓓ $V = 6 \times 7 \times 3$

11. A shipping clerk packs a box of cube-shaped notepads. He packs 8 layers of notepads with 8 rows of 6 notepads in each layer. How many notepads does the clerk pack?

Ⓐ 336   Ⓒ 96

Ⓑ 112   Ⓓ 384

12. The number cubes the fifth-grade math classes use are packed into a box. When the box is full, it has 5 rows of 4 cubes with 6 layers of cubes. Mrs. Benson sees that one layer of cubes is missing from the box. How many number cubes are in the box?

Ⓐ 96   Ⓒ 90

Ⓑ 100   Ⓓ 50

13. **Multi-Step** Alexis uses toy blocks to build a model of a building. Each toy block is 1 cubic inch. The first three floors of the model are made up of 6 rows of 4 blocks. Floors four through eight are made up of 4 rows of 4 blocks. What is the volume of the model?

Ⓐ 104 cu in.   Ⓒ 88 cu in.

Ⓑ 152 cu in.   Ⓓ 136 cu in.

14. **Multi-Step** Aaden is packing boxes into a carton that is 8 inches long, 8 inches wide, and 4 inches tall. The boxes are 2 inches long, 1 inch wide, and 1 inch tall. How many boxes will fit into the carton?

Ⓐ 128   Ⓒ 64

Ⓑ 256   Ⓓ 512

Name _____

9.3 Volume of a Cube

? Essential Question

How can you use formulas to find the volume of cubes?

Connect The base of a rectangular prism is a rectangle. You can use the formulas $V = l \times w \times h$ or $V = Bh$ to find the volume of a rectangular prism.

A cube is a rectangular prism with a square base. A cube has six square faces of the same size. The length, width, and height of a cube are equal. You can use a special form of the formula for the volume of a rectangular prism to find the volume of a cube.

🔑 Unlock the Problem (Real World)

Keyshon built the cube shown at the right using centimeter cubes. What is the volume of the cube? Use centimeter cubes to build Keyshon's cube.

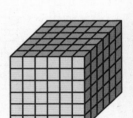

Count the cubes in your model. The base is a square with the length

of _____ centimeters and a width of _____ centimeters. The height

is _____ centimeters.

The volume of the cube is _____ × _____ × _____ or _____ cubic centimeters.
                  length   width   height

You can also use the formula $V = Bh$ to find the volume. The volume of the cube is

_____ × _____ or _____ cubic centimeters.
Base area height

1. **What if** the cube had a length of s centimeters? What would the width and height of the cube be?

   _____

   _____

2. Write a special formula for the volume of a cube with length s centimeters.

   _____

   _____

   _____

Math Talk
Mathematical Processes

Explain how to find the volume of a cube if each side has a length of 3 meters.

Use a formula to find the volume.

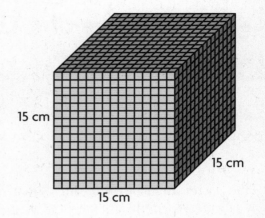

1. The length of the cube is _____. The width is _____

   and the height is _____.

   The volume of the cube is _____ × _____ × _____.
    _s _s _s

   Volume = _____ cubic cm

15 cm

15 cm

15 cm

2.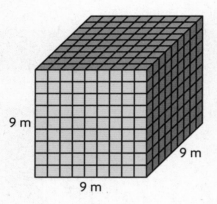

9 m

9 m

9 m

Volume = _____ cubic m

3.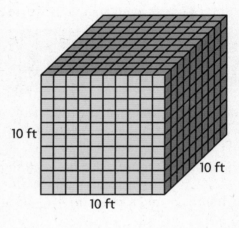

10 ft

10 ft

10 ft

V = _____ cubic ft

Problem Solving

4. **H.O.T.** **Reasoning** Can you use the formula for the volume
of a rectangular prism to find the volume of a cube? **Explain.**

_____

_____

_____

5. **Multi-Step** How much greater is the volume
of the green cube than that of the blue cube?

_____

_____

_____

_____

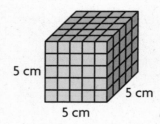

5 cm

5 cm

5 cm

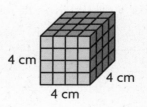

4 cm

4 cm

4 cm

Name _____

H.O.T. **Pose a Problem**

6. Mustafa builds two cubes using 1-cm cubes. The first cube has a side length of 7 cm. The second cube has a side length of 8 cm.

   Use the information about Mustafa's cubes to write a word problem about volume.

Pose a problem.   **Solve your problem.**

7. **H.O.T.** **Multi-Step** Fun Mix cereal comes in two types of boxes. The first box is shaped like a rectangular prism. It is 10 inches long, 5 inches wide, and 12 inches tall. The second box is shaped like a cube with a side length of 9 inches. Which cereal box has a greater volume?

_____

_____

8. **H.O.T.** **Reasoning** A warehouse is shaped like a cube. Its volume is 1,000 cubic meters. The area of the base is 100 square meters. Explain how you can find the height of the warehouse.

_____

_____

Daily Assessment Task

Fill in the bubble completely to show your answer.

9. **Apply** Andy orders a stack of pancakes for breakfast. The pancake stack is in the shape of a cube that has a height of 8 inches. If the cost is $0.02 per cubic inch, what is the cost of his breakfast?

   (A) $10.24

   (B) $5.12

   (C) $12.80

   (D) $6.40

10. A cube has side lengths of 10 inches. What is the volume of the cube?

    (A) 3,000 cubic inches

    (B) 100 cubic inches

    (C) 1,000 cubic inches

    (D) 30 cubic inches

11. **Multi-Step** What is the total volume of the two cubes?

    (A) 16 cubic units

    (B) 34 cubic units

    (C) 30 cubic units

    (D) 152 cubic units

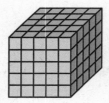

⭐TEXAS Test Prep

12. Which of the following shows the equation for finding the volume of the cube at the right?

    (A) $V = 4 + 4 + 4$

    (B) $V = 4 \times 3$

    (C) $V = 4 \times 4$

    (D) $V = 4 \times 4 \times 4$

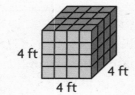

4 ft

4 ft

4 ft

Name _____

9.3 Volume of a Cube

Use a formula to find the volume.

1.

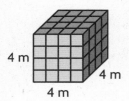

4 m
4 m
4 m

Volume = _____ cubic meters

2.

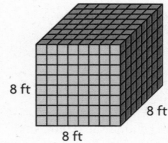

8 ft
8 ft
8 ft

Volume = _____ cubic ft

3.

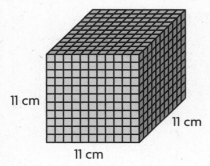

11 cm
11 cm
11 cm

Volume = _____ cubic cm

4.

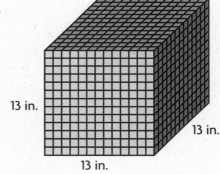

13 in.
13 in.
13 in.

Volume = _____ cubic in.

Problem Solving

5. Karin and Hector build two cubes using 1-in. cubes. Hector's cube has a side length of 12 in. Karin's cube has a side length of 14 in. What is the difference in volume between the two cubes? **Explain.**

_____

_____

_____

6. The office supply store sells erasers that fill the box shown at right. Each eraser is 1 cubic inch. Mr. Williams wants to give one eraser to each of his 365 students. If he buys one box of erasers, will he have enough? **Explain.**

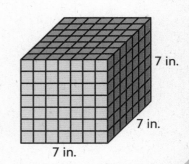

7 in.
7 in.
7 in.

_____

Fill in the bubble completely to show your answer.

7. Use the information in Exercise 6 on the previous page to find the cost of a full box of erasers if one eraser costs $0.05.

Ⓐ $17.15

Ⓑ $2.45

Ⓒ $3.43

Ⓓ $18.25

8. A cube has side lengths of 9 centimeters. What is the volume of the cube?

Ⓐ 81 cubic centimeters

Ⓑ 27 cubic centimeters

Ⓒ 729 cubic centimeters

Ⓓ 162 cubic centimeters

9. Which of the following shows the equation for finding the volume of the cube shown below?

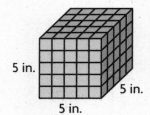

5 in.
5 in.
5 in.

Ⓐ $V = 5 \times 5 \times 5$ Ⓒ $V = 5 \times 3$

Ⓑ $V = 5 + 5 + 5$ Ⓓ $V = 5 \times 5$

10. The total volume of a cube-shaped shipping container is 729 cubic feet. The area of the base is 81 square feet. Which is the length of one side of the container?

Ⓐ 81 feet

Ⓑ 3 feet

Ⓒ 27 feet

Ⓓ 9 feet

11. **Multi-Step** What is the difference between the volume of the rectangular prism and the cube?

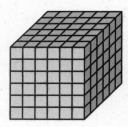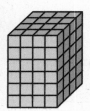

Ⓐ 312 cubic units

Ⓑ 280 cubic units

Ⓒ 120 cubic units

Ⓓ 216 cubic units

12. **Multi-Step** Bethany stacked a cube on top of a rectangular prism to build the model below. What is the total volume of the model?

Ⓐ 27 cubic units

Ⓑ 77 cubic units

Ⓒ 40 cubic units

Ⓓ 120 cubic units

9.4 Apply Formulas

TEKS Algebraic Reasoning—5.4.H
Also 5.6.B
MATHEMATICAL PROCESSES
5.1.B, 5.1.C

? Essential Question

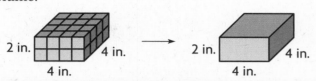

How can you use formulas to solve problems about area, perimeter, and volume?

Connect Both prisms show the same dimensions and have the same volume.

2 in.   4 in.   4 in.   ⟶   2 in.   4 in.   4 in.

🔑 Unlock the Problem (Real World)

Mei Lin builds a jewelry box. The length of the box is 8 inches, the width is 4 inches, and the height is 6 inches. How much velvet does she need to line the bottom of the box?

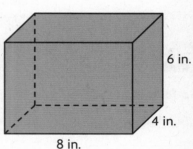

6 in.

4 in.

8 in.

STEP 1 Decide which formula to use.

The jewelry box is a rectangular prism. The base of the prism is a

_____. To find the amount of velvet needed to cover

the base of the prism, you need to find the _____.

What formula should you use to find the area? _____

_____

STEP 2 Find the area.

_____ = _____ × _____

So, Mei Lin needs _____ square inches of velvet.

Remember

You have used these formulas to find area, perimeter, and volume.

$A = l \times w$

$P = 2l + 2w$

$V = l \times w \times h$

Try This!

Choose a formula to find the amount of space the jewelry box will occupy. To find the amount of space, you need to

find the _____.

_____ = _____ × _____ × _____   Write the formula.

_____ = _____ × _____ × _____ = _____   Solve.

So, the jewelry box will occupy _____ cubic inches of space.

Math Talk
Mathematical Processes

What if you only knew the area of the base and the height? **Explain** how you could find the volume.

Connect You can use formulas to find unknown measurements.

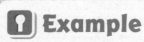 **Example**

Find the unknown measurement.

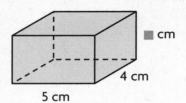

$V = l \times w \times h$

$60 = \underline{\hspace{1cm}} \times \underline{\hspace{1cm}} \times \blacksquare$

$60 = \underline{\hspace{1cm}} \times \blacksquare$

Think: If I filled this prism with centimeter cubes, each layer would have 20 cubes. How many layers of 20 cubes are equal to 60?

So, the unknown measurement is _____ cm.

Share and Show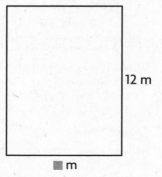

Use a formula to solve.

1. Find the perimeter.

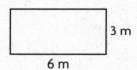

$P = \underline{\hspace{2cm}}$

2. Find the volume.

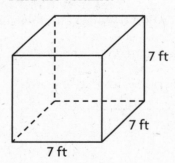

$V = \underline{\hspace{2cm}}$

3. Find the unknown measurement.

$A = 108$ sq m $\quad \blacksquare = \underline{\hspace{1cm}}$ m

Math Talk

Mathematical Processes

Explain how you found the unknown measurement in Exercise 3.

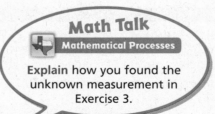

Name _____

4. **H.O.T.** The perimeter of a rectangle is 40 ft. The length is 15 ft.
    Explain how you can find the width of the rectangle.

_____

_____

5. **H.O.T.** **Multi-Step** The area of a square is 64 sq cm. What is the
    perimeter of the square?

_____

_____

Problem Solving Real World

Use the diagram for 6–8.

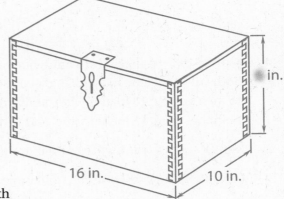

16 in. 10 in. in.

6. Martita uses the diagram to the right to make a cedar chest.
    She wants to add a copper border around of the base of the
    chest. How much of the copper border should she buy?

_____

7. **Multi-Step** Martita wants to line the bottom of the chest with
    felt. She will use two colors of felt so that each color covers half
    of the area. How much felt does she need for each color?

_____

_____

8. **H.O.T.** The instructions for making the chest are smudged.
    Martita cannot read what the height of the chest should be. She knows
    that the volume should be 6,400 cubic inches. **Explain** how you can find
    the height of the chest.

Math on the Spot

_____

_____

_____

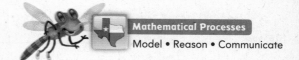

Daily Assessment Task

Fill in the bubble completely to show your answer.

9. A thin plastic cover must be placed on top of this box. How much plastic is needed?

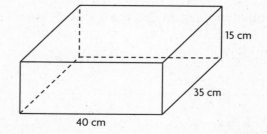

- (A) 525 sq cm
- (B) 1,400 sq cm
- (C) 21,000 sq cm
- (D) 600 sq cm

10. **Representations** Emily wants to put a rosebud wallpaper border on the walls of her room. The border will form a rectangle around the room. Which formula should she use to find the length of wallpaper she needs?

- (A) $V = l \times w \times h$
- (B) $A = l \times w$
- (C) $P = 4s$
- (D) $P = l + l + w + w$

11. **Multi-Step** Spencer and Kamden are comparing the size of their suitcases. Both suitcases are shaped like rectangular prisms. Spencer's suitcase is 15 inches long, 18 inches wide, and 5 inches tall. Kamden's suitcase is 14 inches long, 15 inches wide, and 7 inches tall. Which statement is correct?

- (A) Kamden's suitcase can hold more because it has a greater volume.
- (B) Kamden's suitcase can hold more because it has a greater area.
- (C) Spencer's suitcase can hold more because it has a greater volume.
- (D) Spencer's suitcase can hold more because it has a greater area.

⭐ TEXAS Test Prep

12. Julio's room has a rectangular floor. He covers the floor with 180 square feet of carpet. If the width of the room is 9 feet, what is the length of the room?

- (A) 2 feet
- (B) 20 feet
- (C) 58 feet
- (D) 20 square feet

370

TEKS Number and Operations—5.4.H
Also 5.6.B
MATHEMATICAL PROCESSES 5.1.B, 5.1.C

9.4 Apply Formulas

Use a formula to solve.

1. Find the perimeter.

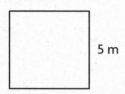

5 m

$P =$ _____

2. Find the volume.

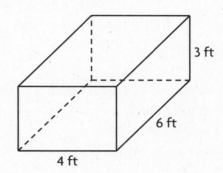

3 ft

6 ft

4 ft

$V =$ _____

Find the unknown measurement.

3.

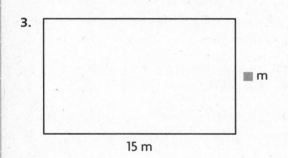

■ m

15 m

$A = 150$ sq m   ■ = _____ m

4.

■ in.

7 in.

$P = 42$ in.   ■ = _____ in.

Problem Solving Real World

5. Yuan is mailing the package shown at right. He needs to find the volume of the package so he can decide what size bag of packing materials to buy to fill the package. What is the volume of the package?

_____

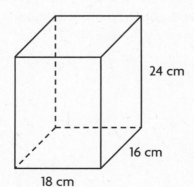

24 cm

16 cm

18 cm

Lesson Check

 **TEXAS Test Prep**

Fill in the bubble completely to show your answer.

6. A classroom floor will be covered with carpet. Which formula is needed to find the amount of carpet needed?

Ⓐ $P = 2l + 2w$

Ⓑ $V = l \times w \times h$

Ⓒ $A = l \times w$

Ⓓ $P = 4s$

7. A storage locker measures 5 feet by 6 feet by 14 feet. How much space in the warehouse will the storage locker occupy?

Ⓐ 420 cubic feet

Ⓑ 154 cubic feet

Ⓒ 1,176 cubic feet

Ⓓ 120 cubic feet

8. The diagram below shows the number of square tiles on a playhouse floor. The length and width of one tile are labeled in inches.

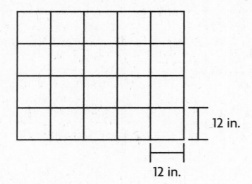

12 in.

12 in.

What is the total area of the playhouse floor?

Ⓐ 144 square inches

Ⓑ 2,304 square inches

Ⓒ 2,880 square inches

Ⓓ 216 square inches

9. **Multi-Step** At Hal's Shipping Store, the cost of mailing a box increases as the size of the box increases. Ming mails a box that measures 11 inches by 12 inches by 9 inches. Eli mails a box that measures 12 inches by 14 inches by 6 inches. Which statement is correct?

Ⓐ Ming's cost is less because her box has less volume.

Ⓑ Ming's and Eli's costs are the same because the boxes have the same volume.

Ⓒ Eli's cost is greater because his box has greater volume.

Ⓓ Ming's cost is greater because her box has greater volume.

10. **Multi-Step** Angela is lining the bottom of some cabinet drawers with paper. How much paper will she need to cover the bottom of three drawers?

Ⓐ 960 sq cm

Ⓑ 480 sq cm

Ⓒ 160 sq cm

Ⓓ 2,880 sq cm

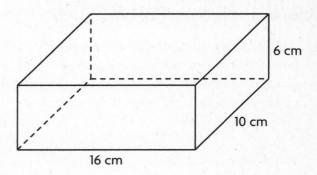

6 cm

10 cm

16 cm

Name _____

 Module 9 Assessment

Vocabulary

Choose the best term from the box.

1. _____ is the amount of space occupied by a solid figure. (p. 355)

2. A _____ is an equation that expresses a mathematical rule. (p. 349)

Concepts and Skills

Use formulas to find the perimeter and area. ➤ TEKS 5.4.H

3.
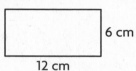

6 cm

12 cm

Perimeter: _____

Area: _____

4.
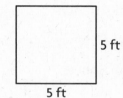

5 ft

5 ft

Perimeter: _____

Area: _____

Use formulas to find the volume. ➤ TEKS 5.4.G, 5.4.H

5.
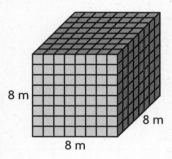

8 m

8 m

8 m

Volume: _____

6.
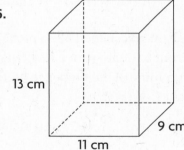

13 cm

9 cm

11 cm

Volume: _____

7. **Find the area of the polygon. Show how you find your answer.** ➤ TEKS 5.4.H

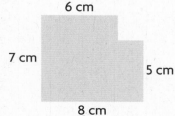

6 cm

7 cm

5 cm

8 cm

Area: _____

_____

_____

_____

8. Which equation shows how to find the volume of the model?  TEKS 5.4.G, 5.4.H

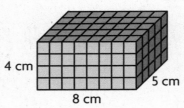

4 cm
5 cm
8 cm

Ⓐ $8 \times 5 = 40$

Ⓑ $(2 \times 8) + (2 \times 5) = 26$

Ⓒ $8 \times 5 \times 4 = 160$

Ⓓ $8 + 5 + 4 = 17$

9. Sanaya has a rectangular bulletin board that is 3 feet long and 2 feet wide. She wants to cover the board with felt and add a satin ribbon around the border of the bulletin board. How much felt and ribbon does Sanaya need? TEKS 5.4.H

Ⓐ 6 feet of felt, 10 feet of ribbon

Ⓑ 6 sq feet of felt, 10 feet of ribbon

Ⓒ 10 sq feet of felt, 6 feet of ribbon

Ⓓ 6 sq feet of felt, 5 feet of ribbon

10. Hicham buys a rectangular sheet of plywood that measures 18 square meters. The sheet of plywood is 3 meters long. What is the perimeter of the sheet of plywood? TEKS 5.4.H

Ⓐ 9 meters

Ⓒ 18 meters

Ⓑ 6 meters

Ⓓ 18 square meters

11. Melinda is making a tin box shaped like a rectangular prism. For the base, Melinda cuts out a square with a side length of 12 inches. If Melinda wants the volume of the tin box to be 1,440 cubic inches, how tall should the box be? TEKS 5.4.H

Ⓐ 12 inches

Ⓒ 10 inches

Ⓑ 6 inches

Ⓓ 8 inches

12. Deval has a rectangular patio that is 15 feet long and 5 feet wide. If Deval uses square tiles with a side length of 1 foot, how many tiles will he need to cover the patio? TEKS 5.4.H

Record your answer and fill in the bubbles on the grid. Be sure to use the correct place value.

⓪	⓪	⓪	.	⓪	⓪
①	①	①		①	①
②	②	②		②	②
③	③	③		③	③
④	④	④		④	④
⑤	⑤	⑤		⑤	⑤
⑥	⑥	⑥		⑥	⑥
⑦	⑦	⑦		⑦	⑦
⑧	⑧	⑧		⑧	⑧
⑨	⑨	⑨		⑨	⑨

10.1 Number Patterns

? Essential Question

How can you generate a number pattern?

Connect A pattern is an ordered set of numbers. You can use a rule or an equation to describe a pattern. When an equation describes the pattern, find the value of the unknowns to make a table or write the pattern.

🔑 Unlock the Problem

Luisa is making flan. For every egg, she can make three flans. The rule $f = 3e$ describes the relationship between the number of flans, f and the number of eggs, e. How many flans can Luisa make if she uses 5 eggs?

You can use an input/output table or a list to show a pattern. When a pattern is shown in a table, it shows the relationship between the inputs and outputs. When a pattern is shown in a list, it only shows the outputs in order.

Complete the input/output table. Replace e in the equation $f = 3e$ with the value shown in the table to find the value of the output f.

Input	Eggs	e	1	2	3	4	5
Output	Flans	f					

The pattern for the number of flans is 3, 6, _____, _____, _____.

The fifth number in the pattern is _____.

So, Luisa can make _____ flans.

Math Talk
Mathematical Processes

Explain how you can use the pattern to find how many flans can be made using 9 eggs.

- **What if** the Luisa changed her recipe to make 4 flans with every egg? How would the pattern change?

_____

_____

_____

🔒 Example Find the pattern.

The rule for the number of circles in a figure is $c = f + 2$ where c is the number of circles and f is the figure number. How many circles will be in Figure 8?

Figure 1   Figure 2   Figure 3

Complete the input/output table.

Input	Figures	f	1	2	3	4	5	6	7	8
Output	Circles	c								

The pattern for the number of circles

is 3, 4, _____, _____, _____, _____, _____, _____.

The eighth number in the pattern is _____.

So, there are _____ circles in Figure 8.

Share and Show

MATH BOARD

Use the rule to complete the table.

1. Rule: $g = n + 6$.

Input	Output
n	g
1	
2	
3	
4	

2. Rule: $p = r \times 12$.

Input	r	2	4	6	8
Output	p				

Problem Solving

Practice: Copy and Solve Use the rule to make an input/output table.
Include four input/output pairs in your table.

3. For input x and output y,
the rule is $y = x + 4$

4. For input s and output a,
the rule is $a = 11s$

5. For input u and output v,
the rule is $v = 7u$

6. For input m and output n,
the rule is $n = m \times 10$

7. **H.O.T.** **Explain** how you can use the formula for the perimeter
of a square, $P = 4s$, to generate a pattern. Use the pattern to find the
perimeter of a square with sides that are 5 cm long.

_____

_____

_____

Problem Solving (Real World)

8. Max makes origami paper cranes for a mobile. He can make 5 cranes
with each sheet of paper. Complete the input/output table to show
the number of cranes Max can make with 6 sheets of paper.

Input	Sheets	s	1	2	3	4	5	6
Output	Cranes	c						

9. **H.O.T.** **Multi-Step** Max decides to make paper owls. He can
make 4 paper owls from each sheet of paper. Complete and use the
input/output table to find how many sheets of paper Max would use
to make 24 paper owls.

Input	Sheets	s					
Output	Owls	o					

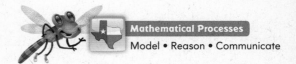
Daily Assessment Task

Fill in the bubble completely to show your answer.

10. **Apply** Matilda is reading a map of the route to her grandfather's house in another state. The equation $m = 25i$ describes the relationship between i, the number of inches on the map, and m, the number of actual miles. How many miles are represented by 12 inches?

   (A) 200 miles   (C) 400 miles

   (B) 600 miles   (D) 300 miles

11. To find the total cost of a field trip, use the equation $c = 4s$, where s is the number of students and c is the cost of the field trip. How much will it cost for 14 students to attend the field trip?

Number of Students (s)	3	6	9	12
Cost of Field Trip in Dollars (c)	12	24	36	48

   (A) $15   (C) $56

   (B) $17   (D) $60

12. **Multi-Step** Robin places 3 roses and 2 daffodils in each vase. How many flowers will she need if she has 6 vases?

   (A) 30

   (B) 12

   (C) 18

   (D) 5

⭐ TEXAS Test Prep

13. Sergei uses the pattern rule $y = 4 + b$ to generate the first three outputs in the pattern. Which of the following is the fifth output in the pattern?

Input	b	1	2	3	4	5
Output	y	5	6	7		

   (A) 5   (C) 8

   (B) 9   (D) 10

378

10.1 Number Patterns

Use the rule to make an input/output table.
Include four input/output pairs in your table.

1. **Rule:** The output is $a + 5$.

2. **Rule:** The output is $3c$.

3. **Rule:** The output is $d \times 6$.

4. **Rule:** The output is $10 + b$.

5. **Rule:** The output is $8e$.

6. **Rule:** The output is $12f$.

7. **Rule:** The output is $8 + g$.

8. **Rule:** The output is $k \times 2$.

Problem Solving Real World

9. Suki uses toothpicks to build a number of separate shapes for her math project. She uses 1 toothpick for each side of a shape. Complete the input/output table to show how many toothpicks Suki needs to make 6 hexagons.

Input	Hexagons	h	1	2	3	4	5	6
Output	Toothpicks	t						

Fill in the bubble completely to show your answer.

10. If c is cups of sugar and b is number of batches of cookies, which rule matches the information in the table?

Input	Batches	b	2	3	4
Output	Cups	c	4	6	8

Ⓐ The output is $b \times 2$.

Ⓑ The output is $c \times 2$.

Ⓒ The output is $b + 2$.

Ⓓ The output is $c + 2$.

11. Tia hangs chili-shaped party lights in her back yard. The rule $c = 14f$ gives the number of chili lights, c, there are for each foot, f, of wire. How many lights are on 8 feet of wire?

Ⓐ 126

Ⓑ 112

Ⓒ 98

Ⓓ 96

12. Harlan uses the pattern rule $l = d + 2$ to represent the number of laps she swims each day for a week. Which is the number of laps she swims on the sixth day?

Input	Day	d	1	2	3
Output	Laps	l	3	4	5

Ⓐ 6

Ⓑ 7

Ⓒ 8

Ⓓ 9

13. Erik uses the equation $e = 25b$ to determine how much he earns for selling hand-carved bowls at the craft fair. If b represents the number of bowls sold and e represents his earnings, how much will Erik earn if he sells 9 bowls?

Number of Bowls	1	2	3
Earnings	$25	$50	$75

Ⓐ $225

Ⓑ $100

Ⓒ $150

Ⓓ $45

14. **Multi-Step** Gina paints beach scenes on notecards. She sells packages of 8 notecards for $8 for one package, $16 for 2 packages, and $24 for 3 packages. Which equation is the rule for the pattern if n is the number of packages and d is the selling price in dollars?

Ⓐ $n = 8d$

Ⓑ $d = 8 + n$

Ⓒ $n = 8 + d$

Ⓓ $d = 8n$

15. **Multi-Step** At his job at the deli, Sam makes 9 sandwiches and 6 salads each hour. Which of the following patterns can you use to find the number of sandwiches he makes in 4 hours?

Ⓐ 9, 18, 27, 36, ...

Ⓑ 6, 12, 18, 24, ...

Ⓒ 9, 15, 21, 27, ...

Ⓓ 8, 16, 24, 28, ...

Name _____

Number Patterns in Tables

? Essential Question

How can you write a rule to describe a pattern?

 Unlock the Problem

When the output in a pattern depends on the input, you can write a rule to describe the relationship between inputs and outputs.

Marcus wants to buy light-up balls for a party. They cost $1 each. The store charges the same shipping fee regardless of how many light-up balls are ordered. So, Marcus has to pay for the light-up balls and pay a shipping fee. The table below shows the cost c for w light-up balls. How much will Marcus pay for 12 light-up balls?

Write a rule to describe the pattern in the table.

Input	w	2	4	6	8
Output	c	4	6	8	10

STEP 1 Describe the relationship between the number of light-up balls and the cost.

Think:

	Input	Output
	↓	↓

$2 + 2 = 4$ 2 light-up balls $+ 2 =$ cost

$4 + 2 = 6$ 4 light-up balls $+ 2 =$ cost

$6 + 2 = 8$ 6 light-up balls $+ 2 =$ cost

$8 + 2 = 10$ 8 light-up balls $+ 2 =$ cost

Math Talk
Mathematical Processes

Explain how you can find the cost for 5 light-up balls.

The output is _____ more than the input.

STEP 2 Decide what operation to use to write a rule.

$c =$ _____ $+$ _____   **Think:** Add 2 to the input to get the output
Since the pattern is additive,
use addition to write a rule.

STEP 3 Use the rule to find the cost of 12 light-up balls.

$c = w + 2$

$c =$ _____ $+ 2$ Replace w with the number of light-up balls.

$c =$ _____   Add to find the cost.

So, the 12 light-up balls cost $ _____.

🔑 Example Find the rule.

Patterns can also involve multiplication.

The output is _____ times the input. The pattern is multiplicative.

The rule is $y =$ _____ × _____.

Think:

1 × _____ = 7

2 × _____ = 14

3 × _____ = 21

4 × _____ = 28

Input	Output
n	*y*
1	7
2	14
3	21
4	28

Share and Show

MATH BOARD

1. Use a rule to describe the pattern in the table.

Input	*s*	1	2	3	4
Output	*t*	9	18	27	36

Multiply by _____.

Rule: _____

Decide if the pattern shown in the table is additive or multiplicative. Write a rule to describe the pattern.

2.

Input	Output
a	*c*
2	5
4	7
6	9
8	11

The pattern is _____.

Rule: _____

3.

Input	*r*	1	2	3	4
Output	*p*	13	26	39	52

The pattern is _____.

Rule: _____

Name _____

4. **Write Math** ▶ **Explain** how you can find a rule for a pattern in a table.

_____

_____

5. **H.O.T.** **Explain** whether the formula for the area of a rectangle can be used to show an additive pattern or a multiplicative pattern.

_____

_____

Problem Solving · Real World

6. **Multi-Step** To make soup, Juan adds 3 cups of hot water to each package of dried soup. Write a rule for the pattern. Make a table to determine how many cups of hot water are needed for 18 packages of dried soup.

_____

_____

7. **H.O.T.** **Multi-Step** Liam and Nora are playing a spelling game. The number of points for each word a player spells correctly is the sum of the number of letters in the word and 3 bonus points for spelling correctly. The table below shows the scoring system. Find the rule and the number of points for spelling an eight-letter word correctly.

Input	Letters	l	3	4	5	6
Output	Points	p	6	7	8	9

_____

8. **H.O.T.** **Apply** Kirk is building a storage cabinet. To be sure of having enough wood, he allows an extra 2 inches on measurements. Write a rule for the pattern. Make a table to find the number of inches that Kirk would measure if he wanted an 11-inch board.

_____

_____

_____

Daily Assessment Task

Fill in the bubble completely to show your answer.
Use the table for 9–10.

Number of Volcanoes	2	3	4	5
Flour (c)	12	18	24	30
Salt (c)	4	6	8	10
Cooking Oil (tbsp)	8	12	16	20

9. **Analyze** Using the recipe shown in the table, how many cups of flour will you need to make 13 model volcanoes?

   (A) 30 cups   (C) 78 cups

   (B) 48 cups   (D) 54 cups

10. If v is the number of volcanoes and s is the number of cups of salt, which of the following rules describes the pattern in the table?

    (A) $v = s + 2$ (C) $s = v + 2$

    (B) $s = v \times 2$ (D) $v = s \times 2$

11. **Multi-Step** The table shows the shipping boxes received by Snazzy Stuff clothing store. Suppose that the store pays $8 for a shirt. How much money does the store pay for 10 boxes of shirts?

Input	Number of Boxes	1	2	3	12
Output	Shirts	12	24	36	144

   (A) $120   (C) $960

   (B) $96   (D) $192

 **TEXAS Test Prep**

12. Which of the following rules describes the pattern in the table?

Input	b	1	2	3
Output	e	4	8	12

    (A) $e = b + 4$ (C) $b = e + 4$

    (B) $e = b \times 4$ (D) $b = e \times 4$

Homework and Practice

Name _____

10.2 Number Patterns in Tables

Find the rule to describe the pattern in the table. Decide if the rule is additive or multiplicative.

1.

Input	Output
m	n
1	11
2	22
3	33
4	44

The rule is _____.

Rule: _____

2.

Input	d	3	5	7	9
Output	f	7	9	11	13

The rule is _____.

Rule: _____

3.

Input	p	2	3	4	5
Output	q	30	45	60	75

The rule is _____.

Rule: _____

4.

Input	Output
s	t
4	10
6	12
8	14
10	16

The rule is _____.

Rule: _____

Problem Solving

5. Marcus pours 12 ounces of cranberry juice into a punch bowl. He uses a container to add sparkling water to the bowl one ounce at a time. Write a rule to show the pattern and use it to calculate how many ounces of liquid Marcus will have in the bowl after adding 8 containers of sparkling water.

_____

_____

_____

Fill in the bubble completely to show your answer.

6. The winning entry in the inventors' competition was a robot made with wheels, gears, and bolts. Using the table shown below, how many bolts are needed to make 7 robots?

Number of Robots	1	2	3	4
Wheels	4	8	12	16
Gears	3	6	9	12
Bolts	8	16	24	32

Ⓐ 40 Ⓒ 28

Ⓑ 21 Ⓓ 56

7. Which of the following rules describes the pattern in the table?

Input	h	3	4	5
Output	j	12	13	14

Ⓐ $j = h + 9$

Ⓑ $j = 9h$

Ⓒ $h = j + 9$

Ⓓ $h = 9j$

8. The equation $c = \$0.75p$ represents the cost of mailing a package for each pound, where c is the cost and p is the number of pounds. If Leila mails a package that weighs 5 pounds, what is the total cost?

Ⓐ $3.00

Ⓑ $4.50

Ⓒ $3.75

Ⓓ $3.55

9. The equation $d = m + 16$ represents the total distance traveled after driving m number of miles. If Mrs. Endo drives 35 miles, what is the total distance traveled?

Ⓐ 41 miles

Ⓑ 21 miles

Ⓒ 51 miles

Ⓓ 19 miles

10. **Multi-Step** Nathanial has a dog walking business. He charges $3 for every 15 minutes of walking. How much will Nathanial charge to walk a dog for one hour?

Ⓐ $18

Ⓑ $45

Ⓒ $60

Ⓓ $12

11. **Multi-Step** The table shows the number of magazines Mr. Gomez receives. He pays $2 for each magazine. How much does Mr. Gomez pay for magazines in 12 months?

Number of Months	1	2	6	12
Magazines	2	4	12	

Ⓐ $24 Ⓒ $12

Ⓑ $48 Ⓓ $36

TEKS Algebraic
Reasoning—5.4.D
Also 5.8.B
MATHEMATICAL PROCESSES
5.1.F, 5.1.G

10.3 Number Patterns in Graphs

? Essential Question

How can you write a rule for a pattern given in a graph?

Number patterns can be represented on a graph. Points on a grid represent the number pairs in the pattern. The first number in the pair is the input and is the distance the point is from 0 on a horizontal number line. The second number is the output and is the distance the point is from 0 on a vertical number line.

Unlock the Problem Real World

Sona has some dimes. Adil offers to give her nickels for her dimes. The graph shows the relationship between the number of dimes Sona gives to Adil and the number of nickels she receives in exchange. Find a rule to describe the pattern.

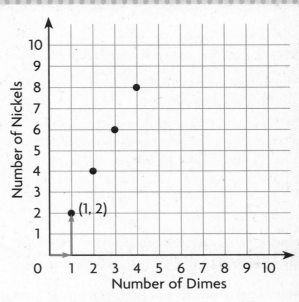

STEP 1 Write number pairs that relate the number of dimes to the number of nickels.

Think: The number of dimes is input. The horizontal distance from 0 for the first point is 1.

(1, _____)

(2, _____)

(3, _____)

(4, _____)

Think: The number of nickels is output. The vertical distance for the first point is _____.

Math Idea

An additive pattern uses addition in its rule. A multiplicative pattern uses multiplication in its rule.

STEP 2 Describe the relationship between the number of dimes and the number of nickels.

The output is _____ times the input. The pattern uses multiplication.

STEP 3 Write the rule. Let *n* stand for number of nickels, and *d* stand for the number of dimes.

$n =$ _____ $\times$ _____

Think: The relationship is multiplicative. Use multiplication to write the rule.

Additive patterns can also be represented in a graph.

Example Find the rule for the pattern shown in the graph.

Jack mails some magazines in a box. The graph shows the relationship between the number of magazines and the total weight of the magazines and the box.

STEP 1 Write number pairs that relate the number of magazines and the total weight.

(1, _____)

(2, _____)

(3, _____)

(4, _____)

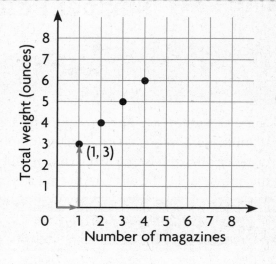

STEP 2 Describe the relationship between the number of magazines and the weight.

The output is the sum of the number of magazines and _____.
The pattern uses addition.

STEP 3 Write the rule. Let w stand for total weight, and m stand for the number of magazines.

$w =$ _____ + _____

Math Talk
Mathematical Processes

Explain what the 2 stands for in $w = m + 2$.

Share and Show

Is the pattern *additive* or *multiplicative*? Find the rule for the pattern.

✓ 1.

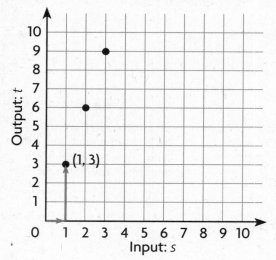

_____

Rule: _____

✓ 2.

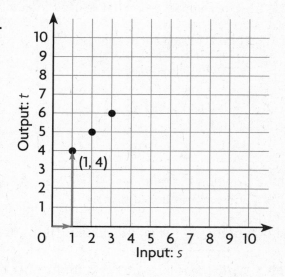

_____

Rule: _____

Name _____

3. **H.O.T.** **Write Math** ▶ **Explain** the differences between the graphs in Exercises 1 and 2.

_____

_____

4. **Write Math** ▶ **Explain** how you can tell whether a pattern shown in a graph is additive or multiplicative.

_____

_____

_____

Problem Solving (Real World)

Use the graph for 5–6.

5. **H.O.T.** **Multi-Step** Maryanne's map uses a scale to show how many miles each inch on the map represents. Use the pattern shown in the graph to find the rule for calculating the actual distance. Use m for number of miles and i for number of inches.

_____

6. **H.O.T.** If the distance on the map is 2.5 inches, how many miles is the actual distance? **Explain** how you calculated the actual distance.

_____

_____

7. **H.O.T.** **Apply** Olivia uses 1 red button for the nose and 2 blue buttons for the eyes for each rag doll she makes. Would the pattern comparing the number of nose buttons to the total number of buttons be multiplicative or additive? **Explain**.

_____

Daily Assessment Task

Fill in the bubble completely to show your answer. Use the graph.

8. The graph shows the number of pounds of fish the seals at an aquarium eat each day. Which statement and equation about the relationship is true?

   (A) additive pattern, $d = p + 3$

   (B) addition pattern, $p = d + 3$

   (C) multiplicative pattern, $p = 10 \times d$

   (D) multiplicative pattern, $d = 3 \times p$

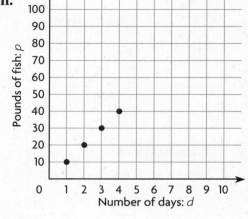

Use the graph for 9–10.

9. The graph shows the relationship between the number of days and the amount of food that a bottlenose dolphin eats. Which point on the graph shows the amount of food that the dolphin consumes in two days?

   (A) point A (C) point C

   (B) point B (D) point D

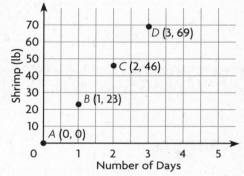

10. **Multi-Step** If s is the amount of food a bottlenose dolphin eats in a day and n is the number of days, which of the following describes the rule for the pattern shown in the graph?

    (A) $s = n + 23$ (C) $n = s \times 23$

    (B) $s = n \times 23$ (D) $n = s + 23$

 TEXAS Test Prep

11. Which of the following rules describes the pattern in the graph?

    (A) $a = 4b$

    (B) $b = 4a$

    (C) $b = 4 + a$

    (D) $a = 4 + b$

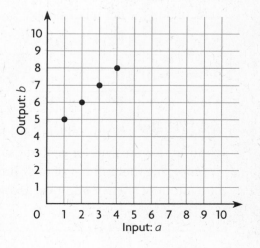

390

10.3 Number Patterns in Graphs

Is the pattern *additive* or *multiplicative*? Write the rule for the pattern.

1.

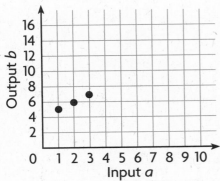

_____

2.

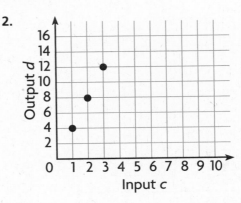

_____

3.

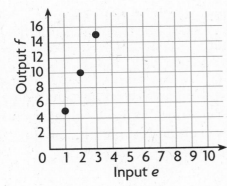

_____

4.

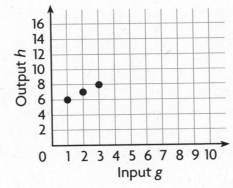

_____

Problem Solving

5. Patrice rents a rowboat for several hours. Use the pattern shown in the graph to write the rule for calculating the cost of renting the rowboat. Use *c* for the cost and *h* for the number of hours.

_____

6. If Patrice rents the boat for 4 hours, what is the cost of the rental?

_____

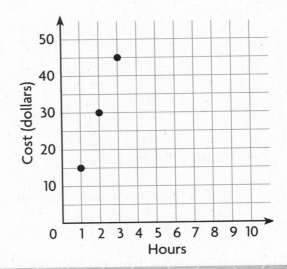

Fill in the bubble completely to show your answer.

7. The graph shows the relationship between the number of hours Ivana bikes and the distance she travels. How many miles does Ivana bike in 4 hours?

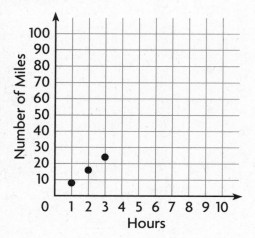

Ⓐ 28 miles   Ⓒ 32 miles

Ⓑ 12 miles   Ⓓ 30 miles

8. Rashid uses cubes to build towers. The graph shows the relationship between the number of towers, t, and the number of cubes, c, he uses. Which equation describes this relationship?

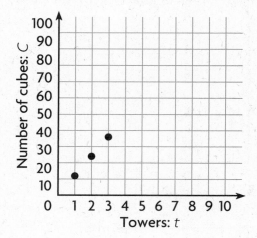

Ⓐ $c = 12 + t$ Ⓒ $t = 12 + c$

Ⓑ $c = 12t$ Ⓓ $t = 12c$

9. **Multi-Step** For every $1 Paula donates to her favorite charity, her mom donates $3. Which of the following identifies the pattern and the amount her mom donates if Paula donates $6?

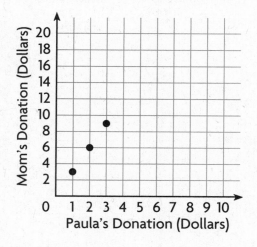

Ⓐ $18, multiplicative   Ⓒ $24, additive

Ⓑ $24, multiplicative   Ⓓ $12, additive

10. **Multi-Step** The graph shows how much time Christina spends making flower arrangements to sell. How many baskets can she make in two hours?

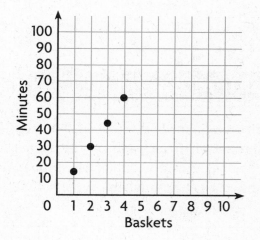

Ⓐ 15   Ⓒ 30

Ⓑ 4   Ⓓ 8

Name _____

10.4 Make Graphs

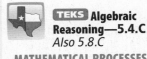
? **Essential Question**

How can you graph a number pattern?

Unlock the Problem

An airport taxi uses the rule $f = m + 2$ to calculate the fare for passengers.
The number of miles, m, is the input, and the output is the fare, f, in dollars.
Graph the pattern.

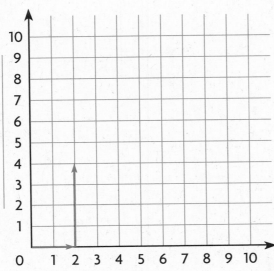

_____

STEP 1 Label the horizontal number line to show that the input is number
of miles. Label the vertical number line to show that the output is
the fare.

_____

STEP 2 Write a number pair and graph it.

For a trip that is 2 miles, the fare will be $_____.

The number pair is (2, _____).

Move right _____ units. Then move up _____ units and draw a
point to represent the number pair.

_____

STEP 3 Graph several number pairs.

Move right _____ units.   (_____, _____)   Move up _____ units.

Move right _____ units.   (_____, _____)   Move up _____ units.

Move right _____ units.   (_____, _____)   Move up _____ units.

Math Talk
Mathematical Processes

Explain what each number in
the number pair represents.

🔑 **Example** Graph a multiplicative pattern.

Celina is counting the number of wheels on tricycles. The rule is $w = 3t$, where t is the number of tricycles and w is the number of wheels. Use the rule to show a pattern on the graph.

STEP 1 Label the horizontal number line to show the input is the number of tricycles. Label the vertical number line to show the output is the number of

_____.

STEP 2 Write a number pair and graph it.

The input _____ times 3 is equal to the output _____.

The number pair is (_____ , _____).

STEP 3 Graph several number pairs.

Move right _____ units.   (_____ , _____)   Move up _____ units.

Move right _____ units.   (_____ , _____)   Move up _____ units.

Move right _____ units.   (_____ , _____)   Move up _____ units.

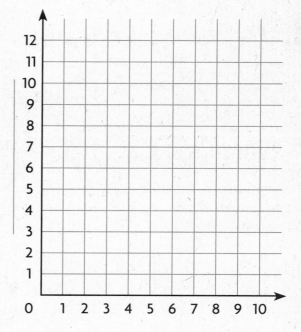

Share and Show

Use the rule to graph a pattern.

✓ **1.** Each doll needs 2 shoes. The rule is $s = 2d$ where d is the number of dolls and s is the number of shoes.

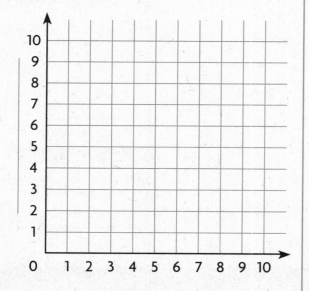

✓ **2.** The score for guessing the correct word is 4 and the number of letters in the word. The rule is $s = 4 + l$ where l is the number of letters and s is the score.

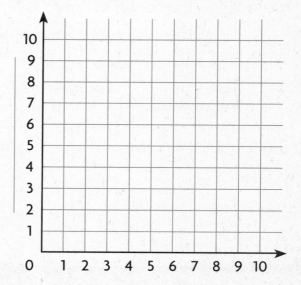

394

Name _____

3. **Write Math** ▶ **Explain** how you can plot a point on the graph to represent a number pair.

_____

_____

_____

4. **H.O.T.** **Write Math** ▶ **Explain** how the first point in your graph for Exercise 2 would change if the rule changes to $s = 5 + l$.

_____

_____

Problem Solving Real World

5. **H.O.T.** **Multi-Step** Rita uses red and blue ribbons in a design. The length of the blue ribbon, b, is always 3 inches greater than the length of the red ribbons, r. Write a rule and plot 4 points on the graph to show the pattern.

_____

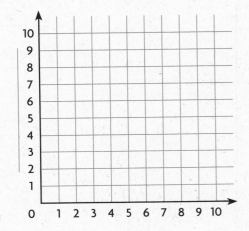

6. **H.O.T.** **Multi-Step** Mina uses green and red ribbons for her design. The length of the green ribbons, g, is always twice the length of the red ribbons, r. Write a rule to describe Mina's design and plot 4 points on the graph to show the pattern.

_____

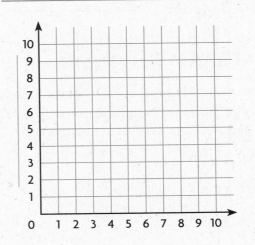

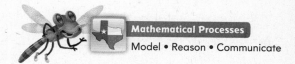
Daily Assessment Task

Fill in the bubble completely to show your answer.

7. A recipe for carrot juice uses the formula $j = 6c$, where j is the amount of juice in ounces and c is the number of pounds of carrots needed. How many pounds of carrots are needed for a 30-ounce glass of carrot juice?

   (A) 5 pounds

   (B) 24 pounds

   (C) 180 pounds

   (D) 36 pounds

8. Harrison uses the rule $y = x + 5$ to complete a table and make a graph. Which number pair will be on the graph?

   (A) (6, 1)

   (B) (4, 8)

   (C) (5, 0)

   (D) (4, 9)

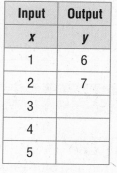

Input	Output
x	y
1	6
2	7
3	
4	
5	

9. **Multi-Step** The rule $d = 12t$ shows the cost in dollars, d, for the number of movie tickets, t. Which two points could be on the graph?

   (A) (0, 12) and (36, 3)

   (B) (1, 11) and (2, 24)

   (C) (0, 0) and (3, 36)

   (D) (0, 12) and (3, 36)

⭐ TEXAS Test Prep

10. Lamar uses the rule $s = 7g$ to show the number of snacks he needs, s, for the number of guests at his party, g. Which number pair shows the number of snacks needed for 4 guests?

    (A) (4, 28)

    (B) (1, 8)

    (C) (4, 14)

    (D) (28, 4)

Name _____

10.4 Make Graphs

Use the rule to graph a pattern.

1. The cost for printing pages at a print shop is a $5 processing fee and $1 for each page. The rule is $c = 5 + p$, where p is the number of pages and c is the total cost.

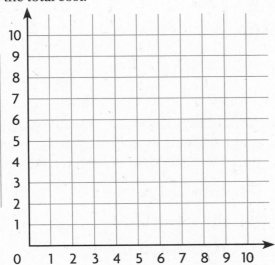

2. Mario uses craft sticks to form triangles. The rule is $c = 3t$, where c represents the number of craft sticks and t represents the number of triangles.

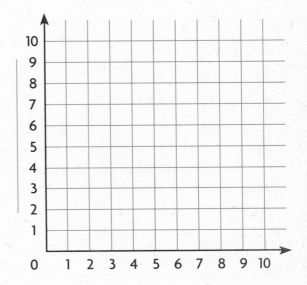

Problem Solving

Use the graph for 3–4.

3. A department store offers free samples of a 2-ounce container of lotion with every fragrance purchase. Write a rule to describe the number of ounces of product for each purchase. Plot 3 points on the graph to show the pattern. Use t for the total number of ounces and f for the ounces of fragrance.

_____

4. Clara buys 6 ounces of fragrance on Monday and returns to buy another 4 ounces of fragrance on Friday. How many ounces of fragrance will she have in all?

_____

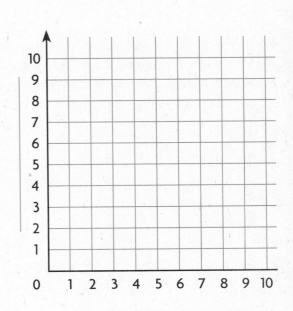

Fill in the bubble completely to show your answer.

5. Duncan uses the rule $b = 4a$ to complete a table and make a graph. Which number pair will be on the graph?

a	2	3	4	5
b	8			

Ⓐ (3, 12)

Ⓑ (3, 7)

Ⓒ (4, 8)

Ⓓ (12, 3)

6. The online music store charges a $6 fee for becoming a member and $1 to download each song. Noriko uses the rule $c = 6 + s$ to calculate her cost. Which number pair shows the cost of 5 songs?

Ⓐ (5, 6)

Ⓑ (5, 11)

Ⓒ (5, 5)

Ⓓ (1, 5)

7. The camp counselors use the equation $c = 8g$ where c is the number of campers and g is the number of groups. Which number pair will not be a point on the graph of the equation?

Ⓐ (0, 0)

Ⓑ (3, 24)

Ⓒ (2, 16)

Ⓓ (8, 1)

8. **Multi-Step** The rule $j = 16p$ shows the number of ounces j for each p pint of orange juice. Which two points will be on the graph?

Ⓐ (2, 32) and (3, 48)

Ⓑ (0, 16) and (1, 32)

Ⓒ (2, 32) and (4, 40)

Ⓓ (1, 8) and (2, 16)

9. **Multi-Step** The rule $g = 5 + y$ shows the relationship of yellow, y, and green, g, split peas in Wendy's soup recipe. Which point on the grid does NOT show the relationship?

Ⓐ (5, 10)

Ⓑ (20, 25)

Ⓒ (15, 10)

Ⓓ (15, 20)

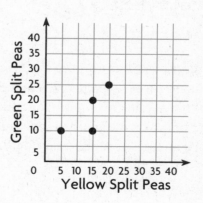

Name _____

 # Module 10 Assessment

Vocabulary

Choose the best term from the box.

1. You can use a graph or an _____ to show a pattern. (p. 375)

2. A _____ is an ordered set of numbers or objects. (p. 375)

Concepts and Skills

Use the rule to complete the table. ♦ TEKS 5.4.C

3. Rule: $m = n + 10$.

Input	Output
n	**m**
1	_____
2	_____
3	_____

4. Rule: $p = s \times 4$.

Input	**s**	2	4	6	8
Output	**p**	_____	_____	_____	_____

Decide if the pattern shown in the table is additive or multiplicative.
Write a rule to describe the pattern. ♦ TEKS 5.4.D

5.

Input	Output
r	**t**
5	7
6	8
7	9

The pattern is _____.

Rule: _____

6.

Input	**a**	1	2	3	4
Output	**p**	7	14	21	28

The pattern is _____.

Rule: _____

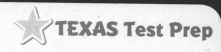

Use the graph for 7–8.

7. The graph shows the relationship between the number of work days and the number of weeks. Which rule best describes the pattern in the graph? ⬇ TEKS 5.4.D

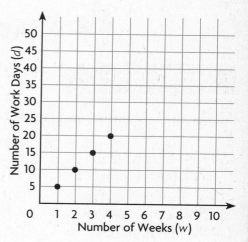

Ⓐ $d = w + 5$

Ⓑ $w = 5d$

Ⓒ $d = 5w$

Ⓓ $w = d + 5$

8. Which of the following number pairs extends the pattern on the graph? ⬇ TEKS 5.4.C

Ⓐ (5, 25)   Ⓒ (25, 5)

Ⓑ (6, 25)   Ⓓ (5, 20)

9. Party favors cost $1, plus $5 for shipping. The rule is $t = 5 + p$, where t is the total cost in dollars and p is the number of party favors bought. Which point on the graph shows the total cost of 4 party favors? ⬇ TEKS 5.4.C

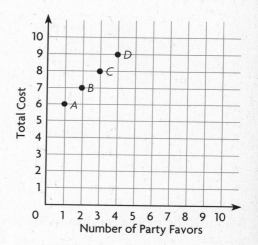

Ⓐ Point A

Ⓑ Point B

Ⓒ Point C

Ⓓ Point D

10. The rule for a pattern is $c = 6w$. What is the output, c, when the input, w, is 6? ⬇ TEKS 5.4.C

Record your answer and fill in the bubbles in the grid. Be sure to use the correct place value.

Name _____

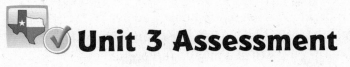

Unit 3 Assessment

Vocabulary

Choose the best term from the box.

Vocabulary
composite number
cubic units
formula
prime number

1. A _____ has more than two factors. (p. 291)

2. Volume is measured using _____. (p. 355)

Concepts and Skills

List all the factor pairs for the number. Tell whether the number is prime or composite. TEKS 5.4.A

3. 69

_____

_____

4. 17

_____

_____

5. 63

_____

_____

Simplify the numerical expression. TEKS 5.4.F

6. $35 - (9 + 6)$

_____

7. $15 + (20 - 4) \div 4$

_____

8. $6 \times [(5 \times 3) - (2 + 9)]$

_____

9. Use formulas to find the area and perimeter. 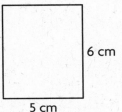 TEKS 5.4.H

6 cm

5 cm

10. Use a formula to find the volume. 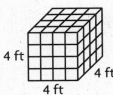 TEKS 5.4.G

4 ft

4 ft

4 ft

Perimeter: _____

Area: _____

Volume: _____

Fill in the bubble completely to show your answer.

11. Moesha has some books. Her mother gives her 5 new books and her father gave her 4 new books. Now Moesha has 11 books. If s stands for the number of books Moesha starts with, which equation represents the problem? ↓ TEKS 5.4.B

Ⓐ $s = 11 + 5$

Ⓑ $11 = 5 \times 4 + s$

Ⓒ $s = 11 \times 5 + 4$

Ⓓ $11 = s + 5 + 4$

12. The graph shows the amount of flour it takes to make croissants. Which rule describes the pattern on the graph?
↓ TEKS 5.4.D

Ⓐ $c = f + 1$

Ⓑ $f = c + 1$

Ⓒ $c = 2f$

Ⓓ $f = 2c$

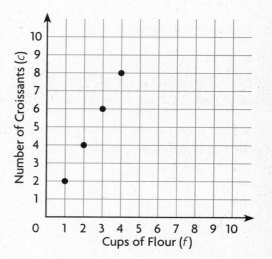

13. Marcello needs to cut a piece of canvas that is 48 sq cm. The width of the sheet of canvas is 8 cm. Which of the following shows the equation Marcello could have used and the length of the canvas? ↓ TEKS 5.4.B, 5.4.H

Ⓐ 64 sq cm, $l = 8 \times 8$

Ⓑ 6 cm, $48 = 8 \times l$

Ⓒ 32 cm, $8 + 8 + 8 + 8 = l$

Ⓓ 12 cm, $48 = 4 \times l$

14. Steve uses the rule $l = 8s$ to determine the number of legs 5 spiders have. What is the value of ■? ↓ TEKS 5.4.C

Spiders	s	2	3	4	5
Legs	l	16	24	32	■

Ⓐ 8

Ⓑ 40

Ⓒ 10

Ⓓ 14

15. An adult elephant eats about 300 pounds of food each day. Which expression shows about how many pounds of food 12 elephants eat in 5 days? ⬇ TEKS 5.4.E

(A) $5 + (300 \times 12)$

(B) $5 \times (300 \times 12)$

(C) $(300 \times 12) \div 5$

(D) $(300 \times 12) - 5$

16. Paula is building a box to store her marble collection. The box is a rectangular prism. The area of the base will be 15 sq inches. She wants the volume of the box to be 150 cu in. Which of the following shows the equation Paula can use and the height of the box? ⬇ TEKS 5.4.B, 5.4.H

(A) $150 = 15h$, 10 in.

(B) $h + 15 = 150$, 135 in.

(C) $h = 15 \times 15$, 225 sq in.

(D) $150 = h \times 15$, 5 in.

17. Ling uses a formula to find the area of her rectangular garden. The garden measures 12 feet by 5 feet. She wants to divide the garden into 10 equal areas. Which equation can Ling use to find out how large each area, t, will be? ⬇ TEKS 5.4.B, 5.4.H

(A) $(12 \times 5) \div t = 10$

(B) $t = 12 \times 5 \times 10$

(C) $t = (12 + 5) \div 10$

(D) $(12 \times 5) \div 10 = t$

18. Amy builds a rectangular prism using centimeter cubes. The length of the prism is 3 centimeters. The width is 2 centimeters and the height is 5 centimeters. Which equation shows a formula for finding the volume of the rectangular prism? ⬇ TEKS 5.4.B, 5.4.G

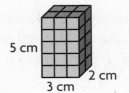

5 cm
2 cm
3 cm

(A) $V = 3 \times 2$

(B) $V = 3 \times 5$

(C) $V = 6 \times 5$

(D) $V = 3 + 2 + 5$

19. Jim wants to put a wallpaper border around a rectangular room. The room measures 14 feet by 10 feet. If the wallpaper border comes in strips that are 20 feet long, how many strips will Jim need? ⬇ TEKS 5.4.H

(A) 48

(B) 2

(C) 3

(D) 140

20. A pack of 8 bottles of olive oil costs $96. Marsha wants to write an equation to calculate the cost of 1 bottle. If b represents the cost of 1 bottle of olive oil, which of the following shows the equation Marsha could use and the cost of 1 bottle? ⬇ TEKS 5.4.B

(A) $96 = b + 8$, $88

(B) $96 = 8b$, $12

(C) Not here

(D) $b = 96 \div 8$, $16

21. Which equation describes the pattern in the table below? ⬇ TEKS 5.4.D

Input	w	2	4	6	8
Output	c	6	8	10	12

(A) $c = w \times 3$

(B) $c = w + 4$

(C) $c = w \times 4$

(D) $w = c \times 3$

22. Drew's weekly allowance is $8. Jan's weekly allowance is $10. Drew spends $3 a week. Jan spends $4 a week. The video game Drew and Jan want to buy costs $55. Write an expression to show how many weeks it will take them to save $55. Then simplify the expression. Describe the steps you used to write and simplify the expression.
⬇ TEKS 5.4.E, 5.4.F

_____

_____

_____

_____

Glossary

Pronunciation Key

a	add, map	f	fit, half	n	nice, tin	p	pit, stop	yo͞o	fuse, few
ā	ace, rate	g	go, log	ng	ring, song	r	run, poor	v	vain, eve
â(r)	care, air	h	hope, hate	o	odd, hot	s	see, pass	w	win, away
ä	palm, father	i	it, give	ō	open, so	sh	sure, rush	y	yet, yearn
b	bat, rub	ī	ice, write	ô	order, jaw	t	talk, sit	z	zest, muse
ch	check, catch	j	joy, ledge	oi	oil, boy	th	thin, both	zh	vision, pleasure
d	dog, rod	k	cool, take	ou	pout, now	th	this, bathe		
e	end, pet	l	look, rule	o͝o	took, full	u	up, done		
ē	equal, tree	m	move, seem	o͞o	pool, food	û(r)	burn, term		

ə the schwa, an unstressed vowel representing the sound spelled a in above, e in sicken, i in possible, o in melon, u in circus

Other symbols:
• separates words into syllables
′ indicates stress on a syllable

A

acute angle [ə•kyo͞ot′ ang′gəl] **ángulo agudo** An angle that has a measure less than a right angle (less than 90° and greater than 0°)
Example:

Word History

The Latin word for needle is *acus*. This means "pointed" or "sharp." You will recognize the root in the words *acid* (sharp taste), *acumen* (mental sharpness), and *acute*, which describes a sharp or pointed angle.

acute triangle [ə•kyo͞ot′ trī′ang•gəl] **triángulo acutángulo** A triangle that has three acute angles

addend [ad′end] **sumando** A number that is added to another in an addition problem

addition [ə•dish′ən] **suma** The process of finding the total number of items when two or more groups of items are joined; the opposite of subtraction

angle [ang′gəl] **ángulo** A shape formed by two line segments or rays that share the same endpoint
Example:

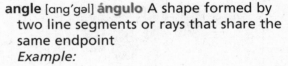

area [âr′ē•ə] **área** The measure of the number of unit squares needed to cover a surface

array [ə•rā′] **matriz** An arrangement of objects in rows and columns
Example:

column
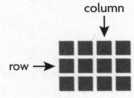
row →

Associative Property of Addition [ə•sō′shē•āt•iv präp′ ər•tē əv ə•dish′ən] **propiedad asociativa de la suma** The property that states that when the grouping of addends is changed, the sum is the same
Example: (5 + 8) + 4 = 5 + (8 + 4)

Glossary H1

Associative Property of Multiplication
[ə•sō′shē•āt•iv präp′ər•tē əv mul•tə•pli•kā′shən]
propiedad asociativa de la multiplicación
The property that states that factors can be grouped in different ways and still get the same product
Example: $(2 \times 3) \times 4 = 2 \times (3 \times 4)$

balance [bal′əns] **equilibrar** To equalize in weight or number

bar graph [bär graf] **gráfica de barras** A graph that uses horizontal or vertical bars to display countable data (p. 557)
Example:

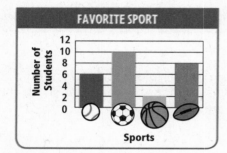

base (geometry) [bās] **base (geometría)** In two dimensions, one side of a triangle or parallelogram that is used to help find the area. In three dimensions, a plane figure, usually a polygon or circle, by which a three-dimensional figure is measured or named
Examples:

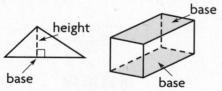

benchmark [bench′märk] **punto de referencia** A familiar number used as a point of reference

budget [bŭj′ĭt] **presupuesto** An organized plan for spending and saving money

capacity [kə•pas′i•tē] **capacidad** The amount a container can hold when filled

Celsius (°C) [sel′sē•əs] **Celsius (°C)** A metric scale for measuring temperature

centimeter (cm) [sen′tə•mēt•ər] **centímetro (cm)** A metric unit used to measure length or distance
    0.01 meter = 1 centimeter

closed figure [klōzd fig′yər] **figura cerrada** A figure that begins and ends at the same point

check [chĕk] **cheque** An order in writing to a bank asking that a certain sum of money be paid out of one's account (p. 635)

common denominator [käm′ən dē•näm′ə•nāt•ər] **denominador común** A common multiple of two or more denominators (p. 213)
Example: Some common denominators for $\frac{1}{4}$ and $\frac{5}{6}$ are 12, 24, and 36.

common factor [käm′ən fak′tər] **factor común** A number that is a factor of two or more numbers

common multiple [käm′ən mul′tə•pəl] **múltiplo común** A number that is a multiple of two or more numbers

Commutative Property of Addition
[kə•myōōt′ə•tiv präp′ər•tē əv ə•dish′ən] **propiedad conmutativa de la suma** The property that states that when the order of two addends is changed, the sum is the same
Example: $4 + 5 = 5 + 4$

Commutative Property of Multiplication
[kə•myōōt′ə•tiv präp′ər•tē əv mul•tə•pli•kā′shən]
propiedad conmutativa de la multiplicación
The property that states that when the order of two factors is changed, the product is the same
Example: $4 \times 5 = 5 \times 4$

compatible numbers [kəm•pat′ə•bəl num′bərz] **números compatibles** Numbers that are easy to compute with mentally

composite number [kəm•päz′it num′bər] **número compuesto** A number having more than two factors (p. 291)
Example: 6 is a composite number, since its factors are 1, 2, 3, and 6.

congruent [kən•grōō′ənt] **congruente** Having the same size and shape (p. 410)

coordinate grid [kō•ôrd′n•it grid] **cuadrícula de coordenadas** A grid formed by a horizontal line called the *x*-axis and a vertical line called the *y*-axis (p. 511)
Example:

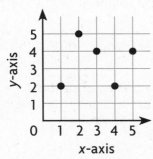

counting number [kount′ing num′bər] **número positivo** A whole number that can be used to count a set of objects (1, 2, 3, 4, . . .)

credit card [krĕd′ĭt kärd] **tarjeta de crédito** An identification card issued by a bank that allows a user to buy items and services immediately and pay the cost at a later time. The bank might charge the user interest in exchange for the use of the money (p. 635)

cube [kyo͞ob] **cubo** A three-dimensional figure with six congruent square faces
Example:

cubic unit [kyo͞o′bik yo͞o′nit] **unidad cúbica** A unit used to measure volume such as cubic foot, cubic meter, and so on (p. 355)

cup (c) [kup] **taza (tz)** A customary unit used to measure capacity
                8 ounces = 1 cup

data [dāt′ə] **datos** Information collected about people or things, often to draw conclusions about them

debit card [dĕb′ĭt kärd] **tarjeta de débito** An identification card issued by a bank that allows a user to immediately remove money from an account (p. 635)

decagon [dek′ə•gän] **decágono** A polygon with ten sides and ten angles
Examples:

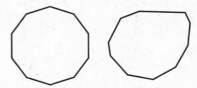

decimal [des′ə•məl] **número decimal** A number with one or more digits to the right of the decimal point

decimal point [des′ə•məl point] **punto decimal** A symbol used to separate dollars from cents in money, and to separate the ones place from the tenths place in a decimal

decimal system [des′ə•məl sis′təm] **sistema decimal** A system of computation based on the number 10

decimeter (dm) [des′i•mēt•ər] **decímetro (dm)** A metric unit used to measure length or distance
                10 decimeters = 1 meter

degree (°) [di•grē′] **grado (°)** A unit used for measuring angles and temperature

degree Celsius (°C) [di•grē′ sel′sē•əs] **grado Celcius (°C)** A metric unit for measuring temperature

degree Fahrenheit (°F) [di•grē′ fâr′ən•hīt] **grado Fahrenheit (°F)** A customary unit for measuring temperature

dekameter (dam) [dek′ə•mēt•ər] **decámetro (dam)** A metric unit used to measure length or distance
                10 meters = 1 dekameter

denominator [dē•näm′ə•nāt•ər] **denominador** The number below the bar in a fraction that tells how many equal parts are in the whole or in the group
Example: $\frac{3}{4}$ ← denominator

difference [dif′ər•əns] **diferencia** The answer to a subtraction problem

digit [dij′it] **dígito** Any one of the ten symbols 0, 1, 2, 3, 4, 5, 6, 7, 8, 9 used to write numbers

dimension [də•men′shən] **dimensión** A measure in one direction

Distributive Property [di•strib′yoo•tiv präp′ər•tē] **propiedad distributiva** The property that states that multiplying a sum by a number is the same as multiplying each addend in the sum by the number and then adding the products (p. 6)
Example: $3 \times (4 + 2) = (3 \times 4) + (3 \times 2)$
$$3 \times 6 = 12 + 6$$
$$18 = 18$$

divide [də•vīd′] **dividir** To separate into equal groups; the opposite operation of multiplication

dividend [div′ə•dend] **dividendo** The number that is to be divided in a division problem
Example: $36 \div 6$; $6\overline{)36}$ The dividend is 36.

divisible [də•vīz′ə•bəl] **divisible** A number is divisible by another number if the quotient is a counting number and the remainder is zero (p. 292)
Example: 18 is divisible by 3.

division [də•vizh′ən] **división** The process of sharing a number of items to find how many equal groups can be made or how many items will be in each equal group; the opposite operation of multiplication

divisor [də•vī′zər] **divisor** The number that divides the dividend
Example: $15 \div 3$; $3\overline{)15}$ The divisor is 3.

dot plot [dät plät] **diagrama de puntos** A graph that records each piece of data along a number line (p. 571)
Example:

Miles Jogged

edge [ej] **arista** The line segment made where two faces of a solid figure meet
Example:

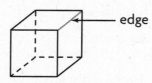

edge

elapsed time [ē•lapst′ tīm] **tiempo transcurrido** The time that passes between the start of an activity and the end of that activity

endpoint [end′ point] **extremo** The point at either end of a line segment or the starting point of a ray

equal to (=) [ē′kwəl too] **igual a (=)** Having the same value

equation [ē•kwā′zhən] **ecuación** An algebraic or numerical sentence that shows that two quantities are equal

equilateral triangle [ē•kwi•lat′ər•əl trī′ang•gəl] **triángulo equilátero** A triangle with three congruent sides (p. 415)
Example:

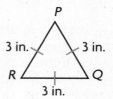

equivalent [ē•kwiv′ə•lənt] **equivalente** Having the same value

equivalent decimals [ē•kwiv′ə•lənt des′ə•məlz] **decimales equivalentes** Decimals that name the same amount
Example: $0.4 = 0.40 = 0.400$

equivalent fractions [ē•kwiv′ə•lənt frak′shənz] **fracciones equivalentes** Fractions that name the same amount or part
Example: $\frac{3}{4} = \frac{6}{8}$

estimate [es′tə•mit] *noun* **estimación (s)** A number close to an exact amount

estimate [es′tə•māt] *verb* **estimar (v)** To find a number that is close to an exact amount

even [ē′vən] **par** A whole number that has a 0, 2, 4, 6, or 8 in the ones place

expanded form [ek•span′did fôrm] **forma desarrollada** A way to write numbers by showing the value of each digit
Examples: $832 = 800 + 30 + 2$
$$3.25 = 3 + 0.2 + 0.05$$

expression [ek•spresh′ən] **expresión** A mathematical phrase or the part of a number sentence that combines numbers, operation signs, and sometimes variables, but does not have an equal sign

face [fās] **cara** A polygon that is a flat surface of a solid figure
Example:

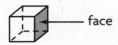
— face

fact family [fakt fam′ə•lē] **familia de operaciones** A set of related multiplication and division, or addition and subtraction, equations
Examples: $7 \times 8 = 56$; $8 \times 7 = 56$;
$\qquad$ $56 \div 7 = 8$; $56 \div 8 = 7$

factor [fak′tər] **factor** A number multiplied by another number to find a product

Fahrenheit (°F) [fâr′ən•hīt] **Fahrenheit (°F)** A customary scale for measuring temperature

fluid ounce (fl oz) [floo′id ouns] **onza fluida (oz fl)** A customary unit used to measure liquid capacity
$\qquad$ 1 cup = 8 fluid ounces

foot (ft) [foot] **pie (ft)** A customary unit used to measure length or distance
$\qquad$ 1 foot = 12 inches

formula [fôr′myoo•lə] **fórmula** A set of symbols that expresses a mathematical rule
Example: $A = b \times h$

fraction [frak′shən] **fracción** A number that names a part of a whole or a part of a group

fraction greater than 1 [frak′shən grāt′ər than wun] **fracción mayor que 1** A number which has a numerator that is greater than its denominator
Example:

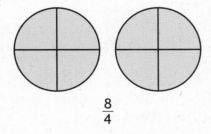

$\dfrac{8}{4}$

frequency [frē′kwən•sē] **frecuencia** the number of times an event occurs (p. 545)

frequency table [fre′kwən•sē tābəl] **tabla de frecuencia** A table that uses numbers to record data about how often something happens (p. 545)
Example:

Favorite Color	
Color	**Number**
Blue	10
Red	7
Green	5
Other	3

gallon (gal) [gal′ən] **galón (gal)** A customary unit used to measure capacity
$\qquad$ 4 quarts = 1 gallon

general quadrilateral [jen′ər•əl kwä•dri•lat′ər•əl] **cuadrilátero general** See *quadrilateral.*

gram (g) [gram] **gramo (g)** A metric unit used to measure mass
$\qquad$ 1,000 grams = 1 kilogram

greater than (>) [grāt′ər than] **mayor que (>)** A symbol used to compare two numbers or two quantities when the greater number or greater quantity is given first
Example: $6 > 4$

greater than or equal to (≥) [grāt′ər than ôr ē′kwəl too] **mayor o igual que (≥)** A symbol used to compare two numbers or quantities when the first is greater than or equal to the second

greatest common factor [grāt′əst käm′ən fak′tər] **máximo común divisor** The greatest factor that two or more numbers have in common
Example: 6 is the greatest common factor of 18 and 30.

grid [grid] **cuadrícula** Evenly divided and equally spaced squares on a figure or flat surface

gross income [grōs ĭn′kŭm′] **ingreso bruto** Income before any taxes are taken out of it (p. 629)

height [hīt] **altura** The length of a perpendicular from the base to the top of a two-dimensional or three-dimensional figure
Example:

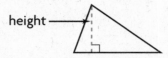

height

heptagon [hep′tə•gän] **heptágono** A polygon with seven sides and seven angles (p. 409)

hexagon [hek′sə•gän] **hexágono** A polygon with six sides and six angles
Examples:

horizontal [hôr•i•zänt′l] **horizontal** Extending left and right

hundredth [hun′drədth] **centésimo** One of 100 equal parts
Examples: 0.56, $\frac{56}{100}$, fifty-six hundredths

Identity Property of Addition [ī•den′tə•tē präp′ər•tē əv ə•dish′ən] **propiedad de identidad de la suma** The property that states that when you add zero to a number, the result is that number

Identity Property of Multiplication [ī•den′tə•tē präp′ər•tē əv mul•tə•pli•kā′shən] **propiedad de identidad de la multiplicación** The property that states that the product of any number and 1 is that number

inch (in.) [inch] **pulgada (pulg)** A customary unit used to measure length or distance
12 inches = 1 foot

income [ĭn′kŭm′] **ingreso** Money earned (p. 617)

income tax [ĭn′kŭm′ tăks] **impuesto sobre el ingreso** Money paid to a city, town, or state government or to the U.S. government based on income (p. 617)

inequality [in•ē•kwôl′ə•tē] **desigualdad** A mathematical sentence that contains the symbol <, >, ≤, ≥, or ≠

interest [ĭn′trĭst] **interés** The additional money paid by a borrower to a lender in exchange for the use of the lender's money. For example, you earn interest from a bank if you have a savings account and you pay interest to a lender if you have a loan

intersecting lines [in•tər•sekt′ing līnz] **líneas intersecantes** Lines that cross each other at exactly one point
Example:

interval [in′tər•vəl] **intervalo** The difference between one number and the next on the scale of a graph

inverse operations [in′vûrs äp•ə•rā′shənz] **operaciones inversas** Opposite operations, or operations that undo each other, such as addition and subtraction or multiplication and division (p. 41)

isosceles triangle [ī•säs′ə•lēz trī′ang•gəl] **triángulo isósceles** A triangle with two congruent sides (p. 415)
Example:

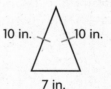

10 in.   10 in.

7 in.

key [kē] **clave** The part of a map or graph that explains the symbols

kilogram (kg) [kil′ō•gram] **kilogramo (kg)** A metric unit used to measure mass
1,000 grams = 1 kilogram

kilometer (km) [kə•läm′ət•ər] **kilómetro (km)** A metric unit used to measure length or distance
1,000 meters = 1 kilometer

least common denominator [lēst käm′ən dē•näm′ə•nāt•ər] **mínimo común denominador** The least common multiple of two or more denominators
Example: The least common denominator for $\frac{1}{4}$ and $\frac{5}{6}$ is 12.

least common multiple [lēst käm′ən mul′tə•pəl] **mínimo común múltiplo** The least number that is a common multiple of two or more numbers

less than (<) [les than] **menor que (<)** A symbol used to compare two numbers or two quantities, with the lesser number given first
Example: $4 < 6$

less than or equal to (≤) [les than ôr ē′kwəl tōō] **menor o igual que (≤)** A symbol used to compare two numbers or two quantities, when the first is less than or equal to the second

line [līn] **línea** A straight path in a plane, extending in both directions with no endpoints
Example:

<------->

line segment [līn seg′mənt] **segmento** A part of a line that includes two points called endpoints and all the points between them
Example:

•———•

linear unit [lin′ē•ər yōō′nit] **unidad lineal** A measure of length, width, height, or distance

liquid volume [lik′wid väl′yōōm] **volumen de un líquido** The amount of liquid in a container

liter (L) [lēt′ər] **litro (L)** A metric unit used to measure capacity
1 liter = 1,000 milliliters

mass [mas] **masa** The amount of matter in an object

meter (m) [mēt′ər] **metro (m)** A metric unit used to measure length or distance
1 meter = 100 centimeters

mile (mi) [mīl] **milla (mi)** A customary unit used to measure length or distance
5,280 feet = 1 mile

milligram (mg) [mil′i•gram] **miligramo (mg)** A metric unit used to measure mass
1,000 milligrams = 1 gram

milliliter (mL) [mil′i•lēt•ər] **mililitro (mL)** A metric unit used to measure capacity
1,000 milliliters = 1 liter

millimeter (mm) [mil′i•mēt•ər] **milímetro (mm)** A metric unit used to measure length or distance
1,000 millimeters = 1 meter

million [mil′yən] **millón** 1,000 thousands; written as 1,000,000

mixed number [mikst num′bər] **número mixto** A number that is made up of a whole number and a fraction
Example: $1\frac{5}{8}$

multiple [mul′tə•pəl] **múltiplo** The product of two counting numbers is a multiple of each of those numbers

multiplication [mul•tə•pli•kā′shən] **multiplicación** A process to find the total number of items made up of equal-sized groups, or to find the total number of items in a given number of groups. It is the inverse operation of division

multiply [mul′tə•plī] **multiplicar** When you combine equal groups, you can multiply to find how many in all; the opposite operation of division

net income [nĕt ĭn′kŭm′] **ingreso neto** Income that is left after taxes are taken out of the gross income (p. 629)

nonagon [nän′ə•gän] **eneágono** A polygon with nine sides and nine angles (p. 409)

not equal to (≠) [not ē′kwəl tōō] **no igual a (≠)** A symbol that indicates one quantity is not equal to another

number line [num′bər līn] **recta numérica** A line on which numbers can be located
Example:

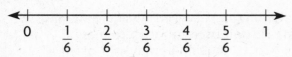

numerator [no͞o′mər•āt•ər] **numerador** The number above the bar in a fraction that tells how many equal parts of the whole or group are being considered
Example: $\frac{3}{4}$ ← numerator

numerical expression [no͞o•mer′i•kəl ek•spresh′ən] **expresión numérica** A mathematical phrase that uses only numbers and operation signs (p. 303)

obtuse angle [äb•to͞os′ ang′gəl] **ángulo obtuso** An angle whose measure is greater than 90° and less than 180°
Example:

obtuse triangle [äb•to͞os′ trī′ang•gəl] **triángulo obtusángulo** A triangle that has one obtuse angle

octagon [äk′tə•gän] **octágono** A polygon with eight sides and eight angles
Examples:

odd [od] **impar** A whole number that has a 1, 3, 5, 7, or 9 in the ones place

open figure [ō′pən fig′yər] **figura abierta** A figure that does not begin and end at the same point

order of operations [ôr′dər əv äp•ə•rā′shənz] **orden de las operaciones** A special set of rules which gives the order in which calculations are done in an expression (p. 309)

ordered pair [ôr′dərd pâr] **par ordenado** A pair of numbers used to locate a point on a grid. The first number tells the left-right position and the second number tells the up-down position (p. 511)

origin [ôr′ə•jin] **origen** The point where the two axes of a coordinate plane intersect (0, 0) (p. 511)

ounce (oz) [ouns] **onza (oz)** A customary unit used to measure weight
16 ounces = 1 pound

overestimate [ō′vər•es•tə•mit] **sobrestimar** An estimate that is greater than the exact answer

pan balance [pan bal′əns] **balanza de platillos** An instrument used to weigh objects and to compare the weights of objects

parallel lines [pâr′ə•lel līnz] **líneas paralelas** Lines in the same plane that never intersect and are always the same distance apart
Example:

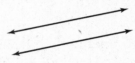

parallelogram [pâr•ə•lel′ə•gram] **paralelogramo** A quadrilateral whose opposite sides are parallel and have the same length, or are congruent
Example:

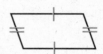

parentheses [pə•ren′thə•sēz] **paréntesis** The symbols used to show which operation or operations in an expression should be done first

partial product [pär′shəl präd′əkt] **producto parcial** A method of multiplying in which the ones, tens, hundreds, and so on are multiplied separately and then the products are added together

partial quotient [pär′shəl kwō′shənt] **cociente parcial** A method of dividing in which multiples of the divisor are subtracted from the dividend and then the quotients are added together

pattern [pat′ərn] **patrón** An ordered set of numbers or objects; the order helps you predict what will come next
Examples: 2, 4, 6, 8, 10

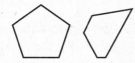

payroll tax [pā′rōl′ tăks] **retención sobre el salario** Money an employer withholds from an employee's earnings (p. 617)

pentagon [pen′tə•gän] **pentágono** A polygon with five sides and five angles
Examples:

perimeter [pə•rim′ə•tər] **perímetro** The distance around a closed plane figure

period [pir′ē•əd] **periodo** Each group of three digits separated by commas in a multi-digit number
Example: 85,643,900 has three periods.

perpendicular lines [pər•pən•dik′yoo•lər līnz] **líneas perpendiculares** Two lines that intersect to form four right angles
Example:

pictograph [pĭk′tə•grăf′] **pictografía** A graph that uses pictures to show and compare information
Example:

HOW WE GET TO SCHOOL	
Walk	✳ ✳ ✳
Ride a Bike	✳ ✳ ✳ ✳
Ride a Bus	✳ ✳ ✳ ✳ ✳ ◗
Ride in a Car	✳ ✳

Key: Each ✳ = 10 students.

pint (pt) [pīnt] **pinta (pt)** A customary unit used to measure capacity
2 cups = 1 pint

place value [plās val′yoo] **valor posicional** The value of each digit in a number based on the location of the digit

plane [plān] **plano** A flat surface that extends without end in all directions
Example:

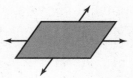

plane figure [plān fig′yər] **figura plana** See *two-dimensional figure*

point [point] **punto** An exact location in space

polygon [päl′i•gän] **polígono** A closed plane figure formed by three or more line segments (p. 409)
Examples:

Polygons   Not Polygons

pound (lb) [pound] **libra (lb)** A customary unit used to measure weight
1 pound = 16 ounces

prime number [prīm num′bər] **número primo** A number that has exactly two factors: 1 and itself (p. 297)
Examples: 2, 3, 5, 7, 11, 13, 17, and 19 are prime numbers. 1 is not a prime number.

prism [priz′əm] **prisma** A solid figure that has two congruent, polygon-shaped bases, and other faces that are all rectangles
Examples:

rectangular prism   triangular prism

product [präd′əkt] **producto** The answer to a multiplication problem

profit [prŏf′ĭt] **ganancia** The amount left after all the expenses are subtracted from the amount of money received from selling an item or service

property tax [prŏp′ər·tē tăks] **impuesto sobre la propiedad** A portion of the value of items that is paid to a city or state government. Property tax can be charged on things such as cars, houses, boats, or land (p. 623)

protractor [prō′trak•tər] **transportador** A tool used for measuring or drawing angles

quadrilateral [kwä•dri•lat′ər•əl] **cuadrilátero** A polygon with four sides and four angles
Example:

quart (qt) [kwôrt] **cuarto (ct)** A customary unit used to measure capacity
2 pints = 1 quart

quotient [kwō′shənt] **cociente** The number, not including the remainder, that results from dividing
Example: 8 ÷ 4 = 2. The quotient is 2.

range [rānj] **rango** The difference between the greatest and least numbers in a group (p. 577)

ray [rā] **semirrecta** A part of a line; it has one endpoint and continues without end in one direction
Example:

rectangle [rek′tang•gəl] **rectángulo** A parallelogram with four right angles
Example:

rectangular prism [rek•tang′gyə•lər priz′əm] **prisma rectangular** A three-dimensional figure in which all six faces are rectangles
Example:

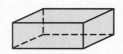

regroup [rē•grōōp′] **reagrupar** To exchange amounts of equal value to rename a number
Example: 5 + 8 = 13 ones or 1 ten 3 ones

regular polygon [reg′yə•lər päl′i•gän] **polígono regular** A polygon in which all sides are congruent and all angles are congruent (p. 410)

related facts [ri•lāt′id fakts] **operaciones relacionadas** A set of related addition and subtraction, or multiplication and division, number sentences
Examples: 4 × 7 = 28   28 ÷ 4 = 7
7 × 4 = 28   28 ÷ 7 = 4

remainder [ri•mān′dər] **residuo** The amount left over when a number cannot be divided equally

rhombus [räm′bəs] **rombo** A parallelogram with four equal, or congruent, sides
Example:

Word History

Rhombus is almost identical to its Greek origin, *rhombos*. The original meaning was "spinning top" or "magic wheel," which is easy to imagine when you look at a rhombus, an equilateral parallelogram.

right angle [rīt ang′gəl] **ángulo recto** An angle that forms a square corner and has a measure of 90°
Example:

right triangle [rīt trī′ang•gəl] **triángulo rectángulo** A triangle that has a right angle
Example:

round [round] **redondear** To replace a number with one that is simpler and is approximately the same size as the original number
Example: 114.6 rounded to the nearest ten is 110 and to the nearest one is 115.

sales tax [sãls tăks] **impuesto sobre las ventas** Money added to the cost of items or services. Sales tax amounts vary from state to state and from city to city (p. 623)

scale [skãl] **escala** A series of numbers placed at fixed distances on a graph to help label the graph

scalene triangle [skã'lēn trī'ang•gəl] **triángulo escaleno** A triangle with no congruent sides (p. 415)
Example:

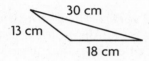

scatter plot [skăt'ər plŏt'] **diagrama de dispersión** A graph that shows a relationship between two sets of data (p. 595)

second (sec) [sek'ənd] **segundo (s)** A small unit of time

60 seconds = 1 minute

simplest form [sim'pləst fôrm] **mínima expresión** A fraction is in simplest form when the numerator and denominator have only 1 as a common factor

simplify [sĭm'plə•fī'] **simplificar** To find the value of a numerical expression (p. 309)

skip count [skip kount] **contar salteado** A pattern of counting forward or backward
Example: 5, 10, 15, 20, 25, 30, . . .

solid figure [sä'lid fig'yər] **cuerpo geométrico** See *three-dimensional figure*

solution [sə•lōō'shən] **solución** A value that makes an equation true

square [skwâr] **cuadrado** A polygon with four equal, or congruent, sides and four right angles

square unit [skwâr yōō'nit] **unidad cuadrada** A unit used to measure area such as square foot, square meter, and so on

standard form [stan'dərd fôrm] **forma normal** A way to write numbers by using the digits 0–9, with each digit having a place value
Example: 456 ← standard form

stem-and-leaf plot [stĕm ənd lēf plŏt] **diagrama de tallo y hojas** A graph that shows groups of data arranged by place value (p. 583)

straight angle [strãt ang'gəl] **ángulo llano** An angle whose measure is 180°
Example:

subtraction [səb•trak'shən] **resta** The process of finding how many are left when a number of items are taken away from a group of items; the process of finding the difference when two groups are compared; the opposite of addition

sum [sum] **suma o total** The answer to an addition problem

tablespoon (tbsp) [tã'bəl•spōōn] **cucharada (cda)** A customary unit used to measure capacity
3 teaspoons = 1 tablespoon

tax [tăks] **impuesto** Money paid to the government in exchange for services, such as road maintenance and police protection (p. 617)

teaspoon (tsp) [tē'spōōn] **cucharadita (cdta)** A customary unit used to measure capacity
1 tablespoon = 3 teaspoons

tenth [tenth] **décimo** One of ten equal parts
Example: 0.7 = seven tenths

thousandth [thou'zəndth] **milésimo** One of one thousand equal parts (p. 11)
Example: 0.006 = six thousandths

three-dimensional [thrē də•men'shə•nəl] **tres dimensiones** Measured in three directions, such as length, width, and height

three-dimensional figure [thrē də•men′shə•nəl fig′yər] **figura de tres dimensiones** A figure having length, width, and height
Example:

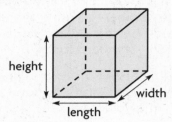

ton (T) [tun] **tonelada (t)** A customary unit used to measure weight
2,000 pounds = 1 ton

trapezoid [trap′i•zoid] **trapecio** A quadrilateral with exactly one pair of parallel sides
Examples:

triangle [trī′ang•gəl] **triángulo** A polygon with three sides and three angles
Examples:

two-dimensional [tōō də•men′shə•nəl] **dos dimensiones** Measured in two directions, such as length and width

two-dimensional figure [tōō də•men′shə•nəl fig′yər] **figura de dos dimensiones** A figure that lies in a plane; a figure having length and width

underestimate [un•dər•es′tə•mit] **subestimar** An estimate that is less than the exact answer

unit cube [yōō′nit kyōōb] **cubo de una unidad** A cube that has a length, width, and height of 1 unit (p. 435)

unit fraction [yōō′nit frak′shən] **fracción unitaria** A fraction that has 1 as a numerator

variable [vâr′ē•ə•bəl] **variable** A letter or symbol that stands for an unknown number or numbers

Venn diagram [ven dī′ə•gram] **diagrama de Venn** A diagram that shows relationships among sets of things
Example:

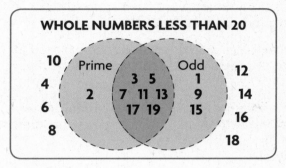

vertex [vûr′teks] **vértice** The point where two or more rays meet; the point of intersection of two sides of a polygon; the point of intersection of three (or more) edges of a solid figure; the top point of a cone; the plural of vertex is vertices
Examples:

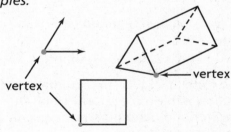

Word History

The Latin word *vertere* means "to turn" and also relates to "highest." You can turn a figure around a point, or *vertex*.

vertical [vûr′ti•kəl] **vertical** Extending up and down

volume [väl′yōōm] **volumen** The measure of the space a solid figure occupies (p. 355)

weight [wāt] **peso** How heavy an object is

whole [hōl] **entero** All of the parts of a shape or group

whole number [hōl num′bər] **número entero** One of the numbers 0, 1, 2, 3, 4, . . . ; the set of whole numbers goes on without end

word form [wûrd fôrm] **en palabras** A way to write numbers in standard English *Example:* 4,829 = four thousand, eight hundred twenty-nine

x*-axis** [eks ak′sis] **eje de la *x The horizontal number line on a coordinate plane (p. 511)

x*-coordinate** [eks kō•ôrd′n•it] **coordenada *x The first number in an ordered pair; tells the distance to move right or left from (0, 0) (p. 511)

yard (yd) [yärd] **yarda (yd)** A customary unit used to measure length or distance
3 feet = 1 yard

y*-axis** [wī ak′sis] **eje de la *y The vertical number line on a coordinate plane (p. 511)

y*-coordinate** [wī kō•ôrd′n•it] **coordenada *y The second number in an ordered pair; tells the distance to move up or down from (0, 0) (p. 511)

Zero Property of Multiplication [zē′rō präp′ər•tē əv mul•tə•pli•kā′shən] **propiedad del cero de la multiplicación** The property that states that when you multiply by zero, the product is zero

Table of Measures

METRIC	CUSTOMARY

Length

METRIC	CUSTOMARY
1 centimeter (cm) = 10 millimeters (mm)	1 foot (ft) = 12 inches (in.)
1 meter (m) = 1,000 millimeters	1 yard (yd) = 3 feet, or 36 inches
1 meter = 100 centimeters	1 mile (mi) = 1,760 yards,
1 meter = 10 decimeters (dm)	or 5,280 feet
1 kilometer (km) = 1,000 meters	

Capacity

METRIC	CUSTOMARY
1 liter (L) = 1,000 milliliters (mL)	1 cup (c) = 8 fluid ounces (fl oz)
1 metric cup = 250 milliliters	1 pint (pt) = 2 cups
1 liter = 4 metric cups	1 quart (qt) = 2 pints, or 4 cups
1 kiloliter (kL) = 1,000 liters	1 gallon (gal) = 4 quarts

Mass/Weight

METRIC	CUSTOMARY
1 gram (g) = 1,000 milligrams (mg)	1 pound (lb) = 16 ounces (oz)
1 gram = 100 centigrams (cg)	1 ton (T) = 2,000 pounds
1 kilogram (kg) = 1,000 grams	

TIME

1 minute (min) = 60 seconds (sec)

1 half hour = 30 minutes

1 hour (hr) = 60 minutes

1 day = 24 hours

1 week (wk) = 7 days

1 year (yr) = 12 months (mo), or
about 52 weeks

1 year = 365 days

1 leap year = 366 days

1 decade = 10 years

1 century = 100 years

1 millennium = 1,000 years

Table of Measures

SYMBOLS

=	is equal to	$\overleftrightarrow{AB}$	line AB
≠	is not equal to	$\overrightarrow{AB}$	ray AB
>	is greater than	$\overline{AB}$	line segment AB
<	is less than	$\angle ABC$	angle ABC, or angle B
(2, 3)	ordered pair (x, y)	$\triangle ABC$	triangle ABC
⊥	is perpendicular to	°	degree
∥	is parallel to	°C	degrees Celsius
		°F	degrees Fahrenheit

FORMULAS

Perimeter		Area	
Polygon	P = sum of the lengths of sides	Rectangle	$A = b \times h$, or $A = bh$
Rectangle	$P = (2 \times l) + (2 \times w)$, or $P = 2l + 2w$		
Square	$P = 4 \times s$, or $P = 4s$		

Volume

Rectangular prism $V = B \times h$, or $V = l \times w \times h$

B = area of base shape, h = height of prism